Kingston upon Hull

Scrooby
Babworth

Gainborough

Nottingham

Cambridge

Leiden

Amsterdam

Delft
Rotterdam

Oxford

Cardiff

Bristol
Bath

London

Southampton

Dartmouth

Plymouth

ENGLISH CHANNEL

J.BROOKS

The Mayflower Pilgrims:

*Roots of Puritan, Presbyterian,
Congregationalist, and Baptist Heritage*

THE
MAYFLOWER PILGRIMS

ROOTS OF PURITAN, PRESBYTERIAN,
CONGREGATIONALIST, AND BAPTIST HERITAGE

DAVID BEALE

AMBASSADOR-EMERALD INTERNATIONAL
GREENVILLE, SOUTH CAROLINA • BELFAST, NORTHERN IRELAND

ISBN: 1-889893-51-X

Published by:
Ambassador-Emerald International
427 Wade Hampton Blvd.
Greenville, SC 29609 USA

and

Ambassador Productions
Ardenlee Street
Belfast, Northern Ireland

Cover design © 2000 Grand Design
Cover design by Matt Donovan and Brad Sherman
Internal design by Matt Donovan
Cover photo of bricks © 2000 Photodisc
Copyediting by Mark Sidwell

Illustration Acknowledgements:
The end sheets (*Mayflower* with map) are by the artist, James Brooks. Illustra-
tions were provided by Boston Guildhall; Gainsborough Old Hall (interior
scene); Pieterskerk (Leiden); Plimoth Plantation (scenes of Plymouth, Plimoth
Plantation, and views of *Mayflower II* with sails); Brian Fernett (*Mayflower II*
docked, statue of William Bradford, and scenes of Forefathers' Monument).
Other miscellaneous scenes are from the author's collection, including some in
London, Cambridge, Austerfield, Gainsborough Old Hall (exterior), Babworth,
Boston, Scrooby, Southampton, Dartmouth, Plymouth, and the Netherlands.

www.emeraldhouse.com

To my mother

CONTENTS

"As one small candle may light a thousand, so the light here kindled hath shone unto many, yea in some sort to our whole nation; let the glorious name of Jehovah have all the praise."

(Bradford, *Plymouth Plantation*, 236)

CHAPTER 1

THE ENGLISH REFORMATION:
THE RISE OF PURITANISM AND SEPARATISM

THE INFLUENCE OF THE ENGLISH BIBLE

John Wyclif: Morning Star of the Reformation

John Wyclif (c. 1320-1384)[1] stood forth as the champion of an open Bible.[2] Although the Roman Catholic Church, at a council held in Toulouse, France, in 1229, had forbidden the use of the Bible to laymen, Wyclif believed that if the common people had the Bible in their own language they would demand a reformation of the church. Wyclif knew no Hebrew and probably no Greek, but he used what he had—the Latin Vulgate. He translated directly from the Latin into the English vernacular to produce the first English Bible. His traveling preachers, called Lollards, were branded as "heretics" and condemned. (See Appendix A for a time chart of English monarchs.) King Henry IV enacted the statute *de Haeretico Comburendo* in 1401, which made such "heresy" a secular crime punishable by burning. However, the demand for the Scriptures far exceeded the supply. There were no printing presses in those days, and copyists had to prepare each Bible by hand. Its influence became so great that ecclesiastical opponents were crying, "The jewel of the clergy has become the toy of the laity." (See Appendix C for an overview of Oxford and its place in Christian history.) A convocation held in Oxford in 1408 instituted and vigorously enforced a penalty of burning for owning or even reading the English Scriptures. No one could translate the Bible into English without a bishop's license. A Roman Catholic papal decree in 1413 banned Wyclif's books, and another law, in 1414, warned that any who

1

should read the English Bible should "forfeite lande, catel, lif, and godes [goods], from theyre heyres [heirs] forever." Finally, the Council of Constance, in 1415, ordered Wyclif's books burned and ordered his bones to be exhumed and burned—a decree carried out in 1428. The Lollards, however, continued to preach.

THE PROVISION OF TOOLS NECESSARY FOR REFORMATION

About 1450, a German named John Gutenberg perfected the first movable-type printing press. Progress in many areas marked the half-century following this invention. The capture of Constantinople by the Turks in 1453 resulted in a great westward movement of Greek scholars with their manuscripts. Numerous events rapidly occurred which were to have tremendous influence upon the future translation and distribution of the Scriptures: the appearance in 1456 of the Latin Gutenberg Bible, the publication in 1476 of the first Greek grammar, the publication in 1480 of the first Greek lexicon, and in 1488 the first printed Hebrew Bible. In 1492 (the year Columbus discovered the New World) Ferdinand and Isabella's expulsion of the Jewish population from Spain sent some 300,000 Jewish exiles all over Europe, many of them becoming teachers, some quite famous for their knowledge of Hebrew and Hebraic culture; also in 1492 (five years before Vasco da Gama rounded the Cape of Good Hope) Oxford University hired its first Greek teacher—Grocyn. In 1506, the first Hebrew lexicon appeared; in 1516 Desiderius Erasmus' Greek New Testament made its debut; and in 1517 (the year in which Luther nailed his *Ninety-five Theses* to the door of the Castle Church in Wittenberg, Germany) the Complutensian Polyglot Bible, with Hebrew, Greek, and Latin texts in parallel columns, appeared. With such tools unlocking the knowledge of the Hebrew and Greek Scriptures, a proliferation of Bibles, translated into vernacular languages, began to appear.

THE TYNDALE BIBLE TO THE GENEVA BIBLE:
HENRY VIII TO BLOODY MARY

William Tyndale (c. 1494-1536)—born about 100 years after John Wyclif's death—early distinguished himself both at Oxford and at Cambridge as a scholar.[3] Early in his life, he accepted the doctrines of the Reformation. Tyndale once remarked to a critic, "If God spare my life, ere many years I will cause the boy that driveth the plough in England to know more of the Scriptures than thou doest." English people everywhere were searching and hoping that God had more for them than a corrupt church. As early as the year 1523, groups of Cambridge students were reported meeting regularly at a secret house, called "The White Horse Inn," to discuss the writings of the German Reformer Martin Luther who, two years earlier, had been condemned as a heretic, at Worms. The little inn at Cambridge was situated where students of King's College, Queen's College, and St. John's College could slip in by the back door. Some who heard of their discussions would, in mockery, call them "Germans." By now, William Tyndale was living in London and beginning his work of translating the Scriptures into English. Forced to flee to Germany, Tyndale, translating from Erasmus' Greek text, completed his English New Testament in 1525. Friends smuggled copies into England in cases of merchandise, as English bishops bought them and burned them at St. Paul's Cross. England's political and religious climate was about to change, however. Within ten years, England would no longer be under the authority of the pope of Rome.

King Henry VIII, distressed about the inability of his wife, Catherine of Aragon, to bear him a male successor, tried to obtain sanction from Pope Clement VII to divorce Catherine and to marry her maid of honor, Anne Boleyn. Catherine had been the widow of Henry's elder brother, and a previous pope had granted a special "dispensation" for Henry to marry her. With his application for an annulment of this marriage, Henry argued from the Bible that "if a man shall take his brother's wife, it is an unclean thing: he hath uncovered his brother's nakedness; they shall be childless" (Leviticus 20:21). Although Pope Clement VII was fond of Henry, he found himself in an awkward position—he was virtually a prisoner of war to Catherine's own nephew, Emperor Charles V, who was angry over a political league the pope had made with Francis I. Proceeding to Rome in 1527, Charles's troops had just stormed and looted the city and had nearly made the pope a prisoner in his own Castle of St. Angelo. Determined, therefore, to remove his kingdom from the jurisdiction of the Roman papacy, Henry VIII, by the Act of Supremacy in 1534, became "the only supreme head in earth of the Church of England." Thomas Cranmer, Archbishop of Canterbury, pronounced Henry's marriage void and Catherine's daughter Mary illegitimate. Only a few days before Cranmer's decision, Henry had married Anne Boleyn, who was already pregnant with Elizabeth. In the same year (1534), the Upper House (Bishops) of Convocation of Cambridge petitioned the Crown to authorize a translation of the Bible into English. Although no immediate results came of this, it became obvious that much of England was now favoring an English Bible.

In 1534 William Tyndale published at Antwerp his translation of the Pentateuch and his revised New Testament. In 1535 Tyndale was seized by the officers of Emperor Charles V and imprisoned in the dungeon of Vilvorde Castle, near Brussels. Here Tyndale continued to work on the Old Testament portion of his translation and passed the manuscripts on to his friend John Rogers, who would incorporate them into the Matthew Bible (1537) after Tyndale's death.[4] In a marginal note at Exodus 32: 15 (the golden calf incident), Tyndale insists that, "The Pope's bull slayeth more than Aaron's calf." But the pope's church found William Tyndale guilty of heresy and handed him over to the secular powers for execution. On October 6, 1536, governmental authorities led him to the stake and strangled and burned him in the prison yard. In a loud voice, his dying words rang out, "Lord, open the King of England's eyes."

Miles Coverdale (1488-1569) had already fled to the Continent and completed his translation of the English Bible. The Coverdale Bible (1535)—the first complete Bible translated into English—was based largely upon William Tyndale's work. Thomas Cromwell, the king's vicar general, entrusted to Miles Coverdale the work of revising the Matthew Bible, striking out controversial notes. In 1539 Coverdale's "Great Bible" appeared. It was so-called for its physical dimensions of sixteen and a half by eleven inches. The Great Bible, the first Bible to be authorized specifically for public use in English churches, provided tremendous incentive for thousands of commoners to learn to read. Cromwell ordered every parson to obtain a copy and to chain it up in some convenient place in his church in order that the parishioners might "resort to the same and read it." Only three years after the martyrdom of William Tyndale, who had promised the plowboy of England a knowledge of the Scriptures, hundreds were listening to the reading of the Holy Bible. Interestingly, the Great Bible was Tyndale's work; it was a simple revision of the Matthew Bible, which was only a slight revision of Tyndale's. Even though Henry completely liquidated all English monasteries in 1539, he was still a Roman Catholic, as his Six Articles of Religion reveal.[5] When King Henry died in 1547, however, at least eight editions of the Great Bible had been printed. Some printers saw it only as an opportunity to make money; but indeed it was the translation of the Bible into English, not Henry VIII, that finally worked a Reformation in England.

Henry's son by the Protestant Jane Seymour, Edward VI, came to the throne at the age of nine. *The Book of Common Prayer* was published in 1549 and revised in 1552. With its publishing, however, came Acts of Uniformity, establishing by law the worship and rituals prescribed in this Prayer Book. The first offense of the Act brought loss of income for a year, and imprisonment for six months. A second offense brought permanent loss of income, and imprisonment for one year. A third offense resulted in imprisonment for life. In 1553 the Protestant Forty-two Articles of Religion were published. Three weeks after signing them Edward died, not yet sixteen years of age, and was soon buried in Westminster Abbey. During these years, John Hooper, bishop of Gloucester, tried to discourage "popish" vestments and ceremonies. Hooper has been called the "Father of Puritanism."

In 1553 King Edward VI's half-sister, Mary, succeeded him to the English throne. She repealed her father's Act of Supremacy and Edward's Acts of Uniformity and restored papal authority to England. "Bloody Mary" prohibited the reading of the English Bible, and in 1554-1555 she burned at the stake the Protestant bishops Hugh Latimer, Nicholas Ridley, and John Hooper. In 1556 Mary proceeded to burn Thomas Cranmer at the stake. (See Appendix B for John Foxe's account of the martyrdom of Hugh Latimer, Nicholas Ridley, and Thomas Cranmer, at Oxford—1555-1556.) This execution was followed by three hundred others, led by the great protomartyr, John Rogers, editor of the Matthew Bible. At the beginning of Mary's reign, approximately eight hundred Protestants left England. The most learned of these exiles went to Geneva, the "holy city of the Alps," and carefully produced the "Geneva Bible," published in 1560 as the first English version ever to be translated entirely from the original languages. Its terse style and pithy notes made it the English household Bible, the Bible of the Puritans—the Bible the Pilgrims would bring to Plymouth.[6] The translators dedicated the new Bible to the twenty-four-year-old daughter of Anne Boleyn, Queen Elizabeth, who ascended the English throne on November 17, 1558.

THE BEGINNINGS OF ORGANIZED ENGLISH PURITANISM AND SEPARATISM

It would not be Elizabeth's policy either to encourage or to discourage the printing of Bibles. Endeavoring to mark out a *via media* between Protestantism and popery,[7] the Queen's first task was to restore the Anglican Church. In order for the bishops of the Church of England to continue claiming a succession from the apostles, many of their ecclesiastics were careful to recognize the Church of Rome as a true church, though corrupt in some points. Elizabeth herself revealed this basic "conservatism" when she began her reign by appointing Matthew Parker as Archbishop of Canterbury. Parker had received his ordination in the Roman Catholic Church in 1527, before England's break with the papacy. To the bishops, therefore, Parker represented a continuity of "apostolic episcopacy." Elizabeth then nullified all the religious restorations of her sister Mary and persuaded Parliament to restore her father's Act of Supremacy, vesting all ecclesiastical jurisdiction in the Crown. For all office holding, in both church and state, it was now necessary to take a solemn oath recognizing the queen as "the only Supreme Governor of this realm . . . in all spiritual and ecclesiastical things." Penalties were provided for those refusing to take the oath. Puritans would be tolerated, but only so long as they took the oath and obeyed the queen. Under her restored Act of Uniformity (1562), ministers failing to subscribe to the *Book of Common Prayer* (Revised 1560) and to the Thirty-nine Articles[8] (to be revised in 1563) would lose their pulpits and be imprisoned! The Act of Uniformity carried severe penalties against anyone who would not conform to the authority and all the rituals of the Church of England. Both Puritans and Roman Catholics would suffer persecution before the Elizabethan age ended. Many were fined or imprisoned for refusing to attend the services of the parish churches. Anyone in London who tried to promote the notion of independent, congregational churches ran the danger of imprisonment or public execution. It was from the passing of Elizabeth's Act of Uniformity that many Puritans began to be called "nonconformists."

The two acts, in part, constituted the "Elizabethan Settlement," which was obnoxious indeed to those who desired reform for the Church of England. In order to ensure uniformity, in 1566, the Queen issued "Advertisements,"[9] which declared null and void all preaching licenses granted prior to 1564. That year would mark the beginning of "Puritanism" as a movement taking organized form. Written by Archbishop Matthew Parker, the Advertisements silenced all preachers, then issued fresh licenses only to "conformable" ministers. Suddenly, thousands of parishes were destitute, with no ministers to preach to them. The vast majority of the Puritans who were deprived of their ministries were Presbyterians, unable to practice according to personal conscience and conviction. One third of London's clergy were suspended for their refusal to submit to Parker's requirements, which included the enforced use of clerical vestments such as the surplice (robe). Puritan ministers cried aloud that clerical vestments belonged not to the ministry of the church of Christ, but to the priesthood of the house of Aaron, or to the "Romish rags of the pope's pagan church!" For eighty years, from 1564 to 1644, a distinct body of Puritans, always in and of the Church of England, dared to speak out against corruption in the Church. The controversy lay deeper than mere outward forms. These Puritans knew from the Scriptures that the very nature and discipline of Christ's church were under attack. Many Puritans were developing increasing Presbyterian convictions on matters of church order. It is from this time, that a definite "Presbytereo-Puritanism became a living force in England."[10] At Cambridge, in a single day in 1565, the Presbyterian Thomas Cartwright and three hundred others threw off their surplices within the walls of St. John's College, Cambridge, while similar occurrences were developing at Trinity and other colleges. (See Appendix D for the University of Cambridge and its influence on the Puritans and the Pilgrims.)

Meanwhile, disappointed over the widespread popular acceptance of the Geneva Bible among the Puritans, Parker directed the translation of the "Bishops' Bible," published in 1568. Parker wrote its preface both to the Old and New Testaments. It was used primarily by the clergy and remained generally unpopular among the common people, a growing number of whom were beginning to voice their opposition to what they saw as an increasingly corrupt church. Many parishes were without any pretense of a ministry; some churches had gone fifteen years without hearing a sermon. Church edifices had deteriorated; inside St. Paul's Cathedral, male youth were stabling their horses and practicing pigeon shooting.

As the Puritans preached eloquently and faithfully, increasing numbers of sincere religious "dissenters" were becoming convinced that they must go beyond Puritanism and worship the Lord outside of England's parish churches. They must become Separatists. While the Puritans were not Separatists, the leading Separatists would remain Puritan in doctrine.[11] In 1567 the sheriff of London uncovered a group of nearly one hundred dissenters gathered in Plumbers' Hall and hearing Separatist preaching from men such as Richard Fitz. They had rented the building for "holding a wedding." About twenty of these Separatists were apprehended and turned over to the Bishop of London, Edmund Grindal, and the inquisitors of the Ecclesiastical Commission; some were imprisoned for over a year. In 1593 seven of them surreptitiously printed "The True Report of our Examination and Conference (as neare as wee can call to remembrance)."[12] This is the earliest surviving document of its kind. The Separatists' "True Report" actually reads like a transcript of a trial under Bloody Mary, as they liken themselves to the "Privy Churches" which met secretly during Mary's reign. The document indicates that the dissenters were keenly familiar with the recent debut of John Foxe's huge folio, *Actes and Monuments of these latter and perillous dayes, touching matters of the Church . . .* (1563).[13] To the Anglican prelates, however, these Separatists were "gospellers" and "heretics."[14]

Meanwhile, in the spring of 1570 Cambridge Professor of Divinity, Thomas Cartwright (1535-1603),[15] called the Father of English Presbyterianism, delivered a series of polemical lectures against "prelacy," the episcopal form of church government. Cartwright was then forced into exile in Geneva, but not before he profoundly influenced two Corpus Christi students—Robert Harrison (d. 1585) and Robert Browne (d. 1633), both of whom would soon leave their permanent mark upon the history of Separatism. Many Separatist assemblies and Puritan preachers' meetings were now holding services which they called "prophesyings," which the reformers John Calvin and Zwingli had practiced on the Continent. The earliest of these "exercises" in England seem to have been held in Northampton. In such meetings, designated speakers preached short expositions on previously-chosen and often difficult passages and topics. Such discourses, regulated by careful rules concerning their length and nature, helped to cultivate the art of preaching and to edify audiences. For their Sunday afternoon and Thursday evening services, the *Mayflower* Pilgrims would later practice prophesyings often, under the careful direction of their Pastor John Robinson. Sometimes allowing laymen to participate, Robinson wrote a treatise in their defense, *The Peoples' Plea For The Exercise of Prophesie . . .* (1618), published by William Brewster's press. The Puritans, however, would limit the prophesyings to the regular ministers except later in New England, where laymen would often be needed in the absence of ordained men. When a time of sickness brought death at Puritan Salem, Massachusetts, *Mayflower* Pilgrim Samuel Fuller, while visiting there, noticed that everyone determined that laymen, "such godly persons that are amongst them," should "make known their godly desire and practice the same, viz solemnly to enter into covenant with the Lord to walk in his ways . . . having men of ability amongst them."[16] With the idea originating among the Puritans themselves, it is safe to conclude that the prophesyings among the English Puritans had a profound influence, even on a "congregationalism" extending far beyond their own day. In England, such practices would advance the growth of Presbyterianism.

In 1571-1572, a group of Puritans submitted "An Admonition to the Parliament" and "A Seconde Admonition to the Parliament," both written by Thomas Cartwright and both opposing the *Book of Common Prayer* as "an imperfect book, culled and picked out of the popish dunghill." Objecting to prelacy, they asserted that "the names archbishops, archdeacons, lord bishops, chancellors, etc., are drawn from the Pope's shop, together with their offices, so the government which they use . . . is anti-Christian and devilish, and contrary to the Scriptures."[17] The queen was so greatly angered that some Puritans ended up in Newgate Prison. Rather than stopping them, however, this prompted them, on November 20, 1572, to establish a Presbyterian Church at the village of Wandsworth (Surrey), just outside of London. (Today, this is near London's Wimbledon.) They erected their own meetinghouse here, on the banks of the Thames. This was the first fully constituted Presbyterian church in England. From the courageous beginning of that "Particular Church," numerous secret meetings of Presbyterians started in private homes in many parts of the kingdom. Vigorous persecution followed, but Presbyterians would not be stopped. The persecution which does not exterminate its foe never fails to strengthen it. In 1575 Archbishop Parker died and was succeeded by Edmund Grindal, who now favored the Puritans. Grindal reported to the queen that due to the ignorance and scarcity of Church of England clergy, the country was in a deplorable spiritual condition. When Archbishop Grindal was ordered to suppress the Puritan prophesyings, or ministers' meetings, he was unable to do so in good conscience. The queen immediately suspended him and sequestered him to his house for six months as a prisoner. Death spared him further suffering in 1583; but from this time, preaching fell into contempt in England, and her national church never recovered. Grindal was succeeded by John Whitgift who, during the first week of his rule, issued his famous articles which include the following: "That all preaching, catechizing, and praying in any private house, where any are present besides the family, be utterly extinguished. . . . That all preachers, and others in ecclesiastical orders, do at all times wear the habits prescribed. That none be admitted to preach, unless he be ordained according to the manner of the Church of England."[18] Wielding almost absolute power with despotic severity, Whitgift suspended many hundreds of clergy from their ministries. For twenty years this man guided the affairs of the Church of England.

Robert Browne (c. 1550-1633)

The sixteenth-century Reformation in England was achieved only through great struggle and conflict. The final form of England's national church, *the* Church of England, established by law, was "episcopal," which means government by bishops. There was no room for those who dissented from this form of church—no room for any freedom of conscience in matters of religion. No one can understand the Pilgrim Fathers and their descendants, as far as their religious heritage is concerned, without an understanding of the religious people known as the independents, at first often called "Brownists." The latter name derived from Robert Browne,[19] who is generally regarded as the first to expound the principles of church government peculiar to independent congregationalism. He probably was not the first to do that, but he did make a strong impact upon the history of Separatism.

Details of his early life are sketchy. Robert Browne was born about the year 1550. He was educated at Corpus Christi College, Cambridge, during the time that the Presbyterian Puritan, Thomas Cartwright, was teaching there. Brown then took holy orders in the Church of England. In 1571 he became chaplain to the Duke of Norfolk and aroused great controversy by

10

the views he expressed "against the calling and authorizing of preachers by bishops." A confrontational visit to Cambridge about 1578 seems to mark his essential break from the Church of England. At Norwich, by 1581, Browne had gathered a small congregation—the pioneer church—and become its pastor. Browne and others of his group were often arrested. He once boasted that he had been committed to thirty-two prisons! Lord Burghley, to whom he was related, often came to Browne's intervention. Sometime in late 1581 or early 1582, he and most of his group of some thirty or forty persons sought refuge in Middelburg, Zeeland (Netherlands).

It was here that Browne wrote and published three treatises, setting forth the tenets with which his name henceforth became associated. These advocated individualism, or independency, in the constitution and establishment of the church, and protests against the interference of all external human powers in matters of religion. These would appear to many people today to be entirely laudable. They were extreme views in his day, however; and it was precisely for this freedom that the Pilgrim Fathers and others left England. Browne's most famous tract, *A Treatise of Reformation Without Tarrying for Any* (1582), found its way to many parts of England.

William Pagett, a brewer's clerk in London, sold Browne's books to members of the English Company of Merchant Adventurers. This prompted a royal proclamation in 1583 declaring Browne's works "seditious, scismaticall and erronious . . . tending to the depraving of the Ecclesiastical government established within this Realme." That same year, two of Browne's followers in England were hanged for distributing his books; forty copies of the books were burned. Independency was completely opposed to the hierarchical system of bishops. Many saw it, however, as something which always leads to extreme individualism and unnecessary factionalism. Indeed, it was dissension which plagued Browne's own church in Middelburg and prompted "Trouble-church Browne" to leave the majority of his congregation in the Netherlands in 1583 or 1584 and go to Scotland. With a handful of his followers, he went to Edinburgh, where his preaching was met with disfavor by the Presbyterians. Within a week, Browne was summoned before the Kirk-Session and imprisoned! On his return to England, Browne was arrested in London and excommunicated in Northampton. Utterly discouraged, Browne recanted and applied for re-admission into the Church of England. His Middelburg church soon ceased to exist.

Browne seems to have been received back into the Establishment late in 1586. From that year until about 1591, he served an appointment as headmaster of St. Olave's School, in London's Southwark area. Browne was then restored to the ministry of the Established Church, holding for the next forty years the position of minister of the parish church of Achurch-cum-Thorpe in Peterborough (Northamptonshire). Other Separatists accused Browne of being an apostate. His writings, however, contain the basic principles of separatist congregationalism: (1) the church is a covenanted community of believers; (2) persons join the local church by voluntary consent, never by coercion; (3) magistrates should have no authority in the spiritual affairs of the church; (4) the local church is a gathered assembly, separate from the authority of parish assemblies. Browne himself has left a description of one of their typical church services:

> In that house where they intend to meet, there is one appointed to
> keepe the doore, for the intent, to give notice if there should be
> any insurrection, warning may be given them. They doe not flocke
> all together, but come 2 or 3 in a company, any man may be admit-
> ted thither, and all being gathered together, the man appointed to
> teach, stands in the midst of the Roome, and his audience gather
> about him. He prayeth about the space of halfe an houre, and part
> of his prayer is, that those which come thither to scoffe and laugh,
> God would be pleased to turne their hearts, by which meanes they
> thinke to escape undiscovered. His Sermon is about the space of
> an houre, and then doth another stand up to make the text more
> plaine, and at the latter end, he intreates them all to goe home sev-
> erally, least the next meeting they be interrupted by those which
> are of the opinion of the wicked, they seeme very stedfast in their
> opinions, and say rather [than] . . . turne, they will burne.[20]

Browne's writings differ with the Church of England in practical matters rather than doctrinal matters. His view of baptism always remained that of the Church of England. Browne, however, had been one of the earliest to espouse an essential congregationalism and independency for the local church. He was the first Englishman to express the doctrine of complete separation of church and state. In this regard, he went beyond the traditional Separatist view which the *Mayflower* Pilgrims would establish.

In the end, being "poor, proud, and unloved," Browne struck the parish constable who had come to collect taxes. Being decrepit, past eighty years of age, and unable to walk, Browne was carried on a feather bed, on a cart, to the Northampton jail, where he died in 1631. While few ever claimed the name "Brownist," Browne's writings would live on among those who claimed the labels "Independent" and "Separatist." Most Separatists, regardless of their estimation of Brown, would never escape the label "Brownist," which remained a synonym for "independent radical."

Origin of the Ancient Church

On October 8, 1587, John Greenwood and twenty-two other Separatists were arrested and thrown into the infamous Clink Prison for holding a private conventicle, meeting in Henry Martin's house in St. Andrews in the Wardrobe, near St. Paul's Churchyard. At least one of these had been a member of John Browne's church in Middelburg (Holland). Greenwood, a Norfolk minister, had attended Corpus Christi College at Cambridge and the Church of England had ordained him. The same church, however, had ousted him from his parish in 1585, making him a Separatist for his refusal to use the *Book of Common Prayer.*

On November 19, 1587,[21] while visiting Greenwood in the Clink, Henry Barrowe[22] was himself arrested, by order of Archbishop Whitgift. Barrowe was from Norfolk and had graduated from Clare College at Cambridge. While still unconverted and pursuing a life of depravity, he had studied law and had been admitted to membership at Gray's Inn, enjoying access to Queen Elizabeth's court. One Sunday, while passing a London church, Barrowe heard the voice of the preacher, stepped inside the church against the sneers of his wicked companions, and was converted to Christ. Immediately, he became a strict Puritan and the complete change that came upon him captured the attention of all who knew him. Drawn into the embrace of Separatism, Barrowe had visited the prison to consult with John Greenwood, only to be arrested. He was taken by boat to Lambeth Palace and interrogated. Barrowe's training in law enabled him to avoid sentencing without an official trial. Finally, he was taken back to the prison and incarcerated with Greenwood. For more than five years, Barrowe and

Greenwood would remain imprisoned—both in the Clink and in the nearby Fleet Prison, situated by the bank of the Fleet stream which enters the Thames near the site of present-day Blackfriars Bridge. While the Fleet Prison no longer stands, the little stream (now covered over) continues its course into the Thames.

From their prisons, Barrowe and Greenwood wrote numerous treatises, pamphlets, letters, and petitions which Separatists smuggled out, a few pages at a time, and sent to Holland for printing. From these writings, says Timothy George, "emerged the most comprehensive statement of Separatist principles set forth in the sixteenth century." George summarizes those principles into four propositions: (1) local church membership should consist only of those who have made a public profession of faith; (2) a "false and antichristian ministrie" has been imposed on the congregations; (3) the false manner of worship, i.e., using the *Book of Common Prayer,* should be forsaken; (4) local churches should have autonomy in the election of their own ministers. George observes that those four Separatist propositions answer to a false membership, a false ministry, a false worship, and a false government.[23]

The printed page indeed became a powerful tool for Separatists. In 1588-1589, an unknown source published seven satirical papers titled the "Marprelate Tracts," written under the pseudonym Martin Marprelate. In attacking episcopacy, the writer refers to the lord-bishops as "petty antichrists, petty popes, proud prelates, enemies to the Gospel, and most covetous wretched priests."[24] With such rhetoric, these tracts fanned the flames of Separatism. To this day no one knows who wrote them, but they spread rapidly all over England, creating a sensation.

In 1588 Francis Johnson (1562-1618),[25] a teaching fellow at Christ's College (Cambridge), preached a sermon from I Peter 5:1-4 favoring the Presbyterian system and was imprisoned for it. The following year, he was expelled after refusing to recant. He was then imprisoned a second time for failing to leave Cambridge quickly enough. Johnson was still a Puritan and not yet a Separatist; in fact he held Separatists in contempt. He traveled to Holland and visited Middelburg (Zeeland), where he accepted the position as chaplain to the English Puritan (Presbyterian) "Church of Merchant Adventurers."[26] In 1591 he learned that a book, written from London's Clink Prison by Henry Barrowe and John Greenwood, was being printed secretly in the Dutch city of Dort. Johnson consulted with the English ambassador and received authority to seize the copies and burn them. Johnson, however, saved two copies—one for a friend to examine and one for himself. He took a copy to his study and began to scrutinize it in order to refute it. The more he read of this *Plain Refutation,* the more he "met with something that began to work upon his spirit, which so wrought with him as drew him to this resolution, seriously to read over the whole book; the which he did once and again."[27] Its contents laid hold of him. Francis Johnson became a Separatist. Soon he would cross the sea and return to London, this time to seek out and confer with Barrowe and Greenwood. Johnson would join the group and become their pastor.[28]

In 1592-1593 an act was passed, titled "An Act for the Punishment of Persons Obstinately Refusing to Come to Church." This Act decreed that "all persons above the age of sixteen, refusing to come to church, or persuading others to deny her Majesty's authority in causes ecclesiastical, or dissuading them from coming to church, or being found present at any conventicle or meeting, under pretense of religion, shall, upon conviction, be committed to prison without bail till they shall conform, and come to church;" and that, should they refuse to recant, "within three months, they shall abjure the realm, and go into perpetual banishment; and that if they do not depart within the time appointed, or if they ever return without the queen's license, they shall suffer death without benefit of clergy." Under the provisions of this cruel act, many Separatists would suffer imprisonment and death.

During the imprisonment of Barrowe and Greenwood, the Welshman John Penry—Morning Star of the Reformation in Wales—joined their little secret church and served even as clerk. Converted and embracing Reformation doctrines, Penry (1559-1593)[29] had graduated from both Cambridge (1584) and Oxford (1586) and served eminently as a Puritan minister. By 1587 he had become a Separatist, pleading in both the spoken and printed word for preachers to take the gospel across Wales. Many had responded to his urgent appeals. Now, the secret church rejoiced at his words of encouragement, as they gathered in private homes to worship.

Francis Johnson, meanwhile, having been persuaded by reading the Separatist book which he had spared from the flames, returned from Holland and, in September 1592, joined the secret church as it gathered in the home of a Mr. Fox on St. Nicholas Lane. In that meeting they selected Johnson as their pastor, celebrated the baptism of seven people, and broke five white loaves for the Lord's Supper. Johnson was soon arrested, then shortly released. During the following weeks the church met in various London homes, at late hours, for safety's sake. John Greenwood, their teacher,[30] was still in prison; he was soon released, though not for long. On December 5, 1592, both Greenwood and Johnson were arrested and conveyed to prison, between one and two o'clock in the morning, for worshipping in the home of Edward Boyes, a haberdasher (retailer), in London's Ludgate Hill area. Boyes himself would suffer and die for the cause of Christ. A walk around Ludgate Hill can still take one back four hundred years. With little houses hugging closely to the ground and narrow lanes running to and fro, Ludgate Hill stands as an aged witness to secret cottage prayer meetings and sudden arrests, when nothing but perfect love could cast away terror. On Sunday, March 4, 1593, as the secret church was "hearing the Word of God truly taught, praying and praising God" in the fields and among the gravel pits of Islington, north of the River Thames, fifty-six of their people were arrested and marched to various prisons.[31]

The secret church then began holding many of its meetings on the south side of the River, in London's Southwark area. During this time, playwright William Shakespeare (1564-1616) lived in Southwark and walked among its familiar landscape of horses, carts and peddlers. Southwark's Globe Theatre (1599) heard his speeches and its Rose Theatre (1592), near Southwark Bridge, saw his first productions. Here in this area, the secret church made a desperate search for a place to worship God. But Southwark could offer no haven of safety or comfort to these Christians. From every direction, they could never escape the daily reminders of disappointment and impending danger. Just to the east of London Bridge stood St. Olave's School, whose headmaster from about 1586 to 1591 was Robert Browne, who had received this position upon his recantation of separatism and return to the Church of England. Close to the River Thames stood Clink Prison adjoining the palace of the wealthy Bishops of Winchester, the guardians of the prison. The palace complex was arranged around two courtyards with extensive gardens. On this site of some eighty acres, known as "The Liberty of the Clink," the bishops made the laws.

This was Southwark's red light district, with worldly amusements and numerous brothels, licensed by the bishop himself. From the twelfth century until its destruction in 1780, the Clink housed inmates ranging from prostitutes, to priests, to pilgrims. Although a warehouse building now occupies much of the site, one can still see remains of the bishops' palace. A portion of a hall has three doorways leading to a kitchen and domestic quarters, with a stone cellar below. A museum called the Clink Exhibition houses crude instruments of torture once used on the prisoners. For the secret church, there were simply no hiding places. On the twenty-second of March, John Penry was arrested and incarcerated in the Clink Prison. The worst was about to come. The next day, Old Bailey court announced a verdict of guilty and a sentence of execution upon John Greenwood and Henry Barrowe.[32]

Tyburn, the place of execution in west London, is memorialized today by a stone in the center of a traffic island at the point where Oxford Street becomes Baywater Road, a short distance from Marble Arch underground station. On April 6, 1593, John Greenwood and Henry Barrowe were brought to Tyburn on a cart and led to the scaffold—the triangular "Tyburn Tree"—some eleven feet high (and capable of dispatching eight victims at a time). From the Clink Prison, John Penry wrote an encouraging letter to Francis Johnson and to the others who were in prison. He addressed it "To the distressed and faithful Congregation of Christ in London, and all the Members thereof, whether in bonds or at liberty." He concludes by signing, "Their loving brother, in the patience and sufferings of the gospel, John Penry—a witness of Christ in this life, and a partaker of the glory that shall be revealed."[33] John Penry's wife, Eleanor, presented a moving petition to the prison keeper for access to her husband. He refused! On May 21, Penry's trial took place. He was transferred to the King's Bench Prison, in Borough High Street (Southwark),[34] to await sentence. In a letter, Penry wrote, "If my blood were an ocean sea, and every drop thereof were a life unto me, I would give them all, by the help of the Lord." On May 29, 1593, John Penry was hanged at St. Thomas a-Watering,[35] near the junction of present-day Albany Road and Old Kent Road in Southwark.[36] He left a young widow and four daughters, the oldest only four years of age.

On a wall at the end of Clink Street a plaque offers this stark reminder:

> Near this site stood
> **THE CLINK PRISON**
> Prisoners for their religion in the
> 16th century in this and other Southwark
> prisons included HENRY BARROWE
> JOHN GREENWOOD JOHN PENRY
> They all three suffered martyrdom in
> 1593. John Penry was imprisoned in the
> King's Bench Prison Southwark, and
> hanged at St. Thomas a watering,
> Old Kent Road
> They were founders of an independent
> Church in Southwark and precursors of
> the movement which led to the
> emigration of the Pilgrim Fathers.

A few days before his walk to the gibbet, Penry had sent a farewell letter to his beloved secret church, advising them to keep together and to go into exile abroad. The secret church of London was soon to become the Ancient Church of Amsterdam. It would be regarded as the "Ancient Church" because it was the earliest of the English Separatist groups to settle in Amsterdam. Postal express riders stopping by Scrooby Manor would soon carry the news of London's latest martyrdom to John Penry's old Cambridge classmate, William Brewster. In another fifteen years, the *Mayflower* Pilgrims would be worshipping with fellow English exile, Francis Johnson, in the Ancient Church of Amsterdam. With religious dissenters in England finding their situation increasingly difficult at the end of Elizabeth's reign, hundreds would flee to Holland from all over England in the years following the turn of the century. Between 1598 and 1617, exiles from twenty-nine English counties and Wales had stopped for spiritual refreshment at the Ancient Church, which grew to a membership of over three hundred.[37]

THE MILLENARY PETITION, THE KING JAMES BIBLE, AND THE ECCLESIASTICAL CONSTITUTIONS AND CANONS

When Elizabeth died on the last day of 1602,[38] the kingdom which she left—so poor and defenseless at the beginning of her reign—had in forty-five years become a rich and mighty realm, the beginning of a vast empire. But Elizabeth left no heir, and the throne of England passed from the Tudors to the Stuarts. James VI of Scotland succeeded her, reigning as James I of England. The Puritans hoped that from him they would receive milder treatment. Archbishop Whitgift, however, had already sent agents to Scotland to assure the king of the loyalty of the Church of England and her bishops; in return, he gave them his complete support. On April 4, 1603, as James was on his way to London, the Puritans presented to him their "Millenary Petition,"[39] unsigned, but expressing the wishes of hundreds of concerned clergymen who desired a true Reformation in the Church of England. In it they set forth in moderate language their desires, including the following amendments to the liturgy:

- that the requirement of the signing of the cross in baptism be discontinued;
- that the requirement of wearing the cap and surplice be discontinued;
- that an examination precede, and a sermon accompany, the communion;
- that certain terms, such as "priest" and "absolution," be discontinued;
- that the Lord's Day be kept, but holiday ceremonies less insisted on;
- that no popish opinion be taught or defended;
- that the reading of the Apocrypha be not required;
- that no ministers be authorized except scripturally qualified men;
- that those in the ministry, who are unable to preach, be charitably removed;
- that beneficed men be restrained from holding additional benefices;
- that non-residence be forbidden;
- that the lawfulness of ministers' marriages be recognized;
- that bishops who hold prebends, parsonages or vicarages, in addition to their bishoprics, relinquish them; and
- that church discipline be administered strictly according to the law of Christ.

There was nothing extreme in the petitions. A fair opportunity was now presenting itself for conciliation. A conference was set, which assembled at Hampton Court Palace,[40] January 14, 16, and 18, 1604, professedly to give due consideration to these matters. James, however, was in no mood for compromise. He could never forgive, for instance, the Puritan notes printed in their Geneva Bible (1560)—especially popular among Scottish Presbyterians. Regarding these marginal notes as "seditious, dangerous and traitorous," James must have hated the one at Exodus 11:19, which depicts the midwives' disobedience to Pharaoh as "lawful." Contrary to James' doctrine of the "divine right of kings" is the note at II Chronicles 15:16, where Asa deposes his wicked mother, Queen Maachah, for her idolatry. The Geneva note says, "Herein [Asa] showed that he lacked zeal: for she ought to have died . . . but he gave place to foolish pity." This sharply offended James, whose own mother was Mary Queen of Scots, whom the fiery John Knox had more than once exhorted and rebuked. James, who for thirty-seven years had been James VI of Scotland, had come to detest any form of representative church government. "I could never yet see a Bible well translated in English; but I think that, of all, that of Geneva is the worst," said King James. Perhaps James had seen such Geneva Bible notes as the one at Revelation 9:3, identifying the locusts which come out of the bottomless pit as "heretics, false teachers, worldly, subtle prelates with monks, friars, cardinals, patriarchs, archbishops, bishops, doctors, bachelors, and masters." James, on the other hand, had acquired a favorite saying, "No bishop, no king!"

Such was the atmosphere at the three-day Hampton Court Conference of January 1604.[41] James had summoned the Archbishop of Canterbury (Whitgift), eight bishops, seven deans, one archdeacon, and a royal chaplain. To represent the Puritans, he had invited only four men. On Saturday the fourteenth, the king, the archbishop, the eight bishops, and four of the deans met alone in the Privy Chamber to discuss the format of the meeting, while the four Puritans and the others waited outside on a bench. James said to his audience that he had lived among Puritans since he was ten years old and that he detested their ways. On Monday the sixteenth, the four Puritan ministers, including the distinguished Dr. John Rainolds (Reynolds)—learned president of Corpus Christi College at Oxford—were called into the Privy Chamber, where the Puritans expressed their concerns under four headings:

purity of doctrine, the ministry, reform of church polity, and changes in the *Book of Common Prayer*. As the Puritans tried to speak, bishops, deans and doctors sneered at them, even for coming before the king "in *Turky gounes, not in their Scholastical habites, suiting to their degrees.*"[42]

During the discussion of polity, the unfortunate use of the word "presbytery" threw James into a rage. He quickly informed the Puritans that a presbytery "as well agreeth with a monarchy as God with the Devil. Then Jack and Tom and Will and Dick shall meet, and at their pleasure censure me and my council, and all our proceedings; then Will shall stand up and say, it must be thus; then Dick shall reply and say, nay . . . but we will have it thus." James then entreated the Puritans not to bring the matter up again for seven years, "and if then you find me pursy and fat and my windpipes stuffed, I will perhaps hearken to you."[43] With that, he broke up the conference for the day. As he was departing, he was heard to mutter, " If this be all they have to say, I shall make them conform, or I will harry [ravage & pillage] them out of the land, or else do worse." All chances of conciliation with the Puritans were gone. On the last day, Wednesday the eighteenth, as the king and the bishops conferred alone, the archbishop of Canterbury replied that he was fully persuaded "that undoubtedly his Majesty spake by the special assistance of God's Spirit." Bishop Richard Bancroft of London fell upon his knees before the king and praised him exceedingly, saying that his "heart melted within" him at the words of such a wise king. His reward would soon come; James appointed him the next Archbishop of Canterbury! The king ended the Hampton Court Conference with an exhortation for obedience and humility from the Puritans. In a letter apparently written the next day, James boasted to a friend that for two days he had "soundly peppered" the Puritans, reducing their scholarship to that of "poore school boyes."[44]

The positive good that came from the conference was the King James Bible. Dr. Reynolds "moved his Majestie, that there might bee a newe translation of the Bible." The king would appoint fifty-four learned men to translate the Bible into English. When the work formally began in 1607, the number of translators actually engaged in the work was about forty-seven, and of these several died before the work's completion. The translators were divided into three groups—Westminster Abbey, Oxford University, and Cambridge University. In the Jerusalem Chamber, the

Westminster group completed Genesis through Second Kings, plus Romans through Jude. The Cambridge group completed First Chronicles through Song of Solomon, plus the entire Apocrypha. The Oxford group completed Isaiah through Acts, plus Revelation. The result was the King James Version of 1611. Separatists, as well as many Puritans, would generally not pay much attention to the king's Bible so long as they could still purchase their beloved Geneva Bibles, which would remain the household English Bible until the 1650's. Some of the Puritan translators themselves, such as Francis Dillingham, continued to use and to quote from the Geneva Bible many years after the King James Version had been published.[45] Ironically, in his endeavor to replace the Geneva Bible because of its hard-hitting notes, the king whom the French called "the wisest fool in Christendom" authorized an unannotated Bible which would encourage independent thought for centuries.

This was an age marked by religious pluralism, non-residence, nepotism and simony. When Puritans and Separatists cried out against such practices, they found that Bishop Richard Bancroft was obsessed with the thought of breaking their backs. In the spring of 1604, the *Ecclesiastical Constitutions and Canons,* edited by Bancroft, were issued in Convocation (presided over by Bancroft), on the strength of Royal Supremacy alone, without Parliamentary consent. These canons, among other things, required the wearing of ministerial surplices, the observance of prescribed religious days, and strict conformity to the *Book of Common Prayer* in worship. The formation of secret conventicles (church meetings) was forbidden as a high crime. The Court of High Commission, authorized by the Act of Supremacy, became the instrument used to enforce such conformity. Archbishop Whitgift was now dead and Bancroft would soon become his successor, surpassing even Whitgift in his severities. Three hundred nonconformist Puritan ministers, in 1604, were silenced, imprisoned, or exiled. The following year, seventeen Nottinghamshire men and women were cited to appear in court for going to Sturton-le-Steeple to hear John Robinson preach. But as William Bradford observed, "the more they afflicted them, the more they multiplied and grew." These persecuted pastors and people would now begin thinking of emigrating to Holland. Concerned Separatist clergymen in the Diocese of Lincoln,[46] in 1605, wrote an *Apology,*[47] setting forth clear and bold reasons for their inability, in good conscience, to obey the 1604 *Ecclesiastical Constitutions and Canons* or to conduct their worship in complete conformity to *The Book of Common Prayer*. The document is important because it constitutes the Separatists' essential grievances—the reasons that the Pilgrims no longer had any choice except to leave the country. The following are concerned with the official *Book of Common Prayer:*

1. Its lectionary (Scripture readings) omits the greater part of the canonical Scriptures, and gives too much honor to the Apocrypha;

2. Its renderings of some Scripture passages are "absurd and senseless;"

3. It contains corrupt popish errors and "humane ceremonies of misticall signification," which are "idolatrous;"

4. It requires the use of the surplice;

5. It requires the use of the sign of the cross in baptism;

6. It requires kneeling at communion, a carry-over from the Roman Catholic practice of kneeling at the adoration of the host at Mass, drawn from the doctrine of transubstantiation;

7. It "appointeth a liturgy which in the whole matter and form thereof is too like unto the Mass-book;"

8. It is also too long and leaves no time for preaching; it sanctions a ministry which lacks the ability to preach;

9. It contains many popish errors, such as calling the minister the priest, commending the observation of holy days and fast days, such as Lent, calling the Friday before Easter Good Friday, and stipulating that each parishioner shall receive communion at Easter;

10. It elevates confirmation by saying that only a bishop can administer it;

11. It makes the marrying and burying of parishioners a ministerial duty, which has no sanction in Scripture; such requirements are carry-overs of the Roman Catholic "sacraments" of matrimony and "last rites;"

12. It advocates confession before a priest, and even absolution, to those troubled in conscience;

13. Its insistence in repeating prayers after the minister, standing for some prayers and kneeling for others, tends to create disorder and confusion; at one service, the Lord's Prayer is repeated eight times and the Gloria Patri twelve times;

14. It perverts Scripture in establishing the orders of bishops, priests and deacons, and it invents such non-biblical offices as those of archdeacons and archbishops.

15. It deprives the local church of the right of giving its consent to the appointment of its ministers;

16. It assumes that magistrates have the divine authority to inflict their decisions on the churches; to the contrary, only what God commands should be obeyed.

ENGLISH PURITANISM AND PRESBYTERIANISM AFTER THE SEPARATISTS' DEPARTURE

In 1660 the Pilgrims had spent twelve years in Holland and forty years in the New World. During those years, great doctrinal transition came over England's established clergy. The England that the Pilgrims left suffered unspeakable turmoil. During the reign of James I, increasing numbers of clergymen began to embrace a semi-Pelagianism of the Roman Catholic type. Emphasizing the abilities of man, it appealed to the moral corruption that had been sweeping the kingdom. The situation only worsened when James died in 1625 and was succeeded by Charles I, who married a French Roman Catholic. Under Charles, the unjust and inhuman proceedings of the Council Table, the Star Chamber, and the High Commission were unparalleled. William Laud, succeeding George Abbot, became archbishop of Canterbury in 1633. During the next seven years the Puritans felt the full force of Laud's fiery zeal, as multitudes of them, ministers and laymen, were driven to Holland and America. As special executive to the king, Laud wielded unbelievable power, driving nonconformists from one diocese to another and even attempting to enforce ritualism on the Presbyterians of Scotland. He instigated exceeding and unmerciful severities, harassing and persecuting Puritans in every corner of the land. Laud put down the Puritan lecturers and suspended anyone who preached against semi-Pelagianism and popish ceremonies. In 1640 the Convocation adopted new Constitutions and Canons, in keeping with Laudian practice and theology. That year, however, ongoing financial crises caused Charles I to convene the Long Parliament. This Parliament, strongly Presbyterian and Puritan in sympathy and conviction, condemned Laud's "superstitious and tyrannical Constitutions and Canons" as "contrary to the fundamental laws of the realm and to the liberty and property of the subject, and as containing things tending to sedition and dangerous consequence." The nation was finally ready to overthrow unmitigated political and ecclesiastical tyranny. Those who were suffering from the arbitrary rule of the king joined with those who were groaning under the despotism of the bishops. In a vast effort, they would overthrow both absolute monarchy and "Anglican popery." On December 18, 1640, the House of Commons impeached Archbishop Laud of treason, and placed him in confinement. The following March, he was sent to the Tower. Three years later, William Laud was beheaded at Tower Hill. A new era had commenced.

"The Age of Puritanism," properly so-called, had ended. After 1644, during England's Civil War (1642-1648),[48] some Puritans were fighting for their king; others were joining with the armies of Oliver Cromwell; and still others were aligning themselves with Presbyterian ranks against Cromwell. The Civil War witnessed the alliance of Parliament with the Scottish army, the adoption of the Solemn League and Covenant, the Westminster Assembly in London, and ended with Oliver Cromwell's Independent army defeating the forces of Charles I and beheading the king. During those years, Puritanism dispersed as a movement. Since 1644, there has not existed in England a body or organized group of people properly called by the name "Puritan." At that time, the Puritans were branching into two major parties, Independents and Presbyterians. The Puritans in New England would manage to keep the movement recognizable there until the end of the 1680's at the latest.

The Protectorate Government, or Interregnum, of Oliver Cromwell and his son, Richard (1649-1660) sent the loyal supporters of the Crown, the "Cavaliers," fleeing to Virginia. Oliver Cromwell died in 1658 and the following year Richard Cromwell was forced to abdicate, as England witnessed the Restoration of the Stuarts, with the ascension of Charles II (1660-1685). At the beginning of the Stuart Restoration, Plymouth Colony was grieving the loss of Governor William Bradford, who died in 1657, having finally put down the pen which had chronicled the intriguing story *Of Plymouth Plantation 1620-1647*. In England, at the Restoration, a Baptist preacher named John Bunyan spent twelve years in a Bedford jail and wrote *Pilgrim's Progress,* as persecution resumed and the great migration of Puritans fled to New England. During the reign of Charles II, the headmaster of a boarding school in Southampton,

25

England, was imprisoned for his devout nonconformist life and views. His wife sat praying on a stone by the prison door, with her infant son at her breast. That boy was Isaac Watts (1674-1748),[49] theologian and hymn writer. Born two years after John Bunyan's release from the Bedford jail, Isaac began studying Latin at the age of four and soon after that began learning Greek and Hebrew. He was educated at an academy for Dissenters in London. After some years as tutor, preacher, and assistant pastor, he became minister of a Dissenting church in London in 1702. His writings, consisting of a wide range of topics, are so numerous that some editions have been up to nine volumes. Watts is best remembered for such works as his *Horae Lyricae* (1706), a collection of religious poems, and his two hymn collections, *Hymns* (1707) and *The Psalms of David* (1719). Among his hymns most loved and sung today are "When I Survey the Wondrous Cross" and "O God, Our Help in Ages Past." Buried in London's Bunhill Fields and memorialized in Westminster Abbey, Isaac Watts is remembered also by his statue, erected in his hometown of Southampton, England, the first city of the *Mayflower's* departure.

The second city of her departure, Dartmouth, is likewise rich in nonconformist history, beginning with the days of Charles II. At the beginning of the Restoration, John Flavel (1630?-1691),[50] nonconformist minister at Dartmouth, was ejected from his church, compelled to move five miles outside the city, and forbidden to preach to his flock. Some of his people met him in woods and thickets to hear his sermons, sometimes interrupted by soldiers. Flavel's own father had died in prison for his nonconformist stance. John was allowed to return to Dartmouth. Not long after preaching his last sermon at Dartmouth, Flavel presided as moderator of the assembly of nonconformist ministers of Devonshire which met at Exeter to unite the Presbyterians and Independents. Having delivered his sermon of praise, which was to be his "dying song," Flavel was stricken with paralysis after supper that same night. His last words were, "I know that it will be well with me." His body was buried in the Dartmouth church. The *Whole Works* of John Flavel were published in London in six volumes in 1820 and are treasured to this day for their deeply spiritual content. Puritanism lives on in such works as these. While theological controversy would disrupt the union, nonconformists would now find some rest from outward persecution. There had been recorded between 1660 and 1688 sixty thousand nonconformists and dissenters who had suffered incarceration in English prisons. More than five thousand of these had died of privation and disease.[51] Following the "Glorious Revolution" of 1688, which deposed James II and brought William and Mary to the throne, times were changing in uniquely different ways on both sides of the Atlantic, with nonconformist worship now legalized in England and Plymouth Colony now merged into the larger Massachusetts Bay Colony (1691). By then, Puritanism as a distinct movement would be a thing of the past, even in New England.

1. Among the numerous works on Wyclif, the best include Lewis Sergeant, *John Wyclif: Last of the Schoolmen and First of the English Reformers* (NY: G. P. Putnam's Sons, 1893); and G. H. W. Parker, *The Morning Star: Wycliffe and the Dawn of The Reformation* (Exeter, England: The Paternoster Press, 1965).

2. For further reading on the history of the English Bible, one might consult Christopher Anderson, *The Annals of the English Bible* (London: Jackson, Walford, and Hodder, 1862); F. F. Bruce, *History of the English Bible* (NY: Oxford University Press, 1978); Charles C. Butterworth, *The Literary Lineage of the King James Bible 1340-1611* (Philadelphia: University of Pennsylvania Press, 1941); Ira Maurice Price, *The Ancestry of Our English Bible* (NY: Harper & Brothers, 1956); Brooke F. Westcott, *A General View of the History of the English Bible* (NY: The Macmillan Co., 1916); and David Beale, *A Pictorial History of Our English Bible* (Greenville, SC: Bob Jones University, 1982).

3. Among the many works on Tyndale, the best include J. F. Mozley, *William Tyndale* (London: Society for Promoting Christian Knowledge, 1937); R. Demaus, *William Tyndale*, revised edition by Richard Lovett, (London: The Religious Tract Society, 1886); and Brian Edwards, *God's Outlaw* (Darlington, Co. Durham, England: Evangelical Press, 1976).

4. John Rogers published the Matthew Bible in 1537 under the pseudonym, "Thomas Matthew." It was largely William Tyndale's translation, but Tyndale's name was in such disfavor with the king that no publisher would use it. The same king whose eyes Tyndale had tried to pray open now licensed the Matthew Bible, without even knowing that this was Tyndale's own work.

5. For example the Six Articles of 1539, which replaced the Ten Articles of 1536, was a "Whip with the Six Strings," sanctioning transubstantiation, oral confession, private masses, monastic vows, celibacy of the clergy, and withholding the cup from the laity.

6. At Pilgrim Hall Museum, in Plymouth, MA, is the Geneva Bible which belonged to Governor William Bradford.

7. A good discussion of the rise of Separatism during Elizabeth's reign is B. R. White, *The English Separatist Tradition: From the Marian Martyrs to the Pilgrim Fathers* (London: Oxford University Press, Ely House, 1971), 20-43.

8. The Thirty-nine Articles were a revision of Edward's Forty-two Articles. Four articles were added to the Forty-two Articles and seven were subtracted, making a total of thirty-nine; seventeen others were modified. The tenth, sixteenth, nineteenth, thirty-ninth, fortieth, forty-first, and forty-second articles were omitted. Articles five, twelve, twenty-nine, and thirty of the Thirty-nine Articles were added. To see the Forty-two Articles, consult Charles Hardwick, *A History of the Articles of Religion* (Cambridge: Cambridge University Press, 1859), 277ff.; for the Thirty-nine Articles, see Philip Schaff, *The Creeds of Christendom, with a History and Critical Notes* (NY: Harper & Brothers 1877), III:486-516.

9. The word "advertisement" meant "a public warning, or solemn proclamation."

10. A. H. Drysdale, *History of the Presbyterians in England: Their Rise, Decline, and Revival* (London: Publication Committee of the Presbyterian Church of England, 1889), 111.

11. As *Mourt's Relation* records, "The Separatist was a Puritan, but the Puritan was not necessarily a Separatist." See G. Mourt (Edward Winslow and William Bradford), *Mourt's Relation: A Journal of the Pilgrims at Plymouth*, ed. Dwight B. Heath (1622; rpt. Bedford, MA: Applewood Books, 1986), 468.

12. The document of the inquisition of the Plumbers' Hall Separatists was originally published as part of a Puritan anthology called *A parte of a register* (1593); it appears in H. C. Porter, ed., *Puritanism in Tudor England* (Columbia, SC: University of South Carolina, 1971), 80-94.

13. For a good evaluation and study of the value of Foxe's writings, along with a discussion of their impact during Foxe's own century, see William Haller, *The Elect Nation: The Meaning and Relevance of Foxe's Book of Martyrs* (NY: Harper & Row, 1963), 118-24 and *passim*.

14. Champlin Burrage, *The Early English Dissenters in the Light of Recent Research* (1550-1641) (Cambridge: Cambridge University Press, 1912), I:80f. Fitz and some others separated from the Plumbers Hall group. Burrage also includes the confession of faith written and agreed upon by Fitz's Separatist congregation (II:9-15).

15. Good sources on Thomas Cartwright include A. F. Scott Pearson, *Thomas Cartwright and Elizabethan Puritanism 1535-1603* (1925; rpt. Gloucester, MA: Peter Smith, 1966); Benjamin Brook, *The Lives of the Puritans* (Pittsburgh, PA: Soli Deo Gloria, 1994), II:136-61; Daniel Neal, *The History of the Puritans, or Protestant Nonconformists; from the Reformation in 1517, to the Revolution in 1688*, 2 vols. (NY: Harper & Brothers, 1843-44), *passim;* Drysdale, *History of the Presbyterians in England,* 111ff.; and Sir Leslie Stephen and Sir Sidney Lee, ed., *The Dictionary of National Biography* (1917; rpt. London: Oxford University Press, 1921-22), III:1135-39.

16. "Governor Bradford's Letter Book," *The Mayflower Descendant 7*, no. 2 (April 1905): 81 (34 vols., compiled and published by George Ernest Bowman, from 1899 to 1937, Massachusetts Society of Mayflower Descendants), on "Mayflower Legacy," 43-vol. searchable CD edition, Wheat Ridge, CO: Search & Research Publishing Corporation, 1998, containing *The Mayflower Descendant With Other New England Town Records.* Perhaps the best source is Nathaniel Morton, *New England's Memorial* (1669; rpt. Boston: Congregational Board of Publications, 1855), 425-27. Morton shows that prophesying was practiced by the churches of John Knox, John Calvin, and the Puritans of both England and New England.

17. There is an excellent discussion of this and other literature of the conflict in Henry Martyn Dexter and Morton Dexter, *The England and Holland of the Pilgrims* (1906; rpt. Baltimore: Genealogical Publishing Co., Inc., 1978), 126ff.

18. Ibid., 129ff.

19. The best sources on Robert Browne include Henry Martyn Dexter, *The Congregationalism of the Last Three Hundred Years as Seen in Its Literature* (NY: Harper and Brothers, 1880), 61-128; B. R. White, *The English Separatist Tradition: From the Marian Martyrs to the Pilgrim Fathers* (London: Oxford University Press, Ely House, 1971), 44-66; Champlin Burrage, *The Early English Dissenters in the Light of Recent Research* (1550-1641), I:94-117; *The Dictionary of National Biography,* III:57-61; Henry Martyn Dexter and Morton Dexter, *The England and Holland of the Pilgrims,* 188-212; and Williston Walker, *The Creeds and Platforms of Congregationalism* (Boston: The Pilgrim Press, 1960), 8-27; Walker includes extracts from Browne's writings and gives a good bibliography of other sources. For a closer investigation of Browne, see Albert Peel and Leland H. Carlson, ed., *The Writings of Robert Harrison and Robert Browne* (London: Allen and Unwin, 1953). Harrison was a colleague of Browne and teacher in Browne's church. Harrison assumed the leadership of the church in Middelburg when Browne left them.

20. Robert Browne, *Book which sheweth the life and manners of all true Christians* (Middelburg, 1582); cited in Horton Davies, *Worship and Theology in England I. From Cranmer to Hooker, 1534-1603 II. From Andrewes to Baxter and Fox, 1603-1690.* 2 vols., 1970, 1975; rpt. Grand Rapids, MI: William B. Eerdmans Publishing Co., 1996 combined edition), I:336.

21. Some sources use the date October 8, 1586 for Greenwood's imprisonment and November 19, 1586 for Barrowe's imprisonment. The year 1587, however, is well-established as correct; see Champlin Burrage, I:128f.

22. The best sources on Henry Barrowe and John Greenwood include Champlin Burrage, *The Early English Dissenters,* I:118f., II:27-61, 97-145; Henry Martyn Dexter, *The Congregationalism of the Last Three Hundred Years, as Seen in Its Literature* (NY: Harper & Brothers, Publishers, 1880), 205-252; and Leland H. Carlson, ed., *The Writings of Henry Barrow: 1587-1590* (London: George Allen & Unwin Ltd., 1962); see also the excellent articles in *The Dictionary of National Biography,* I:1217-18; VIII:527-28.

23. Timothy George, *John Robinson and the English Separatist Tradition* (Macon, GA: Mercer University Press, 1982), 48-53; see also his entire discussion on pp. 9-56.

24. Daniel Neal, *The History of the Puritans,* I:189.

25. The best sources on Francis Johnson include Champlin Burrage, *The Early English Dissenters,* I:136-82, II:134-45; Henry Martyn Dexter, *The Congregationalism of the Last Three Hundred Years,* 263f. and *passim;* Benjamin Brook, *The Lives of the Puritans,* II:89-106; and B. R. White, *The English Separatist Tradition: From the Marian Martyrs to the Pilgrim Fathers* (London: Oxford University Press, Ely House, 1971), 91-115.

26. The Church of Merchant Adventurers had been established about 1575 at Antwerp, then moved to Middelburg in 1583. Thomas Cartwright had been minister of this church (1580-85). Henry Jacob, an Independent, would also minister to these merchants briefly in 1599.

27. William Bradford, *A Dialogue, or the Sum of a Conference Between Some Young Men Born in New England and Sundry Ancient Men that Came Out of Holland and Old England* [Dialogue held in] Anno Domini 1648, published in its entirety in Alexander Young, ed., *Chronicles of the Pilgrim Fathers of the Colony of Plymouth, from 1602 to 1625* (1844; rpt. Baltimore: Genealogical Publishing Co., Inc., 1974), 425.

28. John Brown, *The Pilgrim Fathers of New England and Their Puritan Successors* (London: The Religious Tract Society, 1897), 112-13. Brown and some others point out that Johnson so deeply regretted his former suppression of the books that fourteen years later, in 1605, he personally financed the printing of another edition.

29. The best source on John Penry is William Pierce, *John Penry: His Life, Times and Writings* (London: Hodder and Stoughton, 1923); also valuable are Henry Martyn Dexter, *The Congregationalism of the Last Three Hundred Years,* 246-52; *The Dictionary of National Biography,* XV:791-95; Champlin Burrage, *The Early English Dissenters,* II:62-96; Benjamin Brook, *The Lives of the Puritans,* II:48-68; and Daniel Neal, *The History of the Puritans,* I:356f. There is an excellent discussion of Penry's written works in Donald J. McGinn, *John Penry and the Marprelate Controversy* (New Brunswick, NJ: Rutgers University Press, 1966).

30. In addition to having a pastor and a teacher, the secret church had elders and deacons; see Henry Martyn Dexter, *The Congregationalism of the Last Three Hundred Years,* 232, 259f.

31. Ibid., 266; John Brown gives June 1592 as the time of this arrest, but this seems to be a mistake. Major sources seem to be unanimous in agreement on the March 1593 date.

32. For more details, see John Brown, 37-38, 108, 111.

33. Cited in Benjamin Brook, *The Lives of the Puritans,* II:55.

34. Two and a half centuries later, a similar prison, Marshalsea, also in the Southwark district, won immortality through the writings of Charles Dickens, whose father was an inmate here for debt. Nathaniel Morton, nephew of William Bradford, says that John Smyth was in Marshalsea at the time Penry was in the Clink. See Nathaniel Morton, *New England's Memorial* (1669; rpt. Boston: Congregational Board of Publications, 1855), 446.

35. Named for Thomas à Becket, the place had a refreshing stream where the pilgrims of *Canterbury Tales* watered their horses, as they were leaving the Tabard Inn during their journey to the shrine of Thomas à Becket. Chaucer refers to it as the "watering-place of Saint Thomas." Sometimes it was spelled "Waterings."

36. In April 1593 Parliament passed a statute titled "An Act to retain the Queen's subjects in their due obedience." Greenwood, Barrowe and Penry were being used as examples to show dissenters what could happen to anyone who dared disobey the queen for any reason whatsoever.

37. B. R. White, *The English Separatist Tradition: From the Marian Martyrs to the Pilgrim Fathers* (London: Oxford University Press, Ely House, 1971), 114.

38. Elizabeth died on March 24, 1602 (O.S.), which was the last day of the year according to the Julian Calendar. She died on April 3, 1602 (N.S.).

39. The Puritans had originally hoped for a thousand signatures on the Petition but, realizing that they would probably get no more than 750, they decided to omit the signatures altogether. The name "Millenary" Petition became permanent, however. Indeed, a few men wrote promotional material appealing for support of the Petition. Henry Jacob, for example, wrote a treatise of *Reasons taken out of Gods Word and the best humane Testimonies proving a necessitie of reforming our Churches in England* (1603-4). As late as 1618, there was still lively discussion everywhere on the issues raised by the Petition. William Brewster printed in Leiden *A True, Modest and Just Defence of The Petition for Reformation, Exhibited to The King's Most Excellent Maiestie. Containing An Answere to the Confutation published under the names of some of the Universitie of Oxford etc.* Imprinted 1618. "The Epistle Dedicatory" of this treatise clearly states that no copies of the Petition had been sent out for signatures. An original copy of this printing is in the British Museum.

40. Located near Kingston Upon Thames and little more than ten miles SW of the city of London, Hampton Court Palace was the favorite country residence of Henry VIII (who played tennis here). Five of his wives also lived here! A walk through the palace's rooms and gardens offers a unique taste of nearly five hundred years of history.

41. A day-to-day account of the Hampton Court Conference can be found in Thomas Prince, *Chronological History of New England in the Form of Annals* (Boston: Nathan Hale, ed., 1826), 104ff. For the present study, the edition most often used was a 1736 edition, published in Boston by Kneeland. The first 104 pages are introduction, followed by Part I, which begins new pagination; the Hampton Court Conference begins in Part I, page 8.

42. To his credit, this was the one remark that actually brought a rebuke from James to the bishop who uttered it.

43. J. R. Tanner, ed., *Constitutional Documents of the Reign of James I A.D. 1603-1625 with an Historical Commentary.* (Cambridge: Cambridge University Press, 1930), 67. Two years later, James summoned a group of Presbyterian ministers from Scotland to Hampton Court and ordered them to listen to four English prelates preach to them on the subject of the superiority of bishops over presbyters. The sermons were published as *The Hampton Court Sermons* (1606). There are no records showing that any of the Presbyterian preachers suffered any conviction and repented from such discourses!

44. Cited in Henry Martyn Dexter and Morton Dexter, *The England and Holland of the Pilgrims* (1906; rpt. Baltimore: Genealogical Publishing Co., Inc., 1978), 344.

45. Christopher Anderson, *The Annals of the English Bible* (London: Jackson, Walford, and Hodder, 1862), 478.

46. John Smyth, who was already in Gainsborough, had been deposed from his position as lecturer in Lincoln, because of his "dangerous preaching."

47. *An Abridgement of that Booke which the Ministers off the Lincoln Diocese Delivered to his Maiestie upon the 1st December 1605. Being the First Part of an Apologie for Themselves and Their Brethren That Refuse the Subscription and Conformitie which is required,* cited in Harold Kirk-Smith, *William Brewster 'The Father of New England'—His Life and Times— 1567-1644* (Boston, England: Richard Kay, 1992), 61-63.

48. For excellent background material on this period, see William Maxwell Hetherington, *History of the Westminster Assembly of Divines* (1856; rpt. Edmonton, Canada: Still Waters Revival Books, 1993); and Alexander F. Mitchell, *The Westminster Assembly: Its History and Standards* (1883; rpt. Edmonton, Canada: Still Waters Revival Books, 1992).

49. See Isaac Watts, *The Works of the Reverend and Learned Isaac Watts* (NY: AMS Press, 1971); this includes his sermons and essays, as well as "Memoirs of the Life of the Author," compiled by George Burder; see also David G. Fountain, *Isaac Watts Remembered* (Worthing: Henry E. Walter Ltd., 1974); and Arthur Paul Davis, *Isaac Watts: His Life and Works* (London: Independent Press, Ltd., 1948).

50. John Flavel, *The Works of John Flavel* (London: Banner of Truth Trust, 1968); see also http://www.puritansermons.com/toc.htm

51. John A. Goodwin, *The Pilgrim Republic: An Historical Review of the Colony of New Plymouth With Sketches of the Rise of Other New England Settlements, the History of Congregationalism and the Creeds of the Period* (Boston: Houghton Mifflin Company, 1920), 12.

CHAPTER 2

THE GATHERING OF THE SCROOBY SEPARATISTS

The story begins in the English Midlands, where the counties of Nottinghamshire, Yorkshire, and Lincolnshire meet. Here lie the four East Anglia towns of Babworth, Gainsborough, Austerfield, and Scrooby—all within what residents of the area still call the "Holy Triangle" of *Mayflower* Separatist origins. An imaginary line connecting these towns on a map would form a fair triangle. This is the true starting point of one of the greatest adventures of heroism, religious conviction, and heart-breaking struggle that has ever been told.

BABWORTH

Near the A620 and B6420 junction, Babworth's All Saints' Parish Church (built in 1290) nestles at the end of a beautiful tree-lined bridlepath behind the cottage post office. Here in this church, the Pilgrim movement originated under the teaching of its rector, Richard Clyfton (d.1616), a Christ's College, Cambridge, graduate who was appointed minister here in 1586. It was here that Clyfton the Puritan gradually became Clyfton the Separatist. His preaching soon began to stir many souls in pursuit of purity. William Bradford, who as a teenage orphan from Austerfield had often walked some nine miles to hear him preach, describes Clyfton as "a grave and reverend preacher, who by his pains and diligence had done much good, and under God had been the means of the conversion of many."[1] William Brewster from Scrooby often attended his services with much pleasure. After a nineteen-year ministry at Babworth Church, Clyfton was ejected in 1604, immediately following the famous

Hampton Court Conference, where King James I demanded that all dissenters conform to the Church of England. Some three hundred preachers were removed from their churches for failure to conform. Richard Clyfton, with his wife Ann and their three sons, moved up to Scrooby, six or seven miles away, to live at the Manor House with William and Mary Brewster and their five children, and to become pastor to the Separatists. He would become one of the most effective authors for the Pilgrim Separatists.[2] Clyfton remained with the Pilgrims all the way to Amsterdam, but did not join them in Leiden. He died in 1616 and was buried in Amsterdam's *Zuiderkerk* (South Church). A wicket gate near the south door of the Babworth Church leads through the grove to the Old Rectory where Pastor Clyfton, "a grave and fatherly old man . . . having a Great white beard,"[3] instructed his family and students. One can still tread the ancient path, "the Pilgrim Way," which meanders past Babworth Church. It is the same path taken by Bradford, Brewster, and others as they traveled to Babworth to hear Richard Clyfton's Bible preaching. Of special interest inside the Babworth church is the silver communion chalice which Clyfton used and which William Brewster saw in many of the services. Noteworthy too is the baptismal font, whose cover is made from the same timber used in the construction of *Mayflower II* in Plymouth, Massachusetts. At the time of Clyfton's death, his only living child, Zachary, returned to England and lived first at Richmond, then at Newcastle upon Tyne. Two hundred years later, Zachary Clyfton's family Bible was discovered in an Oxford library; it is a 1599 quarto size Geneva Bible, whose fly-leaf contains vital family history.[4]

GAINSBOROUGH

Situated on the east side of the River Trent, which flows northward into the River Humber, Gainsborough was a river port and a farming center in the seventeenth century, as merchants with sail boats transported local produce such as beans, oats, barley, and rye up and down the busy river. The river here is tidal and there was no bridge until 1791. The Pilgrims from Scrooby would have had to cross by ferry. A place "familiar with forgotten years,"[5] the old north Lincolnshire town already had a long history of befriending and assisting religious dissenters. Perhaps it was only natural that Separatist John Smyth would find refuge here as well.

John Smyth (c. 1570-1612) had trained at Christ's College, Cambridge, where Francis Johnson, who would lead one of the earliest groups of Separatists to Amsterdam, was one of his tutors. Smyth received the B.A. and M.A., remained for a time as a fellow, then received ordination by the Bishop of London.[6] From 1600 to 1602, Smyth held the office of Preacher (or Lecturer) of the City of Lincoln. The word "lecturer," in the sixteenth and seventeenth centuries, referred to teachers appointed by Parliament at the request of parishioners, to give instruction in the Christian faith where there was a scarcity of regular ministers.[7] Many able Puritan preachers often availed themselves of this opportunity. John Smyth was one such Puritan. Becoming increasingly critical of the Church of England, Smyth was deposed for his "strange doctrines" and "forward preaching." With many at Gainsborough attracted to his views, Smyth began holding worship services here in 1602 and became their pastor. When dissenters were outlawed by James I in 1604, Sir William Hickman, the manorial lord, befriended the Smyth group and allowed them to worship in Gainsborough Manor. Hickman had been raised a devout Protestant and had a natural love for religious freedom. His parents, Anthony and Rose Hickman, had given shelter to hunted men, including Presbyterian John Knox, during the reign of Catholic Queen Mary I. The Hickman family had then fled into religious exile in Antwerp, where William was born. They returned to England after the crown passed to Elizabeth. William purchased Gainsborough Manor in 1596. Gainsborough was not an incorporated town, which means that the landlord, the lord of Gainsborough Manor, held considerable power of his own. John Smyth's services in the Manor attracted many people from the villages,[8] since the regular parish priest had been absent for some time. Meanwhile, increasing numbers of nonconformist ministers were being ousted from the churches. In 1606 Smyth attended an important meeting in the Coventry home of Sir William Bowes, whose wife became affectionately known as "Lady Bowes." Here, many ministers who had suffered deprivation discussed what course of action they must take.[9] Accordingly, Smyth broke all ties with the Church of England and was now preaching in the Gainsborough Manor House as the avowed Separatist pastor of a covenanted Separatist church.[10]

Best known as "Old Hall," this grand old manor was erected during the 1470s.[11] King Richard III lodged here one night in 1483. At the center of Old Hall is the "Great Hall," where a fifty-year-old Henry VIII, accompanied by his fifth wife Catherine Howard,[12] held his court and banqueted for four days in 1541 while on his way to York. In 1606, John Smyth and at least sixty to seventy[13] Separatists were banqueting spiritually in this same room whose vast arched roof memorializes the medieval craftsmen who built it. When Sir William Hickman allowed the Separatists to worship in Old Hall, his aging mother, Rose, was still living there. She wrote her life story in her own hand not long before she died.[14] Standing in Old Hall, one can quickly sense the seventeenth-century atmosphere in which Christian Separatists took steps of faith, placing themselves in great physical danger. Here in Old Hall, portraits of Anthony and Rose Hickman and their son William can still be seen, as well as room settings of 1607 and an exhibition devoted to the *Mayflower* story. Pilgrims who attended services here with Smyth included William Bradford, William Brewster, and John Robinson. For their safety and convenience, the Pilgrims, in 1606, began holding their own secret worship services at the Scrooby Manor House. After five years in Gainsborough, Smyth and at least forty of his members moved to Amsterdam, in 1607 or early 1608, to fellowship with Francis Johnson's "Ancient Church" of Separatists. Here, however, he would adopt the practice of "believer's baptism" and chart the course of English Baptist history.[15] Through the centuries that followed, the walls of the Great Hall would hear even more voices of urgency and faith.[16]

AUSTERFIELD

Located in the southern extremity of Yorkshire and just two miles north of Scrooby, Austerfield is the birthplace of William Bradford (1590-1657),[17] who would become governor of Plymouth Plantation in Massachusetts and write his first-hand account of the Pilgrim story in his well-known *Plymouth Plantation*. In fact, he would be the first to apply the term *Pilgrim* to these Separatists. Bradford was the third child and only son of William and Alice Bradford. William Sr., a yeoman farmer, died when Bradford was still an infant. In the village is a sixteenth-century cottage, Austerfield Manor House, believed by many to be the actual birthplace of William Bradford Jr.[18] It stands just down the street from St. Helena's Church. The font from which Bradford was baptized rests in St. Helena's,[19] a quaint and charming stone church building, completed in

Norman architectural style in the twelfth century. When William Bradford was still an infant his father died. His mother remarried a couple of years later. The young William was placed under of the care of his grandfather and two uncles. In those days, Bradford may have often seen a boy named William Butten (1598-1620) playing among the children of Austerfield village. Butten would later appear on the *Mayflower* as a servant of the Samuel Fuller family and would be the first passenger to die on board the ship. Just before land was sighted, Butten died of scurvy and was buried at sea. From an early age, William Bradford had such a deep interest in the Bible that he would walk all the way to Babworth and Gainsborough to hear Separatist preaching, even over the loud objections and scoffing of relatives and neighbors. When the Scrooby congregation began holding meetings in 1606, Bradford loved to go there for fellowship and to listen to the messages. Preaching molded the thinking of this young man, who at the time was unaware of God's plan for his life. When he was seventeen, Bradford moved into the Scrooby Manor House, where William Brewster tutored him in Greek, Hebrew and Latin. Cotton Mather (1663-1728), of Boston, Massachusetts, held Bradford in high esteem and describes his youth in a section of *Magnalia Christi Americana:*

> When he was about a Dozen Years Old, the Reading of the Scrip-
> tures began to cause great Impressions upon him; and those
> Impressions were much assisted and improved, when he came to
> enjoy Mr. Richard Clifton's Illuminating Ministry. . . . Nor could
> the Wrath of his Uncles, nor the Scoff of his Neighbours now
> turn'd upon him, as one of the Puritans, divert him from his Pious
> Inclinations.[20]

SCROOBY

Located on the Great North Road,[21] the quiet hamlet of Scrooby stands on the banks of the River Ryton, within sight of its junction with the River Idle. Scrooby lies about 150 miles north of London and about the same distance from the Scottish border. Its stately, half-timbered and brick Manor House had once belonged to the archbishops of York, who had used it as their palace. Royal records reveal that in 1212 King John himself had stayed at Scrooby Manor. In 1503, fourteen-year-old Margaret Tudor, elder daughter of King Henry VII,[22] stayed here while on her way to Scotland to become the second wife of James IV.[23] In an incredible development of circumstances, Margaret's granddaughter, Mary Stuart, would become Mary Queen of Scots, whose execution would force William Brewster to Scrooby and whose "sniveling son" James I of England (James VI of Scotland) would "harry" Brewster out of Scrooby. For several weeks in 1530, Cardinal John Wolsey made the Manor his home while out of favor with Margaret's younger and temperamental brother, Henry VIII (who spent a night here in 1541).[24] Many others of royal fame rested here; however, the memorial plaque on the Manor House is not to kings, queens, cardinals or archbishops, but rather to a man remembered as a humble Separatist, a man of prayer—a Pilgrim. The dates "1588 to 1608" on the plaque should be 1575 to 1607:[25]

This tablet erected by the Pilgrim Society of Plymouth, Mass., U.S.A., to mark the site of the ancient manor-house where lived, William Brewster

from 1588 to 1608, and where he organized the Pilgrim Church, of which he became the ruling elder, and with which, in 1608, he removed to Amsterdam, in 1609 to Leyden, and in 1620 to Plymouth, where he died

April 16, 1644

William Brewster's life (1566/7-1644)[26] is a memorable illustration of special Providence. Some remarkable events molded young Brewster's life. In 1580 he entered Cambridge's Peterhouse College on the same day as John Penry, the Welshman who would be a Separatist martyr by 1593. Penry's Separatist tracts, published in the late 1580s, would make a profound impact upon young Brewster. Francis Johnson was a fellow at Christ's College while Brewster was at Peterhouse. John Greenwood, who would also become a Separatist martyr of 1593, was still at Cambridge when Brewster arrived. Puritan and Separatist ideas molded his thinking during these years of training. Puritan theologian William Perkins, for example, was completing his studies at Cambridge at about the time Brewster arrived.

From 1584 to 1587 Brewster was in the diplomatic service of William Davison, the British ambassador to the Netherlands. In their struggle to throw off the yoke of Spain, the United Provinces of the Netherlands were seeking diplomatic and financial assistance from England. Davison was a Puritan and Brewster lived with him in The Hague and in other cities such as Leiden, where they witnessed the practice of religious freedom. They even lived for a while in the area where the Pilgrims themselves would live for twelve years. As a close associate, Brewster earned William Davison's complete confidence and personal friendship. As the Assistant Secretary of State under Queen Elizabeth I, Davison became caught up in the intriguing web of circumstances which led to the execution of Mary Queen of Scots (Mary Stuart)—the very episode which would bring Davison's friend and associate, William Brewster, back to his home in Scrooby, England, and prepare him to become the presiding elder of the *Mayflower* Pilgrims.

Henry VII of England had three children—Arthur, Henry, and Margaret. Arthur died at a young age; Henry became the famous Henry VIII; and Margaret married King James IV of Scotland. Their son, James V (Elizabeth's cousin), married the French Mary of Guise (1515-1560) as his second wife; their only child was Mary Stuart (1542-1587), who became Queen of Scots when she was an infant. Her father had died when she was only a few days old. Mary was sent to France at the age of six for her education. In 1558 she married the Dauphin of France who, in 1559, succeeded to the French throne as Francis II, but died the following year. When Mary Stuart finally went to Scotland to take her throne in 1561, she was not only a Roman Catholic, but a nineteen-year-old foreigner who had to use the French language to conduct Scotland's official business. Most importantly, Scotland had just embraced the Reformation. The Scottish Parliament had in 1560 made Protestantism the national religion and adopted the Confession of Faith prepared by John Knox (d. 1572). Knox never hesitated to oppose Mary, whose marriage in 1565 to her own cousin, the Catholic Scottish nobleman Henry Stuart, Lord Darnley, was performed with Roman Catholic rites. Insurrection followed. In 1566, Darnley instigated the murder of Mary's personal secretary, David Rizzio, believing with many others that he was having an affair with Mary. Early in 1567 the house in which Darnley lay sick was blown up by gunpowder. Darnley was discovered strangled close by the scene of the explosion and many suspected that Mary knew of the plot. Incriminating love letters and sonnets, allegedly written by Mary, were found later that year in a silver casket. They were addressed to the Scottish nobleman, James Hepburn, fourth Earl of Bothwell. Bothwell was brought to a mock trial and acquitted; soon afterward, he divorced his wife and married Mary in a Protestant wedding. Later in 1567, however, Mary was forced to sign an abdication in favor of her son (by Lord Darnley) who was crowned five days later as Scotland's King James VI.

Mary went into exile in England, where she spent most of the remainder of her life in prison. She still became involved in various plots to unseat her cousin, Queen Elizabeth I, and to take England's throne. Most famous was the plot of Mary's page, Anthony Babington, to assassinate Elizabeth. The conspiracy was discovered, and in October 1586 Mary was finally brought to trial and sentenced to be beheaded. When Elizabeth resolved to execute Mary Stuart in 1586, William Brewster's superior, the Queen's Assistant Secretary of State, William Davison, was assigned to the legal process and issued the warrant for Mary's execution. Concerned how the execution might influence England's relationship with France, and seeking to avoid being remembered as killing an heir to the English throne, Elizabeth demanded that everything be done so as to relieve her of blame. Elizabeth waited until February 1, 1587 to sign the warrant of execution, which was carried out a week later, outside Mary's prison at Fotheringay Castle, in Northamptonshire. Claiming that William Davison had "deceived" her into signing the warrant by inserting it into a stack of other papers that needed her signature that day, Elizabeth immediately made him the convenient scapegoat. Davison was arrested, tried before the Star Chamber court, fined, and committed to the Tower in 1587. William Brewster attended Davison until a few months prior to his release, then returned to Scrooby to assist his father as town bailiff, royal postmaster, and innkeeper at the Old Manor House. When Elizabeth died on the last day of 1602, she left no Tudor heir to the throne; interestingly enough, Mary Stuart's own son King James VI of Scotland became King James I of England—successor of Elizabeth—the king who within five years would force the Pilgrims, led by William Brewster, out of their homeland.

Following his father's death in 1590, Brewster was appointed as replacement for all of his father's positions in Scrooby. Within two years, he had married his wife Mary, and the two of them were often attending church services in Babworth, listening attentively to Richard Clyfton's preaching. In one of these Babworth services, in 1602, they saw a twelve-year-old boy who had walked all the way from Austerfield to hear Pastor Clyfton. They soon learned that his name was William Bradford; the lad would become a familiar face at these gatherings.

Little did William Brewster realize that Providence had brought him back to Scrooby to prepare him for the humble task of leading a small group of persecuted Separatists to the New World. Never again in this life would this man know royalty or fame. Already Brewster was beginning to acquire Separatist leanings away from the Church of England. Ecclesiastical court records show that he was cited in 1598 for "irregular church attendance" at the parish church of St. Wilfred's. This church, one of the three extant Scrooby buildings which were standing in Brewster's day, was named for a seventh-century archbishop of York. The church's early fifteenth-century square tower supports a tall spire which, with its four pinnacles, symbolizes Christ's five wounds. Its bells called young William Brewster to worship. The south aisle, with its Tudor style windows, dates from the sixteenth century. Near the churchyard, the Old Vicarage, now a private dwelling, also dates from the sixteenth century; but with modern renovation and expansion, it hardly resembles the little thatched-roof cottage of Brewster's day. Brewster and others of similar conviction separated from St. Wilfred's when they began worshipping with John Smyth in Gainsborough in 1602. Two years later, at the Hampton Court Conference, King James I served notice on all dissenters, "I shall make them conform, or I will harry (pillage) them out of the land, or else do worse." He banned private religious meetings and removed those who would not conform to the Church of England. The eight-mile journey to Gainsborough was becoming increasingly dangerous for the Scrooby Separatists. In 1606 they began holding their own secret worship services at Scrooby's Manor House, where Brewster "entertained them with great love," while serving as royal postmaster, and innkeeper. As Moses was brought up in the luxury of the court of Egypt as "the son of Pharaoh's daughter," Brewster had been brought up serving in high places, even in a foreign land, and with the highest officials of his day. And as Moses was called to lead God's people out of Egypt's bondage, Brewster was now prepared to lead his people out of England's bondage. There was a boldness about him, because there was a meekness about him—a meekness which turned his walk and his prayers into constant reminders of God's own glory and presence.

In Scrooby, Richard Clyfton served as pastor, while John Robinson served as teacher. Robinson (1575/6-1625)[27] was the eldest of three children born to John and Ann Robinson at Sturton-le-Steeple in Nottinghamshire. He had entered Corpus Christi College, Cambridge, in 1592, just as Francis Johnson was becoming pastor of the secret church in London. John Greenwood, Henry Barrowe, and John Penry were martyred in London the following year. As John Robinson and his circle of friends and Cambridge instructors discussed such current topics, he was sitting under the direct influence of the well-known Puritan theologian and preacher William Perkins (1558-1602). Converted to Christ from a life of profanity and drink upon "overhearing a woman in the street allude to him as 'drunken Perkins,' holding him up as a terror to a fretful child,"[28] Perkins profoundly molded John Robinson's theology and preaching style. Robinson would publish an edition of Perkins' *Catechism* in 1624, and William Brewster's library inventory would include eleven of Perkins' treatises.

John Robinson graduated with his B.A. in 1596. The following year, he received his ordination and became a fellow in the college, obtaining the M.A. degree in 1599. Resigning his fellowship at Corpus Christi in 1603, he soon became parish minister at St. Andrew's Church at Norwich (Norfolk), where William Perkins was the lecturer. While Perkins personally held little sympathy towards Separatism, St. Andrew's already had a long tradition of nonconformity towards the Church of England. Nonconformist John More had served as pastor of this church until deprived by Queen Elizabeth in 1576 for unlawful preaching and catechizing. Robinson himself was suspended from his position at St. Andrews, probably in 1605, shortly after James I decided to enforce the 1604 *Ecclesiastical Constitutions and Canons,* edited by Archbishop Richard Bancroft. These Canons, among other things, forbade the formation of secret conventicles and "new brotherhoods," and they greatly restricted sermon content. As with most Separatists, Robinson was not arriving at the Separatist position hastily. Only after the fullest consideration did such conviction come to these men and women. It was the intolerance of the Church of England, not the intolerance of the Separatists, which finally sent these Pilgrims into exile. Most recently, the Canons of 1604 were themselves provoking a resurgence of Separatism. The Anglican establishment itself was actually creating the inevitable separation by depriving Richard Clyfton from his Babworth parish, Richard Bernard from Worksop,[29] John Smyth from his lectureship at Lincoln, and now Robinson from his curacy at Norwich. In 1606 those four men, with a number of concerned clergy, attended an urgent meeting held in the home of Lady Bowes of Coventry. Lady Bowes was Isabel, the wife of Sir William Bowes (d. 1611), who was related to John Knox and was a special encouragement to persecuted Christians. Thomas Helwys, who would organize the first Baptist church on English soil, attended the Coventry meeting and would later dedicate his Confession of Faith, *A Declaration of Faith* (1611) to Lady Bowes.[30] Most importantly, at this meeting John Robinson became a convinced Separatist, by both conviction and association. Now, as the teacher of the Scrooby Separatists, John Robinson would rapidly emerge as the theological apologist for what he and the *Mayflower* Pilgrims would regard as consistent Separatism.

Under the able leadership of Clyfton and Robinson, the Scrooby Separatists, "whose hearts the Lord had touched with heavenly zeal for His truth," drew up a Covenant to bind themselves together:

> They shook off this yoke of antichristian bondage, and as the Lord's free people joined themselves (by a covenant of the Lord) into a church estate, in the fellowship of the gospel, to walk in all His ways made known, or to be made known unto them, according to their best endeavors, whatsoever it should cost them, the Lord assisting them.[31]

Bradford's citation is obviously only a short description of the original Covenant. Plymouth Colony later revealed the full version. When the colony, in 1676, requested all churches to renew their covenant before the Lord, the Plymouth Church cited the following as "the substance of that Covenant which their Fathers entered into at the first gathering" of their Scrooby Manor church:

> In the Name of our Lord Jesus Christ & in obedience to his holy will & divine ordinances. Wee being by the most wise & good providence of God brought together in this place & desirous to

unite our selves into one congregation or church under the Lord
Jesus Christ our Head, that it may be in such sort as becometh all
those whom He hath redeemed & sanctifyed to himselfe, wee doe
hereby solemnly & religiously (as in his most holy prescence)
avouch the Lord Jehovah the only true God to be our God & the
God of ours & doe promise & binde ourselves to walke in all our
wayes according to the Rule of the Gospel & in all sincere conformity to His holy ordinances & in mutuall love to & watchfull-
nesse over one another, depending wholy & only upon the Lord
our God to enable us by his grace hereunto.[32]

Today, there is no public access to the Manor House's interior. The landlord explains that they do not have it insured for tourists and that it is not safe
to enter. He uses it for storage. As one stands here today, admiring this quaint
old Manor House, he must imagine a building much larger, occupying six
and a half acres of land, surrounded on three sides by a moat and bounded on
the north side by the River Ryton. A drawbridge led to the outer court. The
present structure is only a remnant of a brick wing of the stately Manor of
Brewster's day. This House once had forty rooms and a chapel. King Charles
I ordered its demolition in 1636-1637; however, the workers spared this
brick remnant. It stands as a silent reminder of the voices these walls once
heard—Brewster, Bradford, Robinson and Clyfton, with their little company—praying and singing, preaching and listening, planning and organiz-
ing, conversing and breaking bread, yet ever so alert lest they be suddenly
interrupted and arrested. Though kings and cardinals, archbishops and
prelates, had feasted within these silent walls, none were so noble and none
left such legacy as the Pilgrims who gathered within these sacred halls. One
who stood at this spot more than a hundred years ago, pondering this ancient
ruin, expresses the profoundness of its simplicity:

All this is not much! No: not much—only that, at some times and
in some places and with regard to some things, a little is more than
much. There is a flavor of the majesty of a mighty past about even
these simplicities; bringing back to us that "golden age of merry
England" which knew not the day of its visitation, and sullied the
splendor of the time of its Spenser and its Shakespeare, its Bacon
and its Milton, by threshing multitudes of the most Christian of its

people with the rods of its Star Chamber and its High Commission, and by carefully gathering much of the chaff into its garners and savagely driving the heaviest of the grain out of the land and over the sea.[33]

Only a few miles to the south is Sherwood Forest, which was far more dense and extensive four hundred years ago. The royal stables of Brewster's day provided fresh horses for the postal express riders traveling from London to Scotland. Although stage coaches were seldom used on the rugged highways of those days, the "Great" North Road—actually a dangerous, ungraded trail, wandering recklessly across miles of fields, bogs, streams, and outlaw-infested woods—brought people to Scrooby village almost daily. Hunt clubs often brought people of royalty; so the Manor House's inn provided refreshment for weary souls of every walk of life. Scrooby's "Pilgrim Fathers Inn"[34] is a later accommodation for travelers and still provides tasty meals for both locals and visiting pilgrims who pass this way.

1. William Bradford, *Of Plymouth Plantation* 1620-1647, ed. Samuel Eliot Morison (1952; rpt. NY: Alfred A. Knopf, 1998), 9-10. This work is hereafter referred to as "Bradford, *Plymouth Plantation*."

2. An important work by Richard Clyfton is *A Plea for Infants and Elder People Concerning Their Baptism,* published in Amsterdam in 1610 as a polemic against John Smyth's views. Smyth, of course, had come to repudiate infant baptism. Clyfton also wrote an *Advertisement* (1612), which describes the Separatists' worship services.

3. *Plymouth Church Records 1620-1859* (1920-23; rpt. Baltimore, MD: Genealogical Publishing Co., Inc., 1975), I:139.

4. For a valuable section on the entries in Zachary Clyfton's Bible, see Edward Arber, ed., *The Story of The Pilgrim Fathers, 1606-1623 A.D; As Told by Themselves, Their Friends, and Their Enemies* (London: Ward and Downey, Limited, 1897), 95-97. One of these entries confirms the arrival of Richard Clyfton and the Pilgrims in Amsterdam as August 1608.

5. Such is one of the descriptions penned by George Eliot (Mary Anne Evans) in her 19th-century novel *Mill on the Floss.* Many believe that the "Floss" is the River Trent; the "Mill" (Dorlcote Mill) was built on the Trent; and the "St. Oggs" of the story is the town of Gainsborough. This classic is presently published by Oxford University Press, 1998.

6. Nathaniel Morton, nephew of William Bradford, says that Smyth suffered in "a wretched dungeon in the Marshalea" Prison in London, at the same time that Francis Johnson and John Penry were imprisoned. See Nathaniel Morton, *New England's Memorial* (1669; rpt. Boston: Congregational Board of Publications, 1855), 446.

7. Some of the lecturers were unordained.

8. Members were also drawn from such surrounding villages as Scrooby, Skegby, Sutton, Sturton-le-Steeple, North Wheatley, Retford, Broxtowe Hall, Mattersey, Worksop, and the Isle of Axholme.

9. Timothy George, *John Robinson and the English Separatist Tradition* (Macon, GA: Mercer University Press, 1982), 82-83. With few and conflicting records, it is now impossible to know exactly how many ministers had been ousted by this time, or even how many attended the Coventry meeting.

10. Records at the Parish Church of Gainsborough reveal that John Smyth's daughter Chara was baptized here in the spring of 1604 (N.S.), and that his daughter Sara was baptized here in March of 1606 (N.S.). So it must have been sometime after Sara's baptism, during 1606, that Smyth attended the Coventry meeting and broke his final ties with the Church of England. Nevertheless, Smyth had been preaching for a dissenting church since 1602. For the baptismal records, see Jennifer Vernon, *Gainsborough Old Hall and the Mayflower Pilgrim Story* (Gainsborough, England: Friends of the Old Hall Association, 1991), 12-15. Vernon also cites the covenant of Smyth's Separatist church: "We covenant with God and with one another, to walk in His ways made known or to be made known unto us, according to our best endeavors, whatsoever it shall cost us, the Lord assisting us."

11. An earlier hall had been built here during the 1460s, but was soon torn down. Many believe that the present Gainsborough Manor was actually built on the site of the palace where King Alfred had been married and where Canute had been proclaimed king of England by the captains of his navy.

12. It was also during his visit to Gainsborough that Henry VIII first met Catherine Parr who would become his sixth wife.

13. There could possibly have been eighty or more Separatists meeting here at Gainsborough Manor; see Harold Kirk-Smith, *William Brewster 'The Father of New England'—His Life and Times—1567-1644* (Boston, England: Richard Kay, 1992), 84. Contrary to Kirk-Smith, however, the number of those who actually left England at this time with Smyth was most likely about forty; Kirk-Smith thinks that seventy to eighty left with Smyth. Actually about half of Smyth's group most likely went to Holland with the Scrooby group, as the number of signatures on the Smyth and Helwys confessions of faith in Holland would suggest.

14. Rose Hickman is buried at the Parish Chute of Gainsborough.

15. See chapter 8 for a continuation of the story of John Smyth.

16. John Wesley preached in the Great Hall in 1759. In his diary, he records his visit of Friday the 3rd: "I preached at Gainsborough, in Sir Nevil Hickman's great hall. . . . At two it was filled with a rude, wild multitude. Yet all but two or three gentlemen were attentive."

17. The best biographical sources on William Bradford include Bradford Smith, *Bradford of Plymouth* (Philadelphia: J. B. Lippincott Company, 1951); and Malcolm Dolby, *William Bradford: His Life and Work* (England: Doncaster Library and Information Services, 1991).

18. There is no absolute proof that the cottage is Bradford's birthplace. John Brown must have been convinced that it was; he even includes a sketch of Austerfield Manor House in his *Pilgrim Fathers of New England and Their Puritan Successors* (London: The Religious Tract Society, 1897), 41.

19. Bradford was baptized on March 29, 1590 (N.S.). The Austerfield parish register contains his baptism and other details of the Bradford family. The register, of course, gives the dates in O.S. There are several conflicting references indicating that the stone baptismal font was discarded in the 1830s and served as a trough for the clerk's poultry. Then it was supposedly discovered and restored to its place in the church during the 1890s. The present font in the building looks like it could well be the real one; but it is probably doubtful that the "poultry story" can be confirmed.

20. Cotton Mather, *Magnalia Christi Americana: or, The Ecclesiastical History of New-England from its first Planting in the year 1620 unto the year of our Lord 1698* (London: T. Parkhurst, 1702 folio), Book II:3-5. The citation above is from the 1702 first edition folio in the Massachusetts History Society. The best reprint editions are NY: Arno Press, 1972; and the Kenneth B. Murdock, edition, Cambridge, MA: Belknap Press, 1977.

21. Prior to 1766 the Great North Road followed Scrooby's present-day Mill Lane, crossed the River Ryton (whose course has since been re-routed), and passed beside St. Wilfred's Parish Church.

22. Margaret was born only four years after her father, Henry Tudor, had killed Richard III at Bosworth, thus bringing at end to the long Wars of Roses.

23. On the previous night, Margaret had stayed at Rushey Inn in Babworth; the inn is now a private home.

24. See Mandell Creighton, *Cardinal Wolsey* (London: Macmillan and Co., Limited, 1921), 195ff. Local tradition has it that, while he was at Scrooby Manor, Cardinal Wolsey "planted a mulberry tree in the grounds. It was on the occasion when he heard the prophecy of Mother Shipton that he would see York but never enter it. The Cardinal laughed and promised to see the hag burned. Nevertheless it proved true. Within sight of York he was recalled by the King and died on the way back to London." Joan Board, *The Old North Road Through Babworth Parish* (Derby, England: J. H. Hall & Sons Limited, 1992), 22. Joan Board was for many years an English instructor in the local area. She is an esteemed authority on the local history and has written popular collections of short stories and poetry. Many have delighted in sharing English cookies and tea while listening to Joan Board tell the most delightful stories and traditions of the beloved Midlands.

25. The dates "1588 to 1608" on the plaque should be 1575 to 1607. William Brewster Sr., resident of Scrooby from 1571, was appointed "Master of the Queen's Postes" in 1575 and began living in the Manor House at that time, when William Jr. was about eight years old. Even though William Jr. would be away from Scrooby for some years before returning here in 1590, this was the place he called home since 1575. It would remain his home until he resigned his post in 1607.

26. William Brewster was born either late 1566 or early 1567. The best sources for studying Brewster include Harold Kirk-Smith, *William Brewster 'The Father of New England'—His Life and Times—1567-1644* (Boston, England: Richard Kay, 1992); Dorothy Brewster, *William Brewster of the Mayflower: Portrait of a Pilgrim* (NY: New York University Press, 1970); Mary B. Sherwood, *Pilgrim: Biography of William Brewster* (Falls Church, VA: Great Oak Press of Virginia, 1982); Ashbel Steele, *Chief of the Pilgrims, or the Life and Time of William Brewster* (Philadelphia, PA: J. B. Lippincott and Company, 1857); William Bradford, *Memoir of Elder William Brewster,* published in its entirety in Alexander Young, ed., *Chronicles of the Pilgrim Fathers of the Colony of Plymouth, from 1602 to 1625* (1844; rpt. Baltimore: Genealogical Publishing Co., Inc., 1974), 459-70; and Edward Arber, ed., *The Story of The Pilgrim Fathers, 1606-1623 A.D; as Told by Themselves, Their Friends, and Their Enemies* (London: Ward and Downey, Limited, 1897), 71-86.

27. The best sources on John Robinson include Robert Ashton, ed., *Works of John Robinson,* 3 vols. (London: John Snow, 1851); Walter H. Burgess, *The Pastor of the Pilgrims: A Biography of John Robinson* (NY: Harcourt, Brace & Howe, 1920); Ozora S. Davis, *John Robinson: The Pilgrim Pastor* (Boston: The Pilgrim Press, 1903); Timothy George, *John Robinson and the English Separatist Tradition* (Macon, GA: Mercer University Press, 1982); and Frederick J. Powicke, *John Robinson* (London: Hodder & Stoughton, Ltd., 1920).

28. Sir Leslie Stephen and Sir Sidney Lee, ed., *The Dictionary of National Biography* (1917; rpt. London: Oxford University Press, 1921-22), XV:892.

29. Bernard soon returned to the Church of England; Clyfton would get no farther than Amsterdam with the Pilgrims; and Smyth would become an Anabaptist.

30. E. Catherine Anwyl, *John Smyth: The Se-Baptist at Gainsborough* (Gainsborough, England: G. W. Belton Ltd., 1991), n.p. Anwyl notices also that John Smyth dedicated his exposition of Psalm 22 to Isabel's brother, Sir William Wray of Glentworth.

31. Bradford, *Plymouth Plantation,* 9.

32. *Plymouth Church Records 1620-1859* (1920-23; rpt. Baltimore, MD: Genealogical Publishing Co., Inc., 1975), I:148.

33. Henry Martyn Dexter and Morton Dexter, *The England and Holland of the Pilgrims* (1906; rpt. Baltimore: Genealogical Publishing Co., Inc., 1978), 250.

34. The Pilgrim Fathers Inn, built in 1771, is situated on the A638.

CHAPTER 3
ESCAPE FROM ENGLAND (1607-1608)

The Pilgrims of Scrooby Inn would soon become the weary souls in search of food and rest. The hosts would become the hunted. The Church of England was not about to tolerate Separatist views. Non-residence, pluralism, nepotism, and simony were widespread among Church of England clergy. The Conventicle Act of 1593 had outlawed unauthorized worship services or "conventicles." The Canons of 1604 had declared that all who rejected the practices of the Church of England had already excommunicated themselves. Every clergyman must accept royal supremacy, the authority of the *Book of Common Prayer* and the Thirty-nine Articles, the use of copes and surplices, and the sign of the cross in baptism. Many Separatists had already suffered imprisonment for their insistence on church purity and simplicity in worship.

At Scrooby Manor, Richard Clyfton served as the pastor; Brewster was the congregation's ruling (presiding) elder; and John Robinson ministered as their teacher. Robinson was born in the nearby village of Sturton-le-Steeple in 1575 or 1576. He had trained and served as Fellow in Corpus Christi College, Cambridge, where he had early acquired strong convictions in Puritan theology and leanings toward Separatist practice. The authorities were now watching the homes of the Scrooby Separatists at night. So intense was the hatred against these Separatists that William and Mary Brewster named their newborn daughter "Fear." All three of these families had small children. Richard and Ann Clyfton had three sons (Zachary, Timothy, and Eleazar) whose ages ranged from about eight to eighteen. John and Bridget Robinson had two small children, John Jr. and

Bridget. William and Mary Brewster had three sons (Jonathan, Love, and Wrestling) and two daughters (Patience and Fear). William Bradford was about eighteen years old now and living with the Brewsters.

Government spies traveling the North Road soon learned from local informers of the Separatist meetings in Scrooby Manor and in Gainsborough Manor. News of these meetings reached the Archbishop of York and the Bishop of Lincoln. It was now impossible for the Separatists to function as normal families in England. Bradford describes their desperate situation:

> After these things they could not long continue in any peaceable condition, but were hunted and persecuted on every side, so as their former afflictions were but as flea-bitings in comparison of these which now came upon them. For some were taken and clapped up in prison, others had their houses beset and watched night and day, and hardly escaped their hands; and the most were fain to flee and leave their houses and habitations, and the means of their livelihood.[1]

In 1607 Elder Brewster resigned his office as Post of Scrooby. Before the end of the year, he was ordered to appear before the Court of High Commission in York for charges of being "disobedient in matters of Religion."[2] Brewster did not appear in court. He was now hiding and the little group was looking for a way to escape to Holland. Emigration without license was prohibited by a statute dating from the reign of Richard II; however, such a license to travel abroad was usually denied to Catholics and Separatists. The Pilgrims could not have even applied for the license, because they were already wanted by the authorities for their refusal to support the state church. In a word, it was not legal for them to stay and worship according to the dictates of their own consciences, submitted as they were to the Bible, nor was it legal for them to escape. Just before he was led to the gallows on London's Old Kent Road in 1593, the Welsh martyr John Penry had written from King's Bench Prison a letter of warning to Separatists urging them to leave the tyranny of England for a more hospitable land.[3] The Scrooby Separatists knew that whatever they did must be in obedience to God. They were well aware that some three hundred Separatists, beginning with Francis Johnson's group in 1593, had already fled to the safety of the Netherlands. They too must now leave by stealth. John Smyth and some forty of his Gainsborough Separatists quietly boarded a ship and sailed across the North Sea. However, the Scrooby group, of perhaps a hundred people,[4] would encounter numerous disappointments in their attempts to escape. Babworth's late rector, Edmund F. Jessup, called it "an adventure to which the only known parallel was the flight of the Children of Israel from Egypt into the wilderness, with the Red Sea between them and the Promised Land. Like the Pharaoh of Egypt who was unwilling to let the people go, so the law forbade these Pilgrims to leave the country."[5]

BOSTON

The Pilgrims decided what possessions they must sell and what they must take with them on their dangerous journey. As quietly and secretly as possible, they negotiated ways to dispose of homes, furniture, farms, and livestock. They found it difficult to keep such transactions hidden from the magistrates. By mid September of 1607, they had negotiated with an English sea captain who agreed to transport them across the sea from Boston to the Netherlands. They set out in small inconspicuous groups southeastward towards the seaport of Boston. Some traveled on foot and some in horse carts. Some went by boats and small barges on the River Idle to the Trent, which took them past Gainsborough and on to Torksey, where they took the Fosse Dyke to Lincoln. From Lincoln they took the River Witham all the way down to Boston.

Boston's Christian history goes back to the seventh century, when the Anglo-Saxon missionary Botolph founded a church here. The place was called Botolph's Stone, later shortened to "Boston." A great distance before the Pilgrims approached Boston, they could see the "Stump," the 272-foot high steeple of beautiful St. Botolph's Church, always the landmark of Boston.[6] The building of the church began in 1309, but was not completed until the 1450s. John Foxe was born in a house which stood where the "Martha's Vineyard" building now stands, at the corner of Church Street and Angel Court. A plaque on the outside of the present building commemorates him with the following inscription: "Here stood the birthplace of John Foxe the martyrologist 1516-1587." During the time of the Pilgrim Separatists, Foxe's eight-volume *Actes and Monuments,* better known as

The Book of Martyrs, had become one of the most widely read books in the English language, second only to the Bible. Ordered to be placed in the churches for public reading, Foxe's work became so popular that thousands of families owned copies. The Pilgrims carried copies to Leiden and eventually brought them to New England. When Foxe died,[7] the future Puritan founder of America's Boston, John Cotton (1584-1652),[8] was just under three years of age. Cotton would begin his ministry at St. Botolph's Church five years after the Pilgrim Separatists' ordeal in Boston. Viewing Cotton's massive wineglass pulpit, with its great sounding board, and pausing to pray in the John Cotton chapel are alone worth a visit.[9] In the spring of 1630, John Cotton left briefly, as he hurried down from the Lincolnshire fens to watch the flagship *Arbella,* carrying Governor John Winthrop (1588-1649), sail out of Southampton seaport to begin the "swarming of Puritans" into New England. Before that year was out, a thousand nonconformist Puritans would arrive in Massachusetts Bay Colony and John Cotton himself would depart from old Boston in 1633, and soon become the "Patriarch of New England." His own son, John, would become the pastor of the Pilgrim Church of Plymouth Colony, in 1669.

When the Pilgrim Separatists arrived in old Boston in 1607, their ship was nowhere in sight! In tiny Scotia Creek, on the seaward side of Boston, they nervously waited until they finally saw the ship creeping into the Wash. The Pilgrims quickly paid the captain his expensive fee for passage. Using small boats, they boarded the ship in the dark of the night and were thanking the Lord for His blessings, when the king's officers suddenly appeared and arrested them all. The ship's captain had betrayed and swindled them without mercy. The Pilgrims watched as officers ransacked their luggage and plundered their books in search of cash. The officers took the Pilgrims by small groups back to the shore and immodestly searched both men and women, to their inner garments, for any valuables that they could find.

A mile south of Boston, at Fishtoft, where the Scotia Creek enters the River Witham, a lone granite obelisk, known as the Pilgrim Fathers' Memorial, stands on the desolate shore at the site of this deplorable episode. Mistakenly, it states that the Pilgrims "set sail":

```
NEAR THIS PLACE
IN SEPTEMBER 1607 THOSE LATER
KNOWN AS THE PILGRIM FATHERS
SET SAIL ON THEIR FIRST ATTEMPT
TO FIND RELIGIOUS FREEDOM
ACROSS THE SEAS


ERECTED 1957
```

The officers took these Separatists into Boston, as "a spectacle and wonder to the multitude which came flocking on all sides to behold them,"[10] then turned them over to the magistrates. Separatist leaders such as Pastor Clyfton, John Robinson, and Elder Brewster were incarcerated in the harsh stone cells of the Boston Guildhall, while the rest of them were made to wander about the area looking for any kind of shelter from the cold and rain. Cotton Mather (1663-1728), pastor at the Second Church of Boston, Massachusetts, describes the scene:

> [When this] great Company of Christians Hired a Ship to Transport them for Holland, the Master perfidiously betrayed them into the Hands of those Persecutors; who Rifled and Ransack'd their Goods, and clapp'd their Persons into Prison at Boston, where they lay for a Month together. But Mr. Bradford being a Young Man of about Eighteen, was dismissed sooner than the rest.[11]

After an entire month, the magistrates released all but seven of the men and ordered the whole group to return to the Scrooby area. The seven who were retained in their cells until they could be "bound over to the assizes [courts]" included Robinson and Brewster. In the Guildhall Museum,[12] on South Street in Boston, one can still visit the courtroom, located directly above the dreadful cells which held the Pilgrim fathers. The two cells[13] are each about six feet wide by seven feet long, and each is secured by an iron-barred gate. Following their trials,[14] the prisoners would have walked down the narrow, winding stairway leading from a trap door of the courtroom down into the gaol area, just to the right of the cells. Winter was coming on now, and the Separatists would have to survive somehow until the spring. It would be too dangerous to attempt another escape before then. They hid with friends and relatives and lived as refugees in secret places until the cold winter was past.

In the late spring or early summer of 1608, the Pilgrims tried once again to escape to the sea. Bradford calls it "an adventure almost desperate," as he describes the giant step of faith and courage taken by these English farmers and villagers crossing a sea to take refuge in a strange land whose people spoke a foreign language and lived almost entirely by industrial manufacturing and commerce:

> Being thus constrained to leave their native soil and country, their lands and livings, and all their friends and familiar acquaintance, it was much; and thought marvelous by many. But to go into a country they knew not but by hearsay, where they must learn a new language and get their livings they knew not how, it being a dear place and subject to the miseries of war, it was by many thought *an adventure almost desperate*; a case intolerable and a misery worse than death. Especially seeing they were not acquainted with trades nor traffic (by which that country doth subsist) but had only been used to a plain country life and the innocent trade of husbandry. But these things did not dismay them, though they did sometimes trouble them; for *their desires were set on the ways of God and to enjoy His ordinances; but they rested on His providence, and knew Whom they had believed.*[15]

IMMINGHAM

This time, they contracted a Dutchman at the port of Hull for the employment of his ship. Today, the official name of this port is Kingston Upon Hull. The man agreed to have them board his vessel near Killingholme, now the site of Immingham Dock but then a remote stretch of coast five miles north of Grimsby, at the mouth of the Humber on the North Sea. The trip to Killingholme would be risky. Seventy-five to a hundred Separatists seen traveling together would surely result in more imprisonments and costly delays. So most of the men traveled by land, while the women, children and goods were placed on a rented barge which took an upstream route thru tributaries—Ryton Water over to Bawtry, then the Idle and the Trent to the Humber. The women and children encountered unspeakable difficulty and discouragement. When they arrived at the mouth of the Humber, they saw neither their men nor their ship. The Humber was so rough at its mouth that many of the women were becoming seasick. They persuaded the boatmen to move the barge into tiny Killingholme Creek, while they waited.

When the ship arrived in the morning, the tide was so low that the barge was bogged tightly in the creek mud. The men had arrived and were pacing the shore. They knew that it would be noon before the tide returned. The ship's captain dispatched a longboat and brought many of the men on board as they waited for the tide. The longboat was returning to pick up the rest of the men when suddenly the sight of a great host of armed English soldiers, approaching on both horse and foot, brought panic to the Dutch captain. Already nervous about taking these refugees out of England, he refused to wait any longer. Swearing his country's oath, *"Sacramente,"* the captain weighed anchor, hoisted sail and away they went. Women and children were now separated from husbands and fathers. A fearful tempest raged upon the ship for days, almost sinking it. With water running into their mouths and ears, sailors were crying, "We sink, we sink." While many prayers ascended to God, the vessel was spared. The storm had swept the ship far to the north, off the coast of Norway. The passengers, including William Bradford, with nothing but the clothes on their backs, reached Holland after fourteen long days. Meanwhile, John Robinson, William Brewster, and Richard Clyfton were with the barge, where mothers looked tearfully into faces of terrified children who were clinging to them, crying, and shivering with cold. The Separatists were brought before magistrate after magistrate, with no one knowing what to do with them. Bradford explains that the authorities "were glad to be rid of them in the end upon any terms, for all were wearied and tired with them. . . . And in the end, notwithstanding all these storms of opposition, they all gat over at length, some at one time and some at another, and some in one place and some in another, and met together again according to their desires, with no small rejoicing."[16] Robinson, Clyfton and Brewster remained with them to the end and finally went over in the last contingent. By August 1608, all of them were united in Amsterdam.

In 1924 the Anglo-American Society of Hull erected a twenty-foot monument commemorating this unforgettable story of the Separatists' final escape from England.[17] The monument, located across from the Church of St. Andrew, in Immingham, contains stones from the shores of Plymouth, Massachusetts and stands as a reminder of faith, bravery, and loyalty to God. It reads:

```
PILGRIM FATHERS
IMMINGHAM TO HOLLAND
1608
TO PLYMOUTH ROCK
NEW ENGLAND
1620


FROM THIS CREEK
THE PILGRIM FATHERS
FIRST LEFT ENGLAND IN 1608
IN SEARCH OF RELIGIOUS LIBERTY


THE GRANITE TOP STONE WAS
TAKEN FROM PLYMOUTH ROCK MASS
```

Perhaps there comes an occasional traveler with the age old question, "What mean these stones?" (Joshua 4:21). Surely the answer to that question is the Separatists' total dedication to the will of God, and their persistence in pursuing His purity for their lives, for their families, and for their churches. Their story will ever remain a source of inspiration and encouragement to serious believers. It would also seem especially appropriate to remember those Pilgrim women and children, as well as the "fathers."

The present-day route of the ferry from Kingston Upon Hull to Rotterdam includes the Pilgrims' *planned* route from Hull to Amsterdam. Today, this pleasant overnight (not fortnight) journey across the North Sea includes comfortable, first-class, two-berth cabins, a fine dinner and a delightful breakfast. As the ferry gets underway, one can look back and see the point of the Pilgrims' departure from Killingholme at Immingham Dock.[18]

1. William Bradford, *Of Plymouth Plantation 1620-1647,* ed. Samuel Eliot Morison (1952; rpt. NY: Alfred A. Knopf, 1998), 10. This work is hereafter referred to as "Bradford, Plymouth Plantation."

2. *High Commissioners Act Book,* vol. 15, Dec. 1, 1607, cited in Harold Kirk-Smith, *William Brewster 'The Father of New England'—His Life and Times—1567-1644* (Boston, England: Richard Kay, 1992), 83.

3. R. Tudur Jones and Alan Tovey, *Some Separatists: The Martyrs of 1593* (Beverley, North Humberside, England: An Evangelical Fellowship of Congregational Churches, 1993), 29-58. The book is the result of the Congregational Studies Conference Papers of 1993, which commemorated four hundred years since the deaths of Henry Barrow, John Greenwood, and John Penry.

4. It is impossible to know precisely how many people escaped England with the Scrooby group; but in Robinson's petition requesting permission from the Leiden magistrates for the group to settle there, he specifically states that they numbered "one hundred persons, or thereabouts, men and woman." The original document is archived in Leiden and cited in H. M. Dexter, *The England and Holland of the Pilgrims* (Boston: Houghton Mifflin Co., 1909), 383. Robinson obviously did not include the children in that figure. Harold Kirk-Smith thinks that the number of these Separatist refugees was smaller, since Scrooby's own population in 1603 numbered only 114, including seventy-one adults over the age of sixteen; see his *William Brewster 'The Father of New England'—His Life and Times—1567-1644,* 57, 89. However, most of the "Scrooby Separatists" actually lived in the neighboring countryside and in nearby villages. Including children and servants, the Scrooby group numbered between forty and seventy, while the Gainsborough group that joined them could well have numbered as many as thirty-five to forty. The total of these who escaped together, therefore, could have been anywhere from seventy-five to one hundred, possibly even a few over a hundred. Samuel Eliot Morison placed the number at "about 125 members of the Scrooby congregation," who went over to Amsterdam; see his footnote in Bradford, 15. The same figure is repeated by Robert Merrill Bartlett, *The Pilgrim Way* (Philadelphia: United Church Press, 1971), 83.

5. Edmund F. Jessup, *The Mayflower Story,* 4th ed. (Retford, England: Whartons Ltd., 1977, 1984), 8.

6. Although no one knows why locals have always affectionately referred to it simply as "the Stump," some think it is because no spire was ever added to the steeple. Ships at sea used it as a landmark. Saint Botolph's is also known as the "Calendar Church," since there are 365 steps to the top of the steeple lantern, 52 windows, 12 pillars supporting the roof, and 7 doors. Actually there are 51 windows now, since they gave one to Trinity Church in Boston, MA in 1879 in honor of its popular minister, Phillips Brooks, who preached at St. Botolph's Church during visits and wrote the carol "O Little Town of Bethlehem."

7. John Foxe is buried in the chancel of London's St. Giles Church, Cripplegate.

8. John Cotton, born in Derby, England, and educated at the University of Cambridge, became "vicar" of Saint Botolph's Church in 1612 and served until 1633, when he was himself forced out of England for his nonconformist views. He arrived in Boston, MA, in September of that year and became teacher of First Church.

9. See H. W. Nicholson, *Boston: the Town, the Church, the People* (Boston, England: Guardian Press Ltd., 1986); Mark Spurrell, *Boston Parish Church* (Boston, England: Ingelow Press, n.d.). Spurrell was lecturer of Boston, England, from 1965 to 1976.

10. Bradford, *Plymouth Plantation,* 12.

11. Cotton Mather, *Magnalia Christi Americana: or, The Ecclesiastical History of New-England from its first Planting in the year 1620 unto the year of our Lord 1698* (London: T. Parkhurst, 1702 folio), Book II:3-5. The citation is from the 1702 first edition folio at the Massachusetts History Society.

12. The Guildhall building, now a museum, predates the Pilgrims by almost two centuries. Until the Reformation, it was the hall of the Guild of St. Mary, which explains its church-like appearance externally. It would later serve as Boston's Town Hall. Besides the courtroom and cells, one can still visit the elegant council chamber, the handsomely beamed banqueting hall, and many exhibits. Especially rewarding is the painting "John Wesley Preaching from his Father's Tomb at Epworth" by George Washington Brownlow (1835-1876). The scene depicts Wesley after being refused the pulpit of the church where his father had labored for years. With the painting, the following inscription from Wesley's *Journal* (June 5, 1742) reads: "I stood near the East end of the Church near my Father's Tombstone, and cried, 'The Kingdom of Heaven is not meat or drink, but righteousness and peace and joy in the Holy Ghost.'"

13. There were probably more than two cells in those days, but only these remain.

14. This is assuming that there were trials. No trial records have survived.

15. Bradford, *Plymouth Plantation,* 11 (italics added).

16. Ibid., 14-15.

17. Until 1970 the memorial stood at the very site of Killingholme Creek, at Immingham Dock. Today, however, that original site is dominated by toiling oil refineries and industrial development.

18. William Penn later made Hull his port of departure. The city is also the birthplace of William Wilberforce, whose residence still stands.

CHAPTER 4

THE YEARS IN HOLLAND (1608-1620)

OVERVIEW OF THE POLITICAL BACKGROUND

Under William the Silent of Orange (1533-1584), the Netherlands had become an asylum of liberty for persecuted people.[1] During the long and desperate struggle with Roman Catholic Spain the provinces of Holland, Zeeland, and Utrecht had united under the "Pacification of Ghent" in 1576. The signing of the Union of Utrecht in 1579 formed an alliance of all northern and a few southern provinces. These Dutch provinces within the Union of Utrecht declared their independence in 1581. Tragedy struck, however, when in the town of Delft, in 1584, William the Silent was assassinated. Realizing the threat that Spain posed to England, Queen Elizabeth immediately offered military assistance to the Dutch, and the Earl of Leicester became the Governor General of the Netherlands in 1585-1586. It was at this time that William Brewster was in the Netherlands, serving in the diplomatic service of William Davison, the British Ambassador. When valuable security keys of the town of Flushing were delivered to Davison in Her Majesty's name, he entrusted them to Brewster, who slept with them under his pillow. Later, as they rode through England, Davison insisted that Brewster wear his gold chain.[2] Long before he returned as a religious refugee in exile, William Brewster would have great fondness for the Netherlands. He was there when the Earl of Leicester, the new Governor General, demonstrated sympathy to Calvinist reformers, such as the Walloon (French-speaking) and Flemish (Dutch-speaking) refugees who were swarming north to Zeeland and Holland, as the Spanish recaptured

59

the southern part of the Low Countries (present-day Belgium), including Antwerp. Many of them fled to England as well. Then the defeat of the Spanish Armada in 1588 seriously curtailed Spain's military capability. Upon Leicester's resignation in 1588, Prince Maurits (Maurice) of Orange-Nassau (son of William of Orange) succeeded him and became Stadholder (chief magistrate and military general). With massive assistance from England, by 1593 he had driven the Spaniards from the northern provinces. During these years the future Pilgrim, Myles Standish, was serving in the Dutch armies. By 1596 both England and France had recognized the United Provinces of the Netherlands as independent. Bringing independence closer to reality for the Dutch people, the States General, in 1609, signed a twelve-year truce with Spain.

This began an era of great commercial prosperity and a Golden Age of Dutch art, represented by such painters as Rembrandt van Rijn and Jan Vermeer. The Netherlands would soon become the foremost commercial and maritime power of Europe, with Amsterdam the financial center of Europe, and Dutch colonial expansion increasing in Africa, the East Indies, and the West Indies. Such was the political climate of the Netherlands when the English Pilgrim refugees arrived in Amsterdam in 1608. The religio-political climate would involve the great controversy between the Remonstrants and the Contra-Remonstrants,[3] climaxing with the 1619 Synod of Dort, just as the Pilgrims would be planning their departure for the New World. The sovereignty of the Dutch Republic of the United Provinces would finally become a reality in 1648 when the Peace of Westphalia marked the end of the Thirty Year's War—actually the Eighty Year's War (1568-1648) for the Dutch and Spanish. The southern provinces eventually became known as Belgium. With the English and the Dutch as the leading maritime and commercial nations of the world, rivalry between them resulted in two Anglo-Dutch wars (1652-1654 and 1665-1667), which resulted in the cessation of Dutch control in New Netherland, which then became New York.

AMSTERDAM

Amsterdam is situated on the river Amstel, which gave it its name— originally "Amstelredam" (dam or dyke of the Amstel). When the Pilgrims arrived in Amsterdam in 1608, the city was rapidly expanding. Its population increased from 50,000 to 120,000 between 1600 and 1630. Strategically situated at the confluence where the Amstel empties into the Zuider Zee (lit. South Sea), Amsterdam quickly became the chief commercial center of northern Europe. The city held this position until the late eighteenth century, when trade declined as a result of the silting of the Zuider Zee, as well as the British blockade before and during the Napoleonic Wars. In 1810 Napoleon incorporated the Netherlands into the French Empire, but after his downfall the Netherlands regained its independence and Amsterdam was made the capital of the country. During World War II, the people suffered great hardship when Amsterdam was occupied by the German army for five years.

The city is divided by canals into about ninety islands, joined by about four hundred bridges. Almost the entire city rests on a foundation of piles driven through peat and sand to a firm substratum of clay. The seat of government is The Hague. Amsterdam is one of the most important commercial centers in Europe. The city is a major port, linked to the North Sea and other European countries by a network of railways and canals, notably the North Sea Canal, which is navigable by oceangoing vessels. Among leading industries in the city are aircraft, shipbuilding, automobiles, sugar refining, publishing, paper products, textiles and clothing, porcelain and glass, chemicals, and the manufacture of heavy machinery. The city is also famous as a center for cutting and polishing diamonds and as the chief financial center of the Netherlands.

As an important center of European cultural life since the seventeenth century, Amsterdam is the site of the National Academy of Art, the Royal Netherlands Academy of Sciences, and the University of Amsterdam (1632). Its *Rijksmuseum* contains one of the largest collections of Dutch and Flemish paintings in the world, and its *Stedelijk Museum* has an extensive collection of modern works. Amsterdam is also noted as the home of the renowned painter Rembrandt; his home is now a museum. The Anne Frank House continues to inspire the thousands who visit it each year. The city has numerous examples of sixteenth- and seventeenth-century architecture. Some of the churches are even earlier, the *Oude Kerk* (Old Church) being built about 1300. In the large Dam Square in the center of the city is *Nieuwe Kerk* (New Church), built in the fifteenth century. John Smyth of Gainsborough was buried in New Church in 1612, next door to the present-day Royal Palace, begun later in the seventeenth century as a much smaller town hall building.

It was in an area of Amsterdam called the *Vloomburg* that many of the Pilgrims lived. Today, the only reminder of Pilgrim homes in Amsterdam is a narrow alley off the *Rembrantsplein* called *Engelse-Pelgrimsteeg* (English Pilgrim Lane). When they arrived in 1608, there were already three English congregations in the city: the English Reformed Church in the Begijnhof; the Ancient Church of Pastor Francis Johnson and teacher Henry Ainsworth; and John Smyth's church.

The English Reformed Church in the Begijnhof[4] seems to have originated as early as 1605, then organized under the pastorate of John Paget, in 1607, as a Presbyterian church of English merchants. The church has occupied the Beguine chapel in the Begijnhof since 1607, when Paget preached his first sermon here from Psalm 51:10, "Create in me a clean heart, O God; and renew a right spirit within me." The Begijnhof chapel is believed to go back to the fifteenth century. An extension was added to it in 1665 to accommodate the influx of English refugees fleeing to Holland following the Restoration of Charles II. The church's silver vessels are on permanent display in Amsterdam's *Rijksmuseum*. These include a baptismal basin, three communion dishes, and two collection boxes (called "poor boxes") of ebony wood set in silver. Such valuables, including the pulpit, were hidden away during the German occupation in 1940. The Nazis hung a swastika from the chancel wall and replaced the Psalmist's words, "Create in me a clean heart, O God," with words they considered more in tune with their own philosophy, *"Das Reich Gottes steht nicht in Worten, sondern in Kraft,"* that is, "The kingdom of God is not in word, but in power" (I Corinthians 4:20).

The Johnson-Ainsworth church was considered the first English-speaking church in Amsterdam (1596); hence, it was called simply the "Ancient Church." While Pastor Francis Johnson and other leaders of the group were still in prison in London, the congregation in 1593 fled to Holland—first to Kampen, then to Naarden, and finally to Amsterdam by 1596. Meeting in the home of Jean de l'Ecluse in an alley on the *Lange Houtstraat,* they were soon joined by Henry Ainsworth (1570-1622),[5] Cambridge man, Separatist preacher, and Hebrew scholar whose much-celebrated *Annotations on Several Books of the Bible* have seen many printings, especially those on the Pentateuch, the Psalms, and the Song of Solomon. The Ancient Church soon produced its statement of faith, *A True Confession,*[6] possibly written by both Ainsworth and Johnson. In 1597 Francis Johnson and his brother George were released from prison in London (Francis from the Clink, George from the Fleet).[7] Arriving in Amsterdam in October, they "hired a great house" near the *Regulierspoort,* with "sundry roomes" which they used as both a "dwelling and [a] preaching house." Here Francis Johnson resumed his duties as pastor. Ainsworth assumed the official position of teacher at about this time, or a little earlier. Their numbers increased from the perhaps fifty to sixty members who first arrived in Amsterdam, to some three hundred strong by 1610, not counting the children and attendees who were not members.[8] In 1607 they built their first building, situated on the *Lange Houtstraat,* ready to welcome the *Mayflower* Pilgrims as they arrived to worship with them the following year. Their officers included Johnson as pastor and Ainsworth as teacher. In addition to these there were "four grave men for ruling elders; and three able and godly men for Deacons; [and] one ancient widow for a deaconess." William Bradford describes this ancient widow as follows:

> [She] did them service many years, though she was sixty years of age when she was chosen. She honored her place and was an ornament to the congregation. She usually sat in a convenient place in the congregation, with a little birchen rod in her hand, and kept little children in great awe from disturbing the congregation. She did frequently visit the sick and weak, especially the women, and, as there was need, called our maids and young women to watch and do them other helps as their necessity did require; and if they were poor, she would gather relief for them of those that were able, or acquaint the deacons; and she was obeyed as a mother in Israel and officer of Christ.[9]

Pilgrim pastor Richard Clyfton, in his *Advertisement* (1612), would pen a firsthand description of the form of worship used in the Ancient Church: (1) prayer and giving of thanks by the pastor or teacher; (2) reading of two or three chapters of the Bible, with brief explanation as time permits; (3) singing of some of the Psalms of David; (4) preaching of the sermon by the pastor or teacher expounding and enforcing some passage of Scripture,

(5) singing again of some of the Psalms of David; (6) sacraments are administered without formal ritual; the Lord's Supper on stated Lord's Days, and baptism whenever there might be a candidate; (7) collection is then made, as each one is able, for the support of the officers and the poor.[10]

This was the same basic order of service used by the Pilgrims in Scrooby and Leiden. Baptism was by sprinkling, but it did not make one a member of the church; membership was by covenant only.[11] Comparing the officers, Bradford says that their own church was not "at all inferior in able men, though they had not so many officers as the other; for they had but one ruling elder [Brewster] with their pastor [Robinson], a man well approved and of great integrity; also they had three able men for deacons [including John Carver and Samuel Fuller]."[12] In their worship, the Pilgrims never tired of singing from Henry Ainsworth's *Book of Psalms: Englished Both in Prose and Metre.* Without a pastor in Plymouth Colony, there would be no administration of the sacraments there for several years; otherwise, Elder Brewster would follow the same basic pattern of worship as did the Ancient Church.

While John Smyth and his group arrived in Amsterdam in 1607 and worshipped with the Ancient Church, they soon left because of Smyth's opposition to the use of English Bible translations (all of them!), as well as the use of hymnbooks. Ainsworth said that Smyth "charged us with synn for using our English Bibles in the worship of God; & he thought that the teachers should bring the originals [of] the Hebrew and Greek, and out of them translate by voice."[13] Smyth's congregation moved into a bakehouse (bakery) which they rented from the Mennonite Jan Munter. They soon became Anabaptists and merged with the Mennonites.[14] With the decline of persecution, some separatists were quickly losing sight of their purpose.

A long period of dissension had been disrupting the Ancient Church itself, even at the time the Pilgrims were arriving. Francis Johnson's brother, George, was in the center of almost every controversy. He even published his "complaints" in *A Discourse of Some Troubles* (1603). He thought, for example, that Henry Ainsworth should be treated as "an apostate," for allegedly attending a Church of England worship service, even though it was conducted by a Puritan minister. George's differences with his brother, Francis, went back to the days when they were in prison in London. Francis had married Thomasine, widow of Edward Boyes, the successful Ludgate Hill haberdasher who had died in prison for his faith. The secret church used to meet sometimes in the Boyes home. Francis Johnson's own personal character was not called into question; his people respected him and esteemed him highly.[15] From the start, the troubles seem to be strictly with George, who resented Thomasine's smart style of dress. He considered her worldly and accused Francis of being "blinded, bewitched and besotted" by the beauty of his wife. George openly criticized Thomasine's use of "lace," her wearing of a "showish" hat and several gold rings, and "shaping" her clothing with whalebone and underpinnings (not an uncommon thing in a day when ladies' clothing was manufactured with no contour at all). He also complained about "scent and starched linen." Starch was "the devil's liquor" to George, who described Thomasine as "bouncy."[16] After members listened to weeks of unsavory discussion, in the end, it was George who was excommunicated from the church. Years later, William Bradford, in a discourse to young men, would speak well of both Francis and Thomasine:

> In our time his wife was a grave matron, and very modest both in her apparel and all her demeanor, ready to any good works in her place, and helpful to many, especially the poor, and an ornament to his calling. She was a young widow when he married her, and had been a merchant's wife, by whom he had a good estate, and was a godly woman; and because she wore such apparel as she had been formerly used to, which were neither excessive nor immodest, for their chiefest exceptions were against her wearing of some whalebone in the bodice and sleeves of her gown, corked shoes, and other such like things as the citizens of her rank then used to wear.[17]

In the midst of this disturbance, a division over church polity developed between Francis Johnson and Henry Ainsworth. Johnson had a bent towards Presbyterian church government, while Ainsworth had more congregationalist leanings. Ainsworth and his contingent left the church in 1610 and he began serving as their pastor. They used a former synagogue two doors down the street. In 1613, the Ainsworth group filed a lawsuit for possession of the Ancient Church's building and won the case. The Johnson group, probably the smaller in number, was ordered to hand over the deed for a settlement of 5,530 guilders. Johnson and his supporters then moved to Emden, Germany. Five years later, their earthly journey would come to a tragic end. After Johnson's death in 1618, most of his congregation set out on a disastrous voyage bound for Virginia. "Packed together like herrings," as William Bradford says, 130 of the 180 people on board died.[18]

Henry Ainsworth led the Ancient Church until his death in the spring of 1622/23. During their entire existence, the Ancient Church had but three church buildings. After their building on the *Lange Houtstraat* burned down in 1662, they found temporary facilities in a building on the *Groenburgwal,* then acquired "a pretty handsome and convenient" building situated behind a narrow alley called the *Bruinistengang* (the Brownists' Alley),[19] just off the *Rembrantsplein.* The Brownists' Alley no longer exists, but it was joined to the present-day *Barndesteeg,* which itself signifies "Place of the Burned." Running parallel to this is a street called *Bloedstraat,* which means Blood Street! These streets were so named because "heretics" were hanged or beheaded here during the sixteenth-century Spanish Catholic rule. To a nineteenth-century pilgrim who was standing before it, the badly deteriorated building was "no comelier than the little home among the boughs which the summer songster has deserted, after autumn winds and winter storms have devastated and fouled it."[20] He was alluding to a poem by Henry Vaughan:

> He that hath found some fledged bird's nest may know
> At first sight if the bird be flown;
> But what fair Dell or Grove he sings in now,
> That is to him unknown.

Today, this area is part of the red light district, called the *Wallen.* Two hundred years after the Ancient Church's dissolution, the building in Brownist Alley would become one of worst places of wickedness and crime in the city. The badly deteriorated building was mercifully torn down in 1910. It had served the Ancient Church until 1701, when the last five members joined the English Reformed Church of the Begijnhof (Presbyterian).

Today, there are plaques at the Begijnhof church commemorating the *Mayflower* Pilgrims, because of the time they worshipped in the Ancient Church. A bronze tablet on the wall to the right of the entrance door reads:

TO THE GLORY OF GOD IN CHRIST JESUS
THIS TABLET IS PLACED HERE BY A COMPANY OF THE
CLERGY OF THE REFORMED CHURCH IN AMERICA
A LINEAL DESCENDANT OF THE CHURCH OF HOLLAND,
AS A TRIBUTE TO
THE PILGRIM FATHERS
WHO SETTLED FIRST IN THE CITY OF AMSTERDAM
IN HOLLAND, THE COUNTRY OF THEIR ASYLUM,
A SHINING EXEMPLAR OF CIVIL AND RELIGIOUS LIBERTY,
MANY OF WHOSE INSTITUTIONS
TRANSMITTED TO AMERICA THROUGH THE
ENGLISH PILGRIMS AND THE DUTCH WHO
SETTLED IN NEW YORK, HAVE GIVEN TO THE
NEW WORLD A DISTINCTIVE CHARACTER
ERECTED A.D. 1927

Inside the church, a tablet on the left wall, near the chancel, reads:

ONE IN CHRIST
1609 - FROM SCROOBY TO AMSTERDAM - 1909
AINSWORTH - JOHNSON - ROBINSON - BREWSTER - BRADFORD
By a joint consent they resolved to go into the Low Countries
where they heard was freedom of Religion for all men
and lived at Amsterdam
(Governor William Bradford: History of Plymouth Plantation)
In grateful remembrance and in Christian brotherhood
The Chicago Congregational Club
rear this Memorial
A.D. 1909

In the center wall of the chancel is a memorial stained-glass window depicting John Robinson committing the Pilgrims to God, as they are about to depart on the *Speedwell* at Delfshaven.

With all the contention in the Ancient Church, it is not at all surprising that the Pilgrims found themselves unable to stay. At one time, half of the

67

congregation excommunicated the other half. The Pilgrims may have been sometimes reminded of the Mennonite, Jan van Ophoorn. After being expelled from his church (in Germany), he "excommunicated" the whole congregation and established a new church "without spot or wrinkle," composed of himself and his wife! Such would not be the Pilgrim way. In 1609, after about nine months in the Ancient Church, the approximately one hundred Pilgrims moved on to Leiden, twenty-five miles to the southwest. The Pilgrims' pastor from Babworth, Richard Clyfton, now serving as teacher for the Johnson group,[21] would remain behind, because of his age and physical condition. William Bradford, in his *Dialogue,* explains:

> [Clyfton] was a Grave and fatherly old man when hee Came first into Holland having a Great white beard and pitty it was that such a Reverend old man should be forced to leave his Country and att those yeers to Goe into exile but it was his Lott and hee bore it patiently much good had hee done in the Country where hee lived and Converted many to God by his faithfull and painfull minnestry both in preaching and cattechising sound and orthodox hee alwaies was and soe Continewed to his end; hee belonged to the Church att Leyden but being setled att Amsterdam and thus aged hee was loth to Remove any more; and soe when they Removed hee dismised to them there and there Remained untill hee died.[22]

LEIDEN

In Leiden, the Pilgrims would now resume their own church under the leadership of Pastor John Robinson. Robinson had a clear view of what he would regard for the rest of his life as biblical ecclesiastical separation. While the Ancient Church, along with John Smyth's church, regarded all ministers of the Church of England as apostate and utterly false, Robinson and the Pilgrims would avoid such rhetoric towards individuals. While they indeed regarded the Church of England as a false church, they would steadily maintain the same judicious, separatist stance that they had taken from the beginning. Furthermore, while the Pilgrims refused state support and practiced more of a congregational polity and ecclesiastical independency, they considered the Presbyterians and other Reformed churches in Leiden to be "true churches," with whom they found themselves compatible and enjoyed close fellowship. By their lives, ministries, and character, these believers would establish their position as traditional and consistently Separatist. In Leiden they would establish themselves in their communities as reasonable, hard working, godly individuals whose convictions were reflected in their adoration of God in the beauty of His holiness, and in their kind regard and treatment towards all people, including other Separatists who considered them as weak or compromising. Their neighbors would take notice of their sacrificial love for one another. The very word *Pilgrim* would become essentially related to words and ideas such as *sacrifice, humility, lovingkindness, consistency, strength, fundamental,* basic, and *separatist.*

Leiden—birthplace of Dutch artists Rembrandt van Rijn, Jan van Goyen, and Jan Steen—is located on the Old Rhine River, near The Hague. On February 12, 1609, the Pilgrims, as a group of "100 persons born in England," petitioned Leiden's city fathers for permission to settle in their city by May 1, "without being however a burden in the least to any one." Although the English ambassador, Sir Ralph Winwood, voiced his protest, the magistrates replied that they "did not refuse any honest persons free and unrestrained ingress, provided they behaved themselves honestly, and submitted to all the laws and ordinances here."[23] Rembrandt, the son of a local miller, was about three years old when the Pilgrims arrived. Before long, he would be studying in the Latin School (which still stands); and when the Pilgrims left the city in 1620, he was a fourteen-year-old student in the University. With about a third of its population consisting of Protestant refugees from the area now called Belgium, Leiden was Holland's second largest city when the Pilgrims arrived. Joining the city's growing population of perhaps more than 35,000,[24] they took up work as woolcombers, weavers, tailors, hatmakers, and glovers, as well as masons, carpenters, tobacco sellers and much more. About half of them worked with textiles. William Bradford, for example, took an apprenticeship with a silk manufacturer and soon became a fustian worker, a weaver of thick twilled cloth which retailed as corduroy or velveteen. Today, Leiden's industries still include textiles, food processing, metal products, printing, and publishing. There was much that the Pilgrims admired about this city whose citizens had successfully withstood a one-hundred-and-twenty-nine-day siege by the armies of Philip II in 1574-1575, during the Dutch revolt against Roman Catholic Spanish rule. During those months, more than six thousand of the city's citizens had died of starvation and epidemics. The Dutch navy finally broke the dikes and sailed in flatboats right up to the city walls to free the people. As a reward for their Dutch Protestant heroism, Prince William I of Orange founded the University of Leiden in 1575, primarily to train Reformed clergy, and since 1600 to train military engineers as well.[25] It became a state institution in the nineteenth century and is now supported by the national government. The main building of the University (erected in 1581) was a familiar sight to the Pilgrims, who would also have walked over the grounds of the present-day *Hortus Botanicus* (botanical gardens), from which tulip bulbs from Turkey, as well as tobacco and tomato plants from the Americas, were first introduced to the rest of Europe. The Leiden American Pilgrim Museum offers a taste of Pilgrim life in the Netherlands. (See the guide provided in Appendix F.)

Although no one knows where the Pilgrims worshipped during their first two years in Leiden, the congregation of the Pieters Kerk (St. Peter's Dutch Reformed Church) probably permitted the Pilgrims to hold their own services at agreed times in their grand building until they could establish their own place of worship.[26] Robinson says, "Touching the Reformed Churches, we account them true churches of Jesus Christ, and both profess and practice communion with them; the sacraments we do administer to their members—if, by occasion, any of them be present with us. Our faith is not negative, nor consists in condemning others."[27] Prior to the Reformation, the Pieterskerk was a Roman Catholic basilica, its present structure built during the late fifteenth century. Its four-hundred-foot spire collapsed in 1512 and was never rebuilt. A tower was erected on the property to house the bell. On October 3, 1574, at the end of the Spanish siege, Leiden's citizens had poured into the Pieterskerk to give thanks for their miraculous relief. The date immediately became Leiden's traditional Thanksgiving Day celebration, which the Pilgrims observed while there, and which continues to be observed today, with local parades, pageants, and fireworks. (Since its deconsecration as a place of worship in 1975, the Pieterskerk has been used for cultural and entertainment purposes.)

For eight thousand guilders, in 1611, the Pilgrims purchased a building just across from the bell tower of the Pieterskerk. The property was located in the Kloksteeg (Bell Alley), which runs from the Pieterskerk down to a bridge and over to the nearby University. The building was known as *De Groene Poort* (Green Close). Robinson and his family lived upstairs and used the ground floor as a meetinghouse for worship and business gatherings. On the plot of land behind the meetinghouse, the Pilgrims built as many as twenty-one small cottages, probably constructed with brick, which was cheaper than wood at that time.[28] Here the Pilgrims lived, as new refugees from England steadily joined them until Robinson's congregation grew to about three hundred. Many of those coming over from England were French Reformed (Walloon) refugees. They had escaped initially to England, where Walloon and Flemish congregations, practically independent of the Church of England, were establishing congregations in locations extending along the east from Kent to Norfolk, including London, Canterbury, Sandwich, and Norwich. With many of the Pilgrims originating from these same areas and already familiar with them, some of the Walloons worshipped with Robinson's congregation in Leiden, where they found themselves in doctrinal agreement.[29] The Pilgrims held three services a week, twice on Sundays and once on Thursday evenings. The Sunday morning worship service would last from eight to noon. Being less formal, the afternoon service would often include the "prophesyings" (lay preaching),[30] with previously selected male members speaking from Scripture texts assigned by the pastor.[31]

THE SYNOD OF DORT

As the largest and most imposing of all previous synods of the Reformed Churches, the Dutch Synod of Dort was one of the most consequential international topics of discussion at the time the Pilgrims were in Holland. Jacobus Arminius (1560-1609),[32] controversial theology professor at the University of Leiden, died in Leiden about six months after the Pilgrims arrived. Arminius's home was on the *Pieterskerkhof* and his burial was in the Pieterskerk. After Arminius's death, his views were championed and further developed and systematized by two men, Simon Episcopius (1583-1643)[33] and Jan Uytenbogaert (1557-1644). In 1610 these men and their supporters sent a petition, called the "Remonstrance" (meaning "reproof"), to the States of Holland and West Friesland. The petition set forth their views in "Five Articles," called the Articles of Remonstrance. In substance these brief Articles teach as follows:[34]

71

1. God has decreed to save through Jesus Christ those of the fallen and sinful race who through the grace of the Holy Spirit believe in him, but leaves in sin the incorrigible and unbelieving. (i.e., election is conditioned by God's foreknowledge of who would respond to the gospel).
2. Christ died for all men (not just for the elect), but no one except the believer has remission of sin.
3. Man can neither of himself nor of his free will do anything truly good until he is born again of God, in Christ, through the Holy Spirit.
4. All good deeds or movements in the regenerate must be ascribed to the grace of God, but His grace is not irresistible.
5. Those who are incorporated into Christ by a true faith have power given them through the assisting grace of the Holy Spirit to persevere in the faith. But it is possible for a believer to fall from grace.

The most practical expressions of Arminianism have included the sermons and hymns of John and Charles Wesley, many of England's eighteenth-century revivals, many of the nineteenth-century American camp meetings, and the continued witness and stand of Fundamentalist Methodists and Free Will Baptists.

The main apologist for the Contra-Remonstrants was Franciscus Gomarus (1563-1641), theology professor and former colleague of Arminius at the University. When all attempts at reconciliation between the two parties failed, a National Synod convened in the city of Dort (Dordrecht), November 13, 1618, to May 9, 1619, with delegates representing each of the Dutch provinces, along with twenty-six invited attendees from several countries, including England, Scotland, the southern provinces of Germany, and Switzerland. Leader of the powerful merchants of Amsterdam, Johan van Oldenbarnevelt, the highest official in the Dutch Republic, shared the Remonstrants' views. Supporting the Counter-Remonstrants' party was Prince Maurice, who had succeeded his father, William of Orange, as the stadholder of the northern provinces. John Robinson, an honorary member of the University since 1615, probably attended some of the sessions, which ended with the condemnation of the Remonstrants. Two hundred ministers were deposed from their pulpits, eighty of whom were sent into exile. There were hundreds of imprisonments, including the theologian Hugo Grotius (1583-1645), who was sentenced for life. He later escaped, but Johan van Oldenbarnevelt was beheaded. The Synod's response to the Five Articles of the Remonstrance came under "Five Heads," known as the Canons of Dort. The doctrines of this creed are sometimes depicted, in their abbreviated form, in an acrostic of the word "tulip." The actual "Heads," however, with each subdivided into several "Articles," occupy almost fifty pages of Philip Schaff's *Creeds of Christendom* and must be studied in their entirety, rather than this mere skeleton outline:[35]

T =Total depravity of the entire human race.

U =Unconditional election of some to salvation.

L =Limited atonement, i.e., Christ died for the elect only.

I =Irresistible grace.

P =Perseverance of every believer.

The atrocities that occurred in the political climate surrounding Dordrecht could not in any way be synonymous with the theology of Calvinism expressed, not only in the articles of Dort, but also in the Heidelberg Catechism, the Belgic Confession, the True Confession of the Separatist Ancient Church (used by the Pilgrims), the Westminster Confession, the Baptist London Confessions, the Philadelphia Baptist Confession, and lives and ministries of Puritans, Presbyterians, and Particular Baptists from Charles Spurgeon to William Carey. The Great Awakenings in America would originate with faithful Dutch Reformed ministers such as Theodore Frelinghuysen and later with the Fulton Street Dutch Reformed Church in New York City.

Although, in time, the Remonstrants would again be allowed the freedom to work and to establish churches and schools in the Netherlands, the immediate results of this National Synod brought unpleasant times for the Pilgrims. While they entertained no dreams of the modern notion of a complete separation of church and state, they had already seen in England the harm that a state church can render to the work of Christ. Now they were beginning to see it again. With the emotion of theological controversy spilling into the streets, lay citizens with no spiritual perception of the nuances of doctrine had begun to look with suspicion and hatred toward anyone who was not a part of the national Dutch Reformed Church. Such people must be "Arminians!" They must be "enemies of the

Dutch Republic!" City officials were forced to erect barricades around City Hall (*Stadhuis*) to protect themselves against rioters.

On April 28, 1619, during the Synod's debates, sixty-three-year-old James Chilton, a Leiden Pilgrim, with his daughter Isabella, was walking from church to his house in *Lange Brug,* when about twenty young fellows surrounded them, shouting that Arminians were gathering illegally in the Chilton home. The boys had confused the Chiltons for the hated Remonstrants. The crowd began throwing stones and Mr. Chilton was hit in the head and knocked to the ground. His doctor later reported to the authorities that Chilton was in danger of death. Professor Jan van Dorsten, of the University of Leiden, notes that "the violence of this incident towards nonconformists in general must have strengthened the resolve of the Pilgrims to leave."[36] As the oldest person on board the *Mayflower,* James Chilton would never see Plymouth; he died while the ship was anchored off Provincetown, Cape Cod.

It was possible, in this climate of misinformation, that some might confuse the Pilgrim Separatists with the followers of John Smyth, who had embraced the heresy of Pelagianism,[37] or with those of Thomas Helwys, who had embraced Arminianism.[38] Even though the Separatist Pilgrims of Leiden wholeheartedly supported the Reformed doctrines of Geneva, with John Robinson expressing his agreement in a *Defence of the Doctrine Propounded by the Synode at Dort* (1624),[39] the controversy had created legal and social problems for the Separatists, especially since they did not possess *official* standing or recognition from the Dutch Reformed Church or the municipal authorities. Professor Jan van Dorsten has called attention to the fact that, in the wake of the Synod of Dort, the Estates General published in Leiden on July 15, 1619 an edict prohibiting the gathering of religious groups outside the Dutch Reformed Church and forbidding such groups from collecting alms for their orphans, their elderly, or their poor. He adds that "the edict was specifically aimed against the Remonstrants, and was never enforced against the Pilgrims." Nevertheless, its very wording "created a legal basis for the possibility of suppressing English language congregations outside the officially recognized English Reformed Church, which was affiliated with the Dutch Reformed Church."[40]

THE PILGRIM PRESS

On *Pieterskerkkoorsteeg* (St. Peter's Choir Alley), walking towards City Hall *(Stadhuis)* from the Pieterskerk, after passing about four buildings on the left, one can see an alley called the *William Brewstersteeg*. (Until 1983, this was called *Stincksteeg,* or Stench Alley). Over the entrance of this alley, a tablet commemorating the "Pilgrim Press" reads:

> Site of the Vicus Choral (or Pilgrim) Press in
> Pieterskerkkoorsteeg (St. Peter's Church Choir Alley)
> Leyden, Netherlands, in the (1609-1620) home of the
> Separatist Pilgrim, elder William Brewster of
> Scrooby, Nottinghamshire, England, the spiritual
> leader of Plymouth in New England until his death in 1643-44.

Halfway down *William Brewstersteeg,* William Brewster in 1609 purchased a house, where he often taught the English language to foreign students, especially Danes and Germans, who attended the nearby University. Adjacent to his home he ran a printing press, located in a corner house on *Pieterskerkkoorsteeg*. From the Pilgrim Press,[41] established in 1616/17, came books which were outlawed in England for their Separatist views. Brewster had three partners in the enterprise: Edward Winslow and John Reynolds, who were printers from London, and Thomas Brewer, who financed the enterprise. In order to establish the press without arousing suspicion, they printed nothing inflammatory in the earliest three titles. These were the only ones that bear the name of William Brewster, but two of them include the publisher's address on the title page. (These would eventually reveal his address to the authorities.) The popular book fairs were excellent places to disseminate literature quickly. Before long, the press was turning out Separatist literature and Brewster was smuggling it into Great Britain, most likely in false bottoms of wine barrels. (See Appendix G for the list of titles that came from the Pilgrim Press.)

The two most-hated of the approximately eighteen titles which came from Brewster's press were *De Regimine Ecclesiae Scoticanae Brevis Relatio* (1618) and *Perth Assembly* (1619), both written by the Scotsman, David Calderwood.[42] Smuggled into Scotland and widely read, these books vigorously attacked the efforts of King James I to force the Church of

England's episcopal form of government (of bishops) upon the Presbyterian Church of Scotland. James believed not only in the divine right of kings, but the divine right of bishops. With his policy meeting fierce opposition, James had called a general assembly of the Church of Scotland, meeting at Perth in 1618, where he hoped to successfully impose his rules upon Scottish Presbyterians. Calderwood urged all Scots to reject James's demands upon Scotland's churches. James's "Five Articles," as described on the title page of the *Perth Assembly*, included (1) kneeling in the act of receiving the Lord's Supper; (2) holy days; (3) bishopping; (4) private baptism; and (5) private communion. Such demands were anathema to Presbyterians, who regarded these things as remnants of Romanism. Calderwood exposed what he regarded as the eternal dangers of such beliefs and practices. He believed that the Church of England retained too much form and substance of the Roman Catholic Church, which insisted that kneeling at the Mass was required because the bread and wine changed into Christ's literal body and blood. "Bishopping" referred to the episcopal form of church government. Private baptism and private communion referred to these ordinances being administered outside the official church, in which many believed, like the Roman Catholic Church, that water baptism washes away original sin.

Informed in a letter from the British ambassador at The Hague, that such books were being printed by "a certain English Brownist of Leyden,"[43] the infuriated James I sent agents to trace the author and the print-type of the forbidden literature. James took these kinds of incidents exceedingly personal, priding himself on being what he considered a theologian and an expert in ecclesiastical matters. Calderwood went into hiding in Leiden, where he secretly worshipped with the Pilgrims. In the spring of 1619, William Brewster was in England with Robert Cushman, negotiating with the Virginia Company for a patent for the Pilgrims to settle in Virginia. In September, agents stormed upon Brewster's property and discovered the Pilgrim Press in Choir Alley. They seized the books, pamphlets, and print-type and proscribed the press. The Dutch authorities, known for allowing a free press, but not wishing to hinder relations with the British, were in a delicate position. Perhaps that might suggest why the records are a little obscure on what happened next. The British ambassador, Sir Dudley Carlton, reported that Brewster had been arrested. Two days later, Carlton confessed that this information turned out to be false, since the bailiff who had been sent to arrest Brewster was a "dull [stupid], drunken fellow" and he had arrested the wrong man. Carlton gladly reported, however, that Brewster's assistant, Thomas Brewer had definitely been arrested. The available evidence allows the following conjecture. Because of the similarity of the names Brewster and Brewer, the drunken bailiff thought that he had apprehended Brewster. With the closing of the Pilgrim Press, Brewster avoided arrest by remaining in England. He would meet the Pilgrims when they arrived.[44] Meanwhile, he continued the negotiations, traveling *incognito* under the name of "Master Williamson," a name which appears in Plymouth Colony records for only a brief time, then disappears without explanation.[45] The name "William Brewster" then suddenly emerges as the elder of Plymouth Church. This may also explain why Brewster was not apprehended when boarding the *Mayflower* in Southampton. Brewster's father's first name was William and it was customary in Holland to call a man by his patronymic. In the Dutch records, for example, Jonathan Brewster's name appears as Jonathan "Willemsz," which means the son of William. Meanwhile, as for Thomas Brewer, he returned to England, where he eventually spent fourteen years in prison.

REASONS FOR LEAVING HOLLAND

With the closing of the Pilgrim Press occurring concurrently with the Remonstrants and Contra-Remonstrants controversies and riots of 1618-1619, the Pilgrims realized that the day was rapidly approaching when their flock could be scattered. Similar fears which had plagued them back in Scrooby once again consumed their thoughts. The walls of their safe haven seemed to be crumbling around them. Proverbs 22:3 says that "a prudent man foreseeth the evil, and hideth himself: but the simple pass on, and are punished." According to William Bradford, the Pilgrims took seriously that advice:

> And therefore according to the divine proverb, that a wise man
> seeth the plague when it cometh, and hideth himself, Proverbs
> xxii.3, so they like skillful and beaten soldiers were fearful either
> to be entrapped or surrounded by their enemies so as they should
> neither be able to fight nor fly. And therefore thought it better to

dislodge betimes to some place of better advantage and less danger, if any such could be found.[46]

The Pilgrims had even more reasons for leaving Holland. Europe's political climate was in growing turmoil. The twelve-year truce between Holland and Roman Catholic Spain was coming to an end. The war known later as the Thirty Years' War had just begun in 1618. With the Pilgrims' brief freedom now threatened, the tide of English Separatist refugees to Holland was ebbing.[47] Coming from rural English villages, many of them were now growing old and weary from the factory life. A heavier burden, however, was the worldly culture which had grown accustomed to Sabbath-breaking. Everywhere, there was that "danger of conscience" which troubled sensitive Christians. Christian youth with adventurous dreams were being lured to far away places. Bradford describes their unbearable yoke:

> But that which was more lamentable, and of all sorrows most heavy to be borne, was that many of their children, by these occasions and the great licentiousness of youth in that country and the manifold temptations of the place, were drawn away by evil examples into extravagant and dangerous courses, getting the reins off their necks and departing from their parents. Some became soldiers, others took upon them far voyages by sea, and others some worse courses tending to dissoluteness and the danger of their souls, to the great grief of their parents and dishonor of God. So that they saw their posterity would be in danger to degenerate and be corrupted.[48]

The future of the traditional English family itself seemed threatened. The Pilgrims, feeling as foreigners in a strange land, desired to preserve their own language and culture, while bringing up their children according to the dictates of their own consciences, submitted as they were to the Bible. Bradford adds that they were concerned, too, for the propagation and advancement of the gospel in regions which had not heard: "Lastly (and which was not least), a great hope and inward zeal they had of laying some good foundation, or at least to make some way thereunto, for the propagating and advancing the gospel of the kingdom of Christ in those remote parts of the world; yea, though they should be but even as stepping-stones unto others for the performing of so great a work."[49]

NEGOTIATING PLANS FOR LEAVING

While the Pilgrims briefly considered going to the fertile and tropical climate of British Guiana, the majority agreed to settle in English North America. They knew that the Virginia Company of London held the right to settle in North America, up to forty-one degrees latitude north, extending as far as Manhattan and most of Long Island, and that they had already planted a colony at Jamestown in 1607. Captain John Smith, the great explorer, had published his *Description of New England* (1616), and the Pilgrims must have read it with great interest. In 1617, they dispatched two agents, John Carver and Robert Cushman, with seven articles expressing a loyal English stance, to solicit a patent from the Virginia Company of London. James I approved of their aim to advance his dominion. Hearing that they planned to make their livelihood by fishing, the king was reported to have said, "So God have my soul, tis an honest trade; twas the Apostles' own calling." The arrangement which the Pilgrims received, however, was very different from that for which they had applied; its terms were hard and its advantages few.

The Pilgrims held a solemn meeting and a day of humiliation to seek the Lord for His direction. After prayers, they waited for their pastor's counsel, which came in a sermon. He took as his text I Samuel 23:3-4, which reads, "And David's men said unto him, Behold, we be afraid here in Judah: how much more then if we come to Keilah against the armies of the Philistines? Then David inquired of the Lord yet again. And the Lord answered him and said, Arise, go down to Keilah; for I will deliver the Philistines into thine hand." From that text, Pastor Robinson "taught many things very aptly and befitting their present occasion and condition, strengthening them against fears and perplexities and encouraging them in their resolutions."[50] The first "resolution" was that they would indeed leave, but on several conditions. Only a part of the church, ideally the youngest and strongest, would go at this time. If a majority decided to go now, Robinson would go also; if only a minority, Elder Brewster would go and Robinson would stay behind. Robinson and others would later join them. If the adventure failed, the voyagers would be welcomed back "to heart and home." In addition, Bradford notes, "those that went should be an absolute church themselves, as well as those that stayed." However, in his last letter before he died (a December 20, 1623, reply to a letter from

Brewster), Robinson strongly discouraged the unordained elder from administering the two ordinances, baptism and the Lord's Supper.[51] Plymouth would not have the sacraments until 1624, and later than that in any regularity. They simply would not consider any other pastor until it was certain that Robinson would not be able to come. Then followed a long and dismal search for the right person.

Still seeking a reasonable patent, Robert Cushman and William Brewster returned to London in the spring of 1619, while a search began for investors to underwrite the cost of the voyage. While the Dutch made them a proposition about settling in New Netherland, Thomas Weston, a London ironmonger, also offered investment support. Weston headed a company of Merchant Adventurers and was searching for financial opportunities. Rejecting the Dutch overture, the Pilgrims instructed their representatives in London to make necessary arrangements with Weston's Merchant Adventurers, who consisted of some seventy people who would invest varying amounts of money in the Plymouth Colony. Consequently, on February 2, 1620, the Virginia Company of London issued to John Peirce, an associate of Weston, a patent granting the Pilgrims permission to settle within their jurisdiction.[52] Unfortunately, Weston at the last minute persuaded Robert Cushman to accept a revised agreement, which omitted a provision allowing the colonists a couple of days a week for their own needs and private enterprises. Even as the Pilgrims were departing for the New World, the issue was not resolved and would ultimately cause great conflict for them at Plymouth Plantation. This problem is discussed in more detail in chapter seven.

JOHN ROBINSON'S INFLUENCE AND LEGACY AS A SEPARATIST

With only about fifty-five of a congregation of over three hundred making the trip at this time, the pastor reluctantly remained behind to continue caring for the larger part of his flock. Highly esteemed in the community, Robinson in 1615 became an honorary member of the University of Leiden. As a defender of Reformed theology, he had participated in the debates leading to the famous Synod of Dort (1619). Bradford describes Robinson as the model pastor, "very profittable in his minnestry and Comfortable to his people. . . . His love was great towards them, and his care was always bent for their good, both soul and body." Timothy George writes, "Robinson's pastoral reputation and the harmony which prevailed at the 'Church of the Green Door' during his tenure—in striking contrast to Separatist squabbling elsewhere—contributed, no doubt, to his popularity and credibility as an apologist for the Separatist way."[53]

Robinson's view of separatism was not quite as stringent as that of John Smyth. In a letter, he exposed the *Prophane Schism of the Brownists,* published in London in 1612. Robinson was willing to fellowship personally with Puritans and Anglicans who lived godly lives. In his *Treatise on the Lawfulness of Hearing the Ministers of the Church of England,* published in Leiden in 1634, "according to the copy that was found in his study after his decease," Robinson allowed for members of Separatist churches to hear sermons preached by godly ministers of the Church of England. Such a milder form of Separatism helps to explain why the New England Pilgrims were not separated enough for Roger Williams and why, on the other hand, they got along so well with the Massachusetts Puritans. Robinson's doctrine of separation was founded squarely upon the biblical doctrine of God's holiness, which he expresses in his *Defence of the Doctrine Propounded by the Synode at Dort,* published in Leiden in 1624. Howbeit, John Robinson never lacked a cutting edge in his biblical convictions. As George himself concludes, Robinson "remained a staunch advocate of Separatist ecclesiology in all of its essentials, and consistently refused to recognize any parish in England as a true visible Church."[54] Separatism has never been a pilgrimage without discouragement. Joseph Hall, a prominent minister in the Church of England wrote the following critical letter to John Robinson, rebuking him for separating from the mother church, the Church of England:

> We hear of your separation, and mourne; yet not so much for you, as for your wrong: you could not do a greater injurie to your mother, than to flie from her. Say shee were poore, ragged, weake; say she were deformed; yet shee is not infectious; or if she were, yet she is yours. This were Cause enough for you, to lament her, to pray for her, to labour for her redresse, not to avoid her: This unnaturalnesse is shameful; and more hainous in you, who are reported, not parties in this evill, but authors . . . . The God of heaven open your eyes, . . . otherwise, your soules shall find too late that it had been a thousand times better to swallow a

Ceremonie, than to rend a Church: yea, that even whoredom and murders shall abide an easier answer than Separation.[55]

Robinson replied, "She is our 'mother,' so may she be, and yet not the Lord's wife!" Robinson reasoned that the Church of England herself had come into being by separating from "her mother, the Church of Rome" and that it was from the Babylonish *Church* of England, not from the *kingdom* of England, that the Pilgrims had separated. Separation, says Robinson, is always "very odious in the eyes of all them from whom it is made." Hence, the "Church of England can better brook the vilest persons continuing communion with it, than any whosoever separating from it." Separation from the world "is the first step to our communion with God, and angels, and good men." If the Separatists have unscripturally offended, let them be blamed, explains Robinson, but "if your church be deeply drenched in apostasy, and you cry Peace, Peace, when sudden and certain desolation is at hand, it is you that do wrong."[56] Robinson's *Justification of Separation from the Church of England,* published in Amsterdam in 1610, stands as one of greatest apologies of all time for the general principles of Separatist ecclesiology.

While many more of the Leiden congregation would come to America during the later 1620s and 1630s, Robinson's own hopes of joining them in the New World would never be realized. After a short illness of eight days, he died peacefully on the first of March, 1625 (same year as King James I and William Hickman of Gainsborough) and was buried three days later, presumably inside the Pieterskerk. No one knows where John Robinson's remains lie. For many years, the church simply removed from the earth, underneath the pavement, the bodies which had been longest interred, in order to make room for others. No one kept any record of the exact location of his grave. At his funeral, however, university professors and Leiden ministers followed his bier into the church, as they bewailed the loss of "that worthy instrument of the Gospel." In 1928 the following memorial tablet was unveiled inside the baptismal chapel in the southwest corner:

In Memory of
JOHN ROBINSON
Pastor of the English Church in Leyden
1609   1625
His Broadly Tolerant Mind
Guided and Developed the Religious Life of
THE PILGRIMS OF THE MAYFLOWER
Of Him These Walls Enshrine All That Was Mortal
His Undying Spirit
Still Dominates the Consciences of A Mighty Nation
In the Land Beyond the Seas
This Tablet Was Erected By the General Society of Mayflower
Descendants in the United States of America   A.D. 1928

On the church's outer wall, a bronze tablet bears this inscription:

In Memory of
Rev. John Robinson, M.A.
Pastor of the English Church Worshipping Over Against
This Spot, A.D. 1609--1625, Whence at his Prompting
Went Forth
THE PILGRIM FATHERS
To Settle New England
in 1620

- - - - - - - - -

Buried under this house of worship, 4 Mar. 1625
Aet. XLIX Years.
In Memoria Aeterna Erit Justus.
Erected by the National Council of the Congregational
Churches of the United States of America
A.D. 1891.

William Bradford left a valuable description of John Robinson:

He was a man learned and of solid judgment, and of a quick and
sharp wit, so was he also of a tender conscience, and very sincere

in all his ways, a hater of hypocrisy and dissimulation, and would be very plain with his best friends. He was very courteous, affable and sociable in his conversation, and towards his own people especially. He was an acute and expert disputant, very quick and ready, and had much bickering with the Arminians, who stood more in fear of him than any of the university. He was never satisfied in himself until he had searched any cause or argument he had to deal in thoroughly and to the bottom; and we have heard him sometimes say to his familiars that many times, both in writing and disputation, he knew he had sufficiently answered others, but many times not himself; and was ever desirous of any light, and the more able, learned, and holy the persons were, the more he desired to confer and reason with them. He was very profitable in his ministry and comfortable to his people. He was much beloved of them, and as loving was he unto them, and entirely sought their good for soul and body. In a word, he was much esteemed and reverenced of all that knew him.[57]

Shortly after Robinson's death, his congregation began dispersing in many directions. This was just what the Pilgrims had feared. Eventually, the meetinghouse and all of the Pilgrim dwellings in Bell Alley were demolished. On that exact spot at No. 21 Kloksteg, there stands an almshouse, erected in 1683 for the benefit of aging members of the Eglise Wallone, a French-speaking Protestant Reformed congregation. The almshouse, known as the Jean Pesijnhof, was built in accordance with the Last Will and Testament of Jean Pesijn and his wife, Maria de Lannoi.[58] At the front entrance of the Jean Pesijnhof facade, a memorial was inscribed:

On this spot lived, taught and died
JOHN ROBINSON 1611 - 1625

The Dutch "hof" is equivalent to the English "close," i.e., a narrow passageway leading from a street to a row of dwellings or apartments. Through the brick-arched entrance of the Pesijnhof, a little porch leads out into the tree-shaded courtyard, once called the *Engelse Poort* (English Close). It was here in this garden that many of the English Separatists lived in their tiny cottages, oftentimes packed with overnight guests. One thing the Pilgrims would appreciate in Plymouth Plantation was space! The Leiden American Pilgrim Museum displays tile fragments dug here and dating from the time of John Robinson. Standing here today, one might imagine hearing the joyful echoes of three hundred saints singing from their Ainsworth *Psalter* (without instruments), "there being many in the congregation very expert in music," or the gentle voice of a pastor praying over his congregation. What ever happened to the congregation's majority who remained behind? What finally moved them away from Bell Alley? Where did they go after the pastor's death? The church existed until about 1635, by which time more than sixty-five more had followed the original fifty-five to leave Leiden and sail to Plymouth Colony. Therefore, a total of approximately 120 of the congregation—including the strongest among them—had made the pilgrimage to New Plymouth by the time of the Bell Alley church's demise. Isaac Robinson,[59] only ten years old in 1620, would become the only child of John Robinson ever to see New England, arriving about 1631/32. Thomas Prince, pastor of the Old South Church in Boston, Massachusetts, recorded in his *Annals* that "Isaac came over to Plimouth Colony, living to above ninety years, a venerable man, whom I have often seen, and has left male posterity in the county of Barnstable."[60] John Robinson would have rejoiced to know that one son, many grandchildren, and untold posterity would actually realize much of his own personal dream of freedom on Cape Cod.

After the dissolution of the Bell Alley church, Robinson's "widow [Bridget], children, and other relatives and friends"[61] joined the Dutch Reformed Church. Bridget died in 1643. Some of the Bell Alley congregation joined the English/Scottish Reformed (Puritan) Church, which at the time was using the chapel of the St. Catherine's Hospital.[62] There is no record of what actually happened to the majority of the Scrooby-Leiden Separatists. Of the Pilgrims' eventual assimilation into Dutch society, Jeremy Bangs points out that Pilgrim descendants who remained in Leiden and in nearby towns became "thoroughly Dutch."[63] As with the Ancient Church, today's world would have scarcely heard of them were it not for the *Mayflower* Pilgrims, who carried the Separatist witness to the New England wilderness. This is the group which preserved the providential workings which had unfolded in England—testimonies of Separatist conviction, persecution, imprisonment, martyrdom for some, and exile for others. Today's church would know little, for example, of the drama which began with Francis Johnson's burning of Separatist books, his being gripped in his soul by a copy which he saved from the flames, his own imprisonments, then the years in Amsterdam and Germany, and his own death, followed by the perishing of his congregation at sea. The Pilgrims themselves never realized that their own lives and convictions would inspire millions to emulate them and to trust and obey the God they adored and worshipped. There is no indication that they entertained the slightest notion that future generations might study them or even know who they were. Thus they would keep few and scanty records (no official land records), during their first fifteen years at Plymouth Plantation! All the more reason to be thankful for William Bradford's pen!

DEPARTURE FROM LEIDEN—"THEY KNEW THEY WERE PILGRIMS"

On July 30, 1620 (N.S.), the Pilgrims were preparing to sail. They had already purchased a Dutch ship, a 60-ton "pinnace" called the *Speedwell,* to accompany the *Mayflower,* a 180-ton vessel which the Adventurer Thomas Weston had contracted and which would be waiting for them at Southampton, England. They planned to use the *Speedwell* permanently for trading in the New World. They gathered early that morning at Pastor Robinson's home in Bell Alley, as Bradford explains, to hear him preach the farewell message from Ezra 8:21, a well-chosen text depicting the Jews in fifth-century B.C. Persia as they longed for their homeland:

> They had a day of solemn humiliation, their pastor taking his text from Ezra viii.21: "And there at the river, by Ahava, I proclaimed a fast, that we might humble ourselves before our God, and seek of him a right way for us, and for our children, and for all our substance" [Geneva Translation]. Upon which [text] he spent a good part of the day very profitably and suitable to their present occasion; the rest of the time was spent in pouring out prayers to the Lord with great fervency, mixed with abundance of tears.[64]

Robinson declared it a day of fasting and prayer to prepare them for the arduous voyage ahead. That farewell service in Pastor Robinson's home quickly became a gathering of genuine praise, prayer, and worship before the eternal throne. That night the whole church gathered for the farewell dinner of goose and pudding. Edward Winslow, twenty-five years later, recalled the occasion: "Pastors house being large, where wee refreshed our selves, after our teares, with the singing of Psalmes, making joyfull melody in our hearts, as well as with the voice, there being many of the Congregation very expert in Musick; and indeed it was the sweetest melody that ever mine eares heard." Winslow also recalls Robinson's farewell address:

> In the next place, for the wholesome counsell Mr. Robinson gave that part of the Church whereof he was Pastor, at their departure from him to begin the great worke of Plantation in New-England, amongst other wholesome Instructions and Exhortations, hee used these expressions, or to the same purpose; We are now ere long to part asunder, and the Lord knoweth whether he should live to see our faces again: but whether the Lord had appointed it or not, he charged us, before God and his blessed angels, to follow him no further than he followed Christ. And if God should reveal anything to us by any other instrument of his, to be as ready to receive it, as ever we were to receive any truth by his Ministry. For he was very confident the Lord had more truth and light to break forth out of his holy Word.[65]

The next morning, from the Nuns Bridge on the Rapenburg, they set out by canal boat, moving through the waters of the Vliet and the Schie twenty-four-miles south to Delfshaven, Rotterdam, where the *Speedwell* was waiting. As Leiden receded into the distance, with its familiar red-tiled roofs, its lofty spires, and its great windmill with white sails slowly turning in the morning breeze, Pilgrim hearts and minds doubtless flooded with tender memories. Some had begun their married lives in Leiden—William and Dorothy Bradford;[66] Edward and Elizabeth Winslow; Isaac and Mary Allerton; Samuel and Bridget Fuller; Degory and Sarah Priest; and others.[67] Many children, such as the Bradford's own son, were staying behind until they could be brought over later, when the beginnings of a settlement would be carved out of a wilderness and there would be actual homes to greet them. Little did they realize that five-year-old John Bradford would never again see his mother and that he would not see his father for seven years and, by then, his father would be remarried. William Brewster was likely already waiting in Southampton for Mary and their two young sons, Love and Wrestling. They were leaving three of their five children behind. It had to be unspeakably difficult for family members to part from one another, with some 3,500 ocean miles and untold dangers separating parents and children, husbands and wives, who loved one another as their own souls. It is at this point that Bradford first describes these Christians as "Pilgrims."

The word *Pilgrim* (παρεπιδημος) in the New Testament means a "stranger," "sojourner," or "exile" residing in a country not his own. The word appears only in Hebrews 11:13, I Peter 1:1 ("strangers" in the KJV), and I Peter 2:11.[68] Bradford plainly refers his readers to the words of Hebrews 11:13: "These all died in faith, not having received the promises, but having seen them afar off, and were persuaded of them, and embraced them, and confessed that they were strangers and pilgrims on the earth." The next verse adds, "For they that say such things declare plainly that they seek a country." The Pilgrim Separatists, with their confidence in God, were departing from Leiden in a great step of faith and courage. Hebrews 11:16 adds, "But now they desire a better country, that is, an heavenly: wherefore God is not ashamed to be called their God: for he hath prepared for them a city." William Bradford's own thoughts transcend to a country far better than any place on earth: "So they left that goodly and pleasant city which had been their resting place near twelve years; but they knew they were pilgrims, and looked not much on those things, but lift up their eyes to the heavens, their dearest country, and quieted their spirits."[69]

Henry Ainsworth and Francis Johnson, in the preface to their 1596 *True Confession* of the Ancient Church in Amsterdam, had likewise described their congregation as "Pilgrims."[70] It was only after 1798, however, that the term *Pilgrims* began to appear in common speech to distinguish the *Mayflower* passengers. Nathaniel Morton first copied the word into the *Plymouth Church Records* of the Old Colony in the seventeenth century.[71] After that, Cotton Mather and other New England historians made a few passing references to it. Then by the end of the eighteenth century, it was beginning to become popular, as evidenced at the 1799 Boston celebration of Forefathers' Day.[72] By 1820 the "Pilgrim Society" was incorporated in Plymouth. In December of that year, Daniel Webster, in his famous speech delivered at the two-hundredth-anniversary celebration of the Pilgrims' landing, freely praises "the Pilgrims." James Thacher, in his 1832

History of the Town of Plymouth, shows frequent usage. And that was the year which witnessed the debut of "America," ("My country, 'tis of thee"), with its "land of the Pilgrim's pride." William Bradford's biblical word had finally become an American household symbol of the faith of the fathers.

DEPARTURE FROM DELFSHAVEN—THE TIDE "STAYS FOR NO MAN!"

Delfshaven (then called Delft Haven) lies in the western section of Rotterdam and was once the harbor for the town of Delft. From Delfshaven's quay in the Voorhaven, the voyagers spent the remainder of the day hauling food and cargo to the *Speedwell.* Apparently, the Pilgrims did not leave unnoticed by the Dutch people. This was an important occasion for them. A new colony might well emerge from this voyage. Jeremy Bangs has brought attention to a painting identified as "The Departure of the Pilgrims from Delfshaven," by the Dutch artist Adam Willaerts (1577-1664). Willaerts signed this painting in 1620. One of the Pilgrims departing Delfshaven in 1620 was Edward Winslow, who had helped Brewster with his printing in Leiden. Winslow would later be called upon to lead in the negotiations of an international peace treaty. The 1654 Treaty of Westminster contains the name Edward Winslow, diplomat appointed by Oliver Cromwell and the Dutch States General. A 1654 engraving depicting the ceremony of the ratification of the Peace of Westminster in White Hall Palace includes Edward Winslow among the dignitaries surrounding Cromwell and the Dutch ambassadors.[73] There is no doubt, however, that one of the most cherished events of Edward Winslow's life was the final evening in Delfshaven with his fellow Pilgrims.

It could have been just a few proximate yards away, in Delfshaven's *Oude Kerk* (Old Church), commonly known now as the "Pilgrim Fathers' Church,"[74] that the Pilgrims gathered that evening for their last worship service before sailing from the continent. In those days, church doors were seldom locked. As a Dutch Reformed Church, its people would no doubt have welcomed the Pilgrims, who indeed needed a place larger than local homes could provide. Friends came from as far away as Amsterdam, nearly fifty miles distance, to see them off. Bradford says that the night "was spent with little sleep by the most, but with friendly entertainment and Christian discourse and other real expressions of true Christian love." Southampton awaited the voyagers, as a fair wind greeted them early the next morning, August 1 (N.S.). It was time for final embraces. Everyone knelt on board the ship's deck, as Pastor John Robinson committed his people to God, in a moving and humble prayer which brought tears to every eye. They knew indeed that they were Pilgrims and they would never again come this way. Bradford recalls:

> What sighs and sobs and prayers did sound amongst them, what tears did gush from every eye, and pithy speeches pierced each heart; that sundry of the Dutch strangers that stood on the quay as spectators could not refrain from tears. Yet comfortable and sweet it was to see such lively and true expressions of dear and unfeigned love. But the tide, which stays for no man, calling them away that were thus loath to depart, their reverend pastor falling down on his knees (and they all with him) with watery cheeks commended them with most fervent prayers to the Lord and His blessing. And then with mutual embraces and many tears they took their leaves one of another, which proved to be the last leave to many of them.[75]

The commemorative tablet on the front of the Pilgrim Fathers' Church, at the end of quayside, reads simply:

This is the startingpoint of the 'Speedwell'
On which the Pilgrim-Fathers sailed to
England on August 1st 1620
They changed the boat there for the
'Mayflower' bound for the New World

Van deze plaats zeilden de Pelgrim-Vaders
Op 1 Augustus 1620 met de 'Speedwell' naar
Engeland en vervolgens met de 'Mayflower'
Naar de Nieuwe Wereld.

To "a salute of small shot and three pieces of ordnance," followed by cheers from the good burghers of Delfshaven, Pilgrim hearts and hands were lifted as the little vessel cast off and sailed down the river. Edward

Winslow adds, "And so, lifting up our hands to each other, and our hearts for each other to the Lord our God, we departed, and found his presence with us in the midst of our manifold straits he carried us through."[76]

1. One of the best sources for this early period is John Lothrop Motley, *The Rise of the Dutch Republic*, 3 vols. (London: Frederick Warne and Co., 1886).

2. William Bradford, *Of Plymouth Plantation 1620-1647*, ed. Samuel Eliot Morison (1952; rpt. NY: Alfred A. Knopf, 1998), 325. This work is hereafter referred to as "Bradford, *Plymouth Plantation*." See the discussion in John A. Goodwin, *The Pilgrim Republic: An Historical Review of the Colony of New Plymouth With Sketches of the Rise of Other New England Settlements, the History of Congregationalism and the Creeds of the Period* (Boston: Houghton Mifflin Company, 1920), 19.

3. These issues are defined and discussed in the present chapter.

4. Good sources on the English Reformed Church in Amsterdam include Alice C. Carter, *The English Reformed Church in Amsterdam in the Seventeenth Century* (Amsterdam: Scheltema & Holkema, 1964); and Keith L. Sprunger, *Dutch Puritanism: A History of English and Scottish Churches of the Netherlands in the Sixteenth and Seventeenth Centuries* (Leiden: E. J. Brill, 1982), 91-122. I was assisted also by helpful miscellaneous materials provided by the church itself.

5. Good sources on Henry Ainsworth include Benjamin Brook, *The Lives of the Puritans* (Pittsburgh, PA: Soli Deo Gloria, 1994), II:299-303; Daniel Neal, *The History of the Puritans, or Protestant Nonconformists; from the Reformation in 1517, to the Revolution in 1688* (NY: Harper & Brothers, 1843-44), I:356f.; Champlin Burrage, *The Early English Dissenters in the Light of Recent Research (1550-1641)* (Cambridge: Cambridge University Press, 1912), I:159-73, *passim;* and Henry Martyn Dexter, *The Congregationalism of the Last Three Hundred Years as Seen in Its Literature* (NY: Harper and Brothers, 1880), *passim.*

6. William L. Lumpkin, *Baptist Confessions of Faith* (Valley Forge: The Judson Press, 1969), 79-97. The Particular Baptists would later use the *True Confession* as a model for their First London Confession (1644).

7. Francis and George Johnson planned to establish a Separatist colony in Canada, but this ended in failure; see B. R. White, *The English Separatist Tradition: From the Marian Martyrs to the Pilgrim Fathers* (London: Oxford University Press, Ely House, 1971), 97-98; and John Brown, 113.

8. Henry Martyn Dexter and Morton Dexter, *The England and Holland of the Pilgrims* (1906; rpt. Baltimore: Genealogical Publishing Co., Inc., 1978), 423, 445.

9. William Bradford, *A Dialogue, or the Sum of a Conference between some Young Men born in New England, and sundry Ancient Men that came out of Holland and Old England* [Dialogue held in] Anno Domini 1648, published in its entirety in Alexander Young, ed., *Chronicles of the Pilgrim Fathers of the Colony of Plymouth, from 1602 to 1625* (1844; rpt. Baltimore: Genealogical Publishing Co., Inc., 1974), 455-56.

10. Cited in Henry Martyn Dexter and Morton Dexter, 541-43; see also Horton Davies, *The Worship of the English Puritans* (Westminster: Dacre Press, 1948), 166, 244, and *passim.*

11. Nathaniel Morton, *New England's Memorial* (1669; rpt. Boston: Congregational Board of Publications, 1855), 424.

12. William Bradford, *Dialogue,* published in its entirety in Alexander Young, ed., *Chronicles,* 456.

13. *Differences of the Churches of the Separation,* 12, published in 1608; cited in Henry Martyn Dexter and Morton Dexter, 447.

14. The John Smyth church is discussed more fully in chapter 8, on the Baptists, in this book.

15. The church did suffer from rumors and scandals among its members.

16. For further discussion of the problems within the Ancient Church, see Champlin Burrage, *The Early English Dissenters in the Light of Recent Research* (1550-1641) (Cambridge: Cambridge University Press, 1912), I:167-82; and Timothy George, *John Robinson and the English Separatist Tradition* (Macon, GA: Mercer University Press, 1982), 86-87.

17. William Bradford, *Dialogue,* published in its entirety in Alexander Young, ed., *Chronicles,* 446.

18. Bradford, *Plymouth Plantation,* 357.

19. See Keith L. Sprunger, *Dutch Puritanism: A History of English and Scottish Churches of the Netherlands in the Sixteenth and Seventeenth Centuries* (Leiden: E. J. Brill, 1982), 51. In derision, the Ancient Church was called the Brownist Church.

20. Alexander Mackennal, *Homes and Haunts of the Pilgrim Fathers* (London: The Religious Tract Society, 1899), 123-24.

21. Richard Clyfton supported the Johnson group during the split in the Ancient Church. He replaced Ainsworth as their teacher and served until the group departed for Germany. He died in 1616 and was buried in Amsterdam's *Zuiderkerk* (South Church). This beautiful church was built in 1603, a masterpiece of Dutch Renaissance architecture, with its pale stone tower and its red and gold clock. At this writing, this prominent landmark is being used primarily as a center for "urban renewal."

22. *Plymouth Church Records 1620-1859* (1920-23; rpt. Baltimore, MD: Genealogical Publishing Co., Inc., 1975), I:139.

23. The text of the original document is in D. Plooij and J. Rendel Harris, *Leyden Documents Relating to the Pilgrim Fathers* (Leyden: E. J. Brill, 1920), iff.; see also D. Plooij, *The Pilgrim Fathers from a Dutch Point of View* (1932; rpt. NY: AMS Press, Inc., 1969), 42ff.

24. Joke Kardux and Eduard van de Bilt, *Newcomers in an Old City: The American Pilgrims in Leiden 1609-1620* (Leiden: Uitgeverij Burgersdijk & Niermans, 1998), 27. This excellent book shows that with religious refugees coming to Leiden from England, France and other countries, the city's population grew from "about 12,000 people in 1574 to 26,000 in 1600 and 45,000 in 1622." Some older works are probably mistaken in citing such high 1609 population numbers as "one hundred thousand;" for example, see Edward Arber, ed., *The Story of The Pilgrim Fathers, 1606-1623 A.D; as Told by Themselves, Their Friends, and Their Enemies* (London: Ward and Downey, Limited, 1897), 143.

25. Motley, *The Rise of the Dutch Republic,* II:516-58.

26. The Pilgrims were in doctrinal agreement and on friendly terms with the Dutch Reformed Protestants. The Pilgrims' simplicity, rather than formality, in public worship was the major difference. Of course, the Pilgrims would not have especially liked such Dutch Reformed practices as celebrating marriages as church ceremonies and celebrating Christmas, Easter, and Ascension Day. The Pilgrims, of course, would not have had sufficient space in their own homes to accommodate general worship services. They probably held cottage prayer meetings at times, but for church services they most likely used the Pieterskerk.

27. Cited by William Bradford's nephew, Nathaniel Morton, *New England's Memorial* (1669; rpt. Boston: Congregational Board of Publications, 1855), 424-25.

28. For a view of everyday Pilgrim life in Leiden, see Jeremy D. Bangs, "A Real Leiden Pilgrim House," in *The Pilgrims in the Netherlands: Recent Research,* ed. Jeremy D. Bangs, (1985; rpt. Leiden: Leiden American Pilgrim Museum, 1998), 44-50; Ozora S. Davis, *John Robinson: The Pilgrim Pastor* (Boston: The Pilgrim Press, 1903), 139. Davis correctly states that twenty-one homes were erected and the arrangement had no resemblance whatsoever to "communistic schemes" of living together; see also Henry Martyn Dexter and Morton Dexter, *The England and Holland of the Pilgrims* (1906; rpt. Baltimore: Genealogical Publishing Co., Inc., 1978), 532.

29. Jeremy D. Bangs, *Pilgrim Life in Leiden* (Leiden: Leiden American Pilgrim Museum, 1997), 18.

30. See chapter one for the meaning and origin of prophesyings.

31. Nathaniel Morton, *New England's Memorial* (1669; rpt. Boston: Congregational Board of Publications, 1855), 425-27.

32. The best study of Arminius is Carl Bangs, *Arminius: A Study in the Dutch Reformation* (Eugene, OR: Wipf and Stock Publishers, 1998). Bangs provides an excellent historical context for the Pilgrims in Holland.

33. John Robinson challenged Episcopius in debate and won much recognition for his knowledge and skills.

34. Philip Schaff, *The Creeds of Christendom, with a History and Critical Notes* (NY: Harper & Brothers, 1877), III:545-49.

35. Ibid., III:550-97.

36. Jan van Dorsten, "Why the Pilgrims Left Leiden," in *The Pilgrims in the Netherlands: Recent Research*, ed. Jeremy D. Bangs, 34.

37. William L. Lumpkin, *Baptist Confessions of Faith* (Valley Forge: The Judson Press, 1969), 100.

38. Ibid., 118-19; Thomas Helwys also wrote *A Short and Plaine Proofe by the Word and Workes of God that Gods Decree is Not the Cause off Anye Mans Sinne or Condemnation and that All Men are Redeamed by Christ,* (Amsterdam, 1612).

39. See the excellent discussion in Timothy George, *John Robinson and the English Separatist Tradition* (Macon, GA: Mercer University Press, 1982), 169-237.

40. Jeremy D. Bangs, *The Pilgrims in the Netherlands,* 34; see also Bangs, *Pilgrim Life in Leiden,* 44.

41. There is a valuable discussion, with accompanying documents, of Brewster and the Pilgrim Press in Edward Arber, ed., *The Story of The Pilgrim Fathers, 1606-1623 A.D: as Told by Themselves, Their Friends, and Their Enemies* (London: Ward and Downey, Ltd., 1897), 195-247; see also the following helpful chapters in Jeremy D. Bangs, ed., *The Pilgrims in the Netherlands: Recent Research,* including Theo Bögels, "Govert Basson, English Printer at Leiden," 18-23; R. Breugelmans, "The Pilgrim Press and How Its Books were Sold," 24-28; and Paul Hoftijzer, "A Continuing Tradition: English Puritan Booksellers in the Second Half of the Seventeenth Century in Amsterdam," 29-33.

42. The most valuable source is Rendel Harris and Stephen K. Jones, *The Pilgrim Press: A Bibliographical & Historical Memorial of the Books Printed at Leyden by the Pilgrim Fathers* (Cambridge: W. Heffer and Sons, 1922).

43. Edward Arber, ed., *The Story of The Pilgrim Fathers, 1606-1623 A.D: as Told by Themselves, Their Friends, and Their Enemies,* 198.

44. Such a conjecture agrees with the records provided in Henry Martyn Dexter and Morton Dexter, *The England and Holland of the Pilgrims* (1906; rpt. Baltimore: Genealogical Publishing Co., Inc., 1978), 580 and *passim.* Some records suggest that Brewster was hiding away during this time in the Dutch village of Leiderdorp, a few miles to the northeast of Leiden, but this is not conclusive.

45. See G. Mourt (Edward Winslow and William Bradford), *Mourt's Relation: A Journal of the Pilgrims at Plymouth,* ed. Dwight B. Heath (1622; rpt. Bedford, MA: Applewood Books, 1986), 56.

46. Bradford, *Plymouth Plantation,* 23.

47. Ibid., 27.

48. Ibid., 25.

49. Ibid.

50. Ibid., 36.

51. See Bradford, *Plymouth Plantation,* 377; Robinson's advice was in harmony with the Confession of the Ancient Church of Johnson and Ainsworth; see Williston Walker, *The Creeds and Platforms of Congregationalism* (Boston: The Pilgrim Press, 1960), 70. There is a helpful discussion of this in Timothy George, *John Robinson and the English Separatist Tradition,* 156-57, n. 263.

52. The original text of this first patent has not survived.

53. Timothy George, *John Robinson and the English Separatist Tradition,* 90.

54. Ibid., 241.

55. John Robinson, *Works of John Robinson with a Memoir and Annotations,* ed. Robert Ashton (London: John Snow, 1851), III:401-420, *passim;* also cited in part in Henry Martyn Dexter and Morton Dexter, *The England and Holland of the Pilgrims,* 450-51.

56. Robinson, *Works,* III:401-420 *passim.* No copy of Robinson's reply has survived, except in Joseph Hall's *Works,* which Ashton used to extract it into his edition of Robinson's *Works.*

57. William Bradford, *Dialogue,* published in its entirety in Alexander Young, ed., *Chronicles,* 452.

58. The name "De Lannoi" is preserved in the middle name of Franklin Delano Roosevelt.

59. The Leiden poll tax register of October 15, 1622, states that John and Bridget Robinson had six children: John, Bridget, Isaac, Mercy, Fear, and Jacob. John matriculated at Leiden University in 1633 and became a medical doctor, soon returning to England.

60. Cited in Alexander Young, ed., *Chronicles of the Pilgrim Fathers of the Colony of Plymouth, from 1602 to 1625* (1844; rpt. Baltimore: Genealogical Publishing Co., Inc., 1974), 453-54, n. 2; Young cites Thomas Prince, *Chronological History of New England in the Form of Annals* (Boston, 1826), 238. The quotation does not appear in the 1736 edition, but Prince, who died in 1758, added it to the later edition.

61. D. Plooij, *The Pilgrim Fathers from a Dutch Point of View* (1932; rpt. NY: AMS Press, Inc., 1969), 91, 93-94.

62. Today, the former St. Catherine's Hospital is a Walloon Church. In the Pilgrims' day, however, the hospital's chapel was being used by Leiden's English/Scottish Reformed Church, first led by pastors Robert Dury (Durie) and Hugh Goodyear. This church was a counterpart to Amsterdam's Begijnhof church and had originated between 1607 and 1609, about the time of the Pilgrims arrival in Leiden. Both were recognized as "official" churches, in harmony with the Dutch Reformed churches. In 1644, the one at Leiden began using the former Falijde Begijnhof Chapel on the Rapenburg. It stood close to the Bell Alley property and John Robinson's congregation had used this building on occasions. See Joke Kardux and Eduard van de Bilt, *Newcomers in an Old City: The American Pilgrims in Leiden 1609-1620* (Leiden: Uitgeverij Burgersdijk & Niermans, 1998), 29, 37; and Plooij, *The Pilgrim Fathers,* 47-49, 82-99.

63. Bangs, *Pilgrim Life in Leiden,* 43-44.

64. Bradford, *Plymouth Plantation,* 47.

65. Edward Winslow, *Hypocrisie Unmasked,* published in its entirety in *The Mayflower Descendant* 27, no. 2 (April 1925): 59, 65 (34 vols., compiled and published by George Ernest Bowman, from 1899 to 1937, Massachusetts Society of Mayflower Descendants), on "Mayflower Legacy," 43-vol. searchable CD edition, Wheat Ridge, CO: Search & Research Publishing Corporation, 1998, containing *The Mayflower Descendant With Other New England Town Records.* The sections cited above are Winslow's *Hypocrisie Unmasked* (London, 1646), 91, 97. The same work was reissued in 1649, under the title, *The Danger of Tolerating Levellers in a Civil State;* see also Timothy George, *John Robinson and the English Separatist Tradition,* 91; and Daniel Neal, *The History of the Puritans, or Protestant Nonconformists; from the Reformation in 1517, to the Revolution in 1688* (NY: Harper & Brothers, 1843-44), I:476-77.

66. William Bradford was twenty-three years old and Dorothy May was sixteen when they were married. Dorothy May's family belonged to Amsterdam's Ancient Church as late as 1613; see D. Plooij and J. Rendel Harris, ed., *Leyden Documents Relating to the Pilgrim Fathers* (Leyden: E. J. Brill, 1920), iv, xvii, lxx.

67. The Pilgrim marriages in Leiden are registered at the *Stadhuis* (City Hall).

68. The Old Testament word *pilgrimage* usually refers to one's sojourn on earth; hence, the patriarch Jacob says to Pharaoh, "The days of the years of my pilgrimage are an hundred and thirty years: few and evil have the days of the years of my life been, and have not attained unto the days of the years of the life of my fathers in the days of their pilgrimage" (Genesis 47:9). Likewise, the Psalmist exclaims, "Thy statutes have been my songs in the house of my pilgrimage" (Psalm 119:54). The word "stranger," in Genesis 17:8, however, denotes an idea similar to the New Testament word.

69. Bradford, *Plymouth Plantation*, 47.

70. Williston Walker, *The Creeds and Platforms of Congregationalism*, 58.

71. *Plymouth Church Records 1620-1859*, I:43.

72. Cited in "Reports from the State Societies," *The Mayflower Descendant* 1, no. 2 (April 1899): 114.

73. Jeremy D. Bangs, "Towards a Revision of the Pilgrims: Three New Pictures," *The New England Historical and Genealogical Register* 153, no. 609 (January 1999): 3-28. The article includes photocopies of the two scenes mentioned above.

74. The Old Church (Pilgrim Fathers' Church) of Delfshaven was built about 1417. It converted to Protestantism in 1574. In 1761 it was completely rebuilt into its present appearance. It has plaques and a window commemorating the Pilgrims. Of the Pilgrim Fathers' Church in Delfshaven, Bangs says that the building "is now owned by the non-profit Foundation for Old Churches in Holland, which leases it to the congregation for its normal uses, and which prefers to call the building the 'Pilgrim Fathers' Church' in an attempt to raise funds for the laudable goal of maintaining this ancient medieval monument" (ibid., 14).

75. Bradford, *Plymouth Plantation*, 48.

76. Edward Winslow, *Hypocrisie Unmasked*, published in its entirety in Alexander Young, ed., *Chronicles of the Pilgrim Fathers of the Colony of Plymouth, from 1602 to 1625*, 384.

CHAPTER 5

THE SAILING OF THE MAYFLOWER
FROM OLD ENGLAND

ROTHERHITHE

In London's Rotherhithe section, on the south bank of the River Thames, was the *Mayflower*'s home berth, where Captain Christopher Jones (spelled "Jonas" by Bradford) had received his orders to meet the *Speedwell* at Southampton and together make the voyage to the New World. At Rotherhithe's Mayflower Court, the "Mayflower Public House," a sixteenth-century seafarers inn, originally called the Spread Eagle, is nestled by the jetty on which Captain Jones and his crew stepped to board their ship. The sea dog skipper and his crew had no doubt shared many a spine-tingling tale of the sea in this old pub. Born at Maldon and married at Harwich, Jones had moved to Rotherhithe in 1611 when it was a village. He was the *Mayflower*'s master and quarter-owner.[1] On the corner of St. Marychurch and Rotherhithe Streets, opposite the pub, is the parish church of St. Mary's, where Jones is buried in an unknown spot somewhere underneath the parking lot.

Although not Separatists themselves, the *Mayflower*'s captain and crew would have no doubt been previously acquainted with the Separatist movement. The Rotherhithe section is less than two miles down the river from Southwark, where Separatists had been meeting openly since 1616, when Henry Jacob established an Independent church there. Separatists John Greenwood, Henry Barrow, and John Penry had been thrown into Southwark's Clink Prison and hanged in 1593. Jones's master mate and pilot, John Clarke,[2] had grown up in Rotherhithe and had been baptized and married in the parish church. Since 1611, the church's rector had been the famous Puritan author Thomas Gataker (1574-1654), who had just returned from the Netherlands and who would become a prominent member of the Puritans' Westminster Assembly in 1643. The church records show that two of Jones's children were baptized here in St. Mary's Church. The present building of St. Mary's was erected in 1715, largely replacing the smaller twelfth-century building of Jones's day. On July 25, 1620, as Jones and his crew navigated the *Mayflower* from the little jetty at the Spread Eagle pub for the trip to Southampton, little did the captain realize that on March 5, 1622 (N.S.), his weather-beaten body would be returned to the dust of St. Mary's churchyard. The trip would take its toll upon crew and passengers alike.

SOUTHAMPTON

Situated near the head of Southampton Water (inlet of the English Channel), on the Itchen and Test rivers, the city of Southampton was an important port even in the Middle Ages and is still perhaps the major trading port on the southern coast of England. As early as the eighteenth century it became a fashionable resort town. It still has passenger traffic to the Continent, but its transatlantic passenger traffic has actually declined from that of earlier centuries. During World War II German bombs heavily damaged the port. There is a memorial of tribute to the D-day Allies who sailed from Southampton to Gold Beach for the liberation of Normandy on June 6, 1944. The principle industries today are shipbuilding and the manufacture of motor vehicles.

Waiting for the *Mayflower* when it arrived at Southampton on July 29 was John Alden, who joined the voyage as the ship's cooper. Alden's fame rests chiefly on the romantic and fictional tale written by the American poet Henry Wadsworth Longfellow, "The Courtship of Myles Standish" (1858). In the poem, Alden, deeply in love with Priscilla Mullins, proposes to her on behalf of his shy friend Myles Standish, whereupon she inquires, "Why don't you speak for yourself, John?" In 1623 Alden did indeed marry Priscilla Mullins and the Alden home in Duxbury, Massachusetts stands today. John Alden lived longer than any of the other signers of the *Mayflower Compact*.

On Wednesday, August 5, as the *Speedwell* sailed into Southampton, her passengers saw the *Mayflower* for the first time. Captain Christopher Jones had her prepared and waiting, probably off the north end of the West Quay. It is remarkable that neither William Bradford's *Plymouth Plantation* nor Mourt's *Relation* mentions the name of the *Mayflower* (or of the *Speedwell*). Except for entries in the London Public Records of vessels sailing at that time, the name of the ship does not appear in any source until the Land Division of 1623 in Plymouth Colony. They divided the land that year partly according to the year that each family had arrived on three ships—the *Mayflower* (1620), the *Fortune* (1621), and the *Anne* (1623). In what is probably William Bradford's own handwriting, the record begins with those who "came first over in the May-Floure."[3] The earliest published mention of the vessel's name is in *New England's Memorial* (1669) by Nathaniel Morton, who was raised by his uncle, William Bradford. Morton would have accurately known the ship's name; he also gives the name and size of the *Speedwell*.[4]

Patient research has made it possible to have a near accurate picture of the *Mayflower*.[5] In Pilgrim Hall Museum in Plymouth, Massachusetts, there is a *Mayflower* model, carefully researched and constructed by marine archeologist, R. C. Anderson. Also in Plymouth, there is *Mayflower II,* the full-scale replica built at Upham's Yard in Brixham (Devon), England. This ship made the voyage from Plymouth, England in 1957. The *Mayflower* was a cargo ship which, according to Bradford in his history, "was hired at London, of burthen about 9 score."[6] This is about 181 tons by modern standards. The *Mayflower* had three masts and six sails. Five were big and square—fore and main courses, fore and main topsails, and a spritsail on the bowsprit. Then there was a smaller triangular mizzen (aft) sail. The ship was steered with a whipstaff attached to the tiller. Her length was a little over a hundred feet from the back rail to the end of the bowsprit beak; that would be perhaps up to ninety feet at the waterline. Her keel was about sixty-four feet and her board width was about twenty-five feet. She was armed with twelve cannon (eight "minions" and four "sakers"). Also on board was a four-ton shallop (over thirty feet long), brought over in pieces and put together on the beach of Cape Cod Harbor (Provincetown). The *Mayflower* would have also carried a twenty-foot longboat (or work boat).

Passengers and crew together totaled about 120. The captain's cabin was at the after end of the half-deck. There were probably four mates, four quartermasters, a surgeon, a carpenter, a cooper, and cooks, along with the boatswains and gunners. There are records of the *Mayflower*'s voyages from 1609,[7] indicating that Christopher Jones was her captain. By 1612, its owners were Christopher Nichols, Richard Child, Thomas Short, and Christopher Jones. Never carrying passengers, she had transported cargo such as salt, hops, vinegar, hats, hemp, wine, and cognac to Baltic ports such as Norway, and returned with tar, deals (pine planks), and fish. She had often carried cloth to Rochelle and Bordeaux and returned with cargos of French wine. She was now ready to carry treasures far more priceless, including Elder Brewster's library of perhaps as many as three hundred volumes, including his beloved *Geneva Bible,* which would be a school-book for the children.

In Southampton, one can still walk along the old city walls and exit the fourteenth-century West Gate, through which the Pilgrims passed to board their ships for the New World. With the building of the current docks, dry land now covers the actual site of the ships' anchorage. Southampton's *Mayflower* Memorial Column, erected in 1913, stands in front of the walls, near the base of the Royal Pier. The Memorial is a tall pillar surmounted by a crescent of fire under a canopy, like those used prior to the days of light-houses. At the top of the column stands a bronze model of the *Mayflower.* Below are tablets dedicated to William Brewster, John Alden, and Edward Winslow. The following tablets, using N.S. dates, commemorate the August 15, 1620, departure of the ships:

THE PILGRIM FATHERS MEMORIAL, SOUTHAMPTON, HAMPSHIRE, ENGLAND. THE SEPARATIST CONGREGATION FROM BABWORTH, NOTTINGHAMSHIRE (1586-1604), WHICH MOVED TO SCROOBY IN 1606, TO AMSTERDAM, NETHER-LANDS, IN 1608, AND TO LEYDEN IN 1609. SAILED FROM DELFT HAVEN IN THE SPEEDWELL, ON AUGUST 1 (NEW STYLE), 1620, TO JOIN THE MAYFLOWER, WITH ITS LONDON COLONISTS, HERE BOTH SHIPS SAILED ON AUGUST 15 (N.S.), 1620, FOR THE NEW WORLD. AFTER TURNING BACK TO DARTMOUTH, AND A SECOND TIME TO PLYMOUTH FOR REPAIRS, THE SPEEDWELL WAS ABANDONED AND ON SEPTEMBER 16 (N.S.), THE MAYFLOWER ALONE SAILED TO PLYMOUTH, NEW ENGLAND, WITH 102 PASSENGERS.

THE GENERAL SOCIETY OF MAYFLOWER DESCENDANTS (U.S.A, 1897)

IN GRATEFUL MEMORY OF
THOSE PILGRIMS OF THE "MAYFLOWER"
who crossed the Atlantic in the year 1620,
and became the founders
of the first of those settlements
which afterwards developed into the colonies
of New England
This tablet is placed here by the
Massachusetts Society of the Colonial Dames
of America.

On the 15th of August 1620
From the West Quay near this spot
The famous MAYFLOWER began her voyage
Carrying the little company of
PILGRIM FATHERS
Who were destined to be the founders
of the New England States of America.

Just inside the West Gate, a fifteenth-century merchants' hall stands as a reminder of life in Tudor England. The little building was moved here from St. Michael's Square. In the Pilgrims' day, a fish market occupied its lower arcades, while the upper floor accommodated woolen cloth trading. As the Pilgrims packed their possessions on board, they must have felt mixed emotions for this country which had been their native home—a land whose leaders had rejected the pope but who would still not tolerate New Testament churches. It was at this time that the Pilgrims read two farewell letters, bearing the date July 27, from Pastor John Robinson in Leiden. One is addressed to Robinson's brother-in-law, John Carver, the man destined to become the first governor of Plymouth Plantation. Robinson concludes his letter to Carver with these words: "And the Lord in whom you trust and whom you serve ever in this business and journey, guide you with His hand, protect you with His wing, and show you and us His salvation in the end, and bring us in the meanwhile together in this place desired, if such be His good will, for His Christ's sake. Amen."[8] There was a powerful bond

between the Pilgrims and John Robinson. They would long for his antici-
pated arrival in Plymouth Colony, then mourn the devastating news of his
death in Leiden in 1625. Robinson addressed his second letter to the entire
Pilgrim group. This insightful and revealing "farewell letter" is provided in
its entirety in Appendix H of this book.

DARTMOUTH

The Pilgrims were hardly three days at sea when the *Speedwell* was
taking water. In preparation for the voyage, the tiny ship had been refitted
with taller masts and larger sails so that it could keep up with the
Mayflower, three times the *Speedwell*'s size. The two ships turned back
and anchored at Dartmouth, England on August 23, for the *Speedwell*'s
repair. A major fishing harbor in the Pilgrims' day, Dartmouth was mainly
known for her strategic naval port, with its fine shipwrights. Incredibly, on
June 4, 1944, 485 vessels of the United States amphibious forces steamed
out of this same port to participate in the largest seaborne invasion in history, as 2,700 ships and hundreds of small craft transported some 176,000
troops for the successful invasion and liberation of Normandy, France, on
D-day, June 6.

The picturesque and charming resort village is renowned for its yacht-
ing facilities, its fruitful fields, and its little hillsides dotted with houses
overlooking the river, where small ferryboats link traffic with Kingswear.
At Bayard's Cove one can view distant castles guarding the mouth of the
River Dart, which pleasantly greeted the *Mayflower* and the struggling
Speedwell. The quay wall at the Cove is capped with a "Mayflower Stone,"
carrying these words (with an O.S. date):

TO COMMEMORATE
THE SAILING OF THE PILGRIM FATHERS
FROM THIS PORT IN THE MAYFLOWER &
SPEEDWELL ON THE 20TH AUGUST 1620

Underneath the stone and attached to the wall is a large plaque,
placed here by the General Society of Mayflower Descendants (U.S.A.
1897). It recalls the story of the two Pilgrim ships and the English towns,
such as Dartmouth, which shared the history of the desperate attempts to

begin their mission across the Atlantic. The plaque uses N.S. dates and reads as follows:

DARTMOUTH, DEVON, ENGLAND

Here, off Bayard's Cove, The Mayflower (180 tons) with London Colonists, and the Speedwell (60 tons) with Leyden Pilgrims—some 122 in all—lay at anchor from August 23 (New Style) to about August 31, 1620. These ships had sailed from Southampton on August 15. They put in at Dartmouth to repair the leaking Speedwell. They sailed from Dartmouth for America.

When about 300 miles w.s.w. of Land's End, the unseaworthiness of the Speedwell made it necessary to put back to Plymouth, Devon, on September 7. The Speedwell was abandoned and on September 16 the Mayflower alone set sail again for America, with 102 passengers. Their spiritual leader was Elder William Brewster. The Mayflower cast anchor in Cape Cod Harbor, New England, on November 21, 1620, off what is now Provincetown, arriving at Plymouth on December 26.

On November 21 the Mayflower Compact, a charter of self government —The first American Constitution—was made law by 41 signatories. Thus Dartmouth took part in establishing civil and religious liberty in the New World.

The *Speedwell* was thoroughly examined from stem to stern. Some leaks were found and mended; after more than a week, they set sail again about August 31. Approximately three hundred ocean miles later, Captain Reynolds of the *Speedwell* announced that his vessel was still taking water and was now as "leaky as a sieve." Again the ships turned back, this time to Plymouth, where they anchored on September 7.

PLYMOUTH

Plymouth, in County Devon,[9] is situated on the sound at the Rivers Plym and Tamar. It is still a fine natural harbor, a fishing port and the site of the Royal Naval Dockyard. English navigator Sir Francis Drake sailed from Plymouth in 1588 to defeat the *Spanish Armada.* It was here, on the "Hoe," at the top of the cliff overlooking the Barbican, where Drake was playing bowls when Admiral Howard reported to him that Spanish ships were just off the Lizard. Legend has it that Drake retorted, "There's plenty of time to win this game and to thrash the Spaniards too."

The Pilgrims knew Plymouth for her fine shipwrights, who found nothing wrong with the *Speedwell*'s hull. But the voyagers could take no further chances with it. Bradford and others suspected that the *Speedwell*'s captain, desiring to get out of his contract which required him to remain in the New World for a year, had deliberately crowded on too much sail, bulging the seams and forcing the ship to take water. Of course, no one could fully test such suspicions. It was reported that the ship continued in service for several more years, but it could have been for coastal service. It is tempting to imagine what *might* have occurred had the *Speedwell* not had her "misfortunes!" The two ships might then have arrived sometime in October at the Hudson River—not Cape Cod! To the Pilgrims, however, the God of heaven is always in control, able even to make the wrath of man to praise Him and to bring fulfillment to His own holy decrees. Perhaps this is what prompted Edward Arber of London's King's College to say that "the overmasting of the *Speedwell* [was] one of the Turning Points of modern history."[10] The Pilgrims quietly committed their desperate situation to God and His divine protection. Repair costs had already forced them to sell some of their precious supplies. So now they sold the ship and combined its passengers and cargo with the *Mayflower.* Some twenty passengers willingly dropped out. Bradford reflects that the Pilgrims were like Gideon's army. Their small number was divided, as if God by "His Providence, thought these few too many for the great work He had for them to do." It was as William Stoughton put it: "God sifted a whole nation, that He might send choice grain into this wilderness." In those days, ships made most of their Atlantic crossings from early spring to mid summer, avoiding the late summer and autumn storms at sea. Since wooden ships could easily break apart in the storms, they seldom sailed alone. By now, however, the Pilgrims had consumed all the provisions which they had planned for the entire voyage. Now they were eating food that they might well need to stay alive in the New England wilderness. Regarded by many Anglican authorities as outlaws, they could not turn back. Having sold their homes and possessions, they had no place else to go. The 102 names of the passengers, grouped by families and including the family servants, are recorded on a sign outside the Island House, in which some of them, it is believed, would have spent their last night in England.

From this Elizabethan section called the Barbican (in Sutton Pool), on September 16, 1620, the *Mayflower* sailed out alone. The wall of the West Pier of Sutton Harbor holds plaques commemorating a number of historic voyages. Most prominent, however, is the bronze *Mayflower* Memorial tablet, placed here in 1891, sheltered by a portico which was placed over it in 1934. The tablet carries the inscription provided below. On the seventh line of the text, the word "Cawsey" (*Causeway* in modern English) refers to the cobblestone path that once ran along an earlier pier that was completely absorbed by the present "*Mayflower* Pier," built in 1791 to provide protection for the many small boats that always anchored in Sutton Pool. When the old cawsey disappeared, so did the flight of steps belonging to the old pier. The *Mayflower* Memorial does stand, however, within just a few feet of where the historic craft was moored. The text of the tablet (with its O.S. date) reads:

> On the 6th of September 1620, in the Mayoralty of Thomas Fownes, after being "kindly entertained and courteously used by divers Friends there dwelling," the Pilgrim Fathers sailed from Plymouth in the MAYFLOWER, in the Providence of God to settle in NEW PLYMOUTH, and to lay the Foundation of the NEW ENGLAND STATES—The ancient Cawsey whence they embarked was destroyed not many Years afterwards, but the Site of their Embarkation is marked by the Stone bearing the name of the MAYFLOWER in the pavement of the adjacent Pier. This Tablet was erected in the Mayoralty of J. T. Bond, 1891, to commemorate their Departure, and the visit to Plymouth in July of that Year of a number of their Descendants and Representatives.

Today's pilgrim can not only know where the *Mayflower* once docked, but he can also enjoy the same delightful harbor that the Pilgrims viewed with such alarm, as each day was bringing them closer towards winter. One can look out over this ancient harbor at the same landscape that the Pilgrims would have seen as they viewed Plymouth Sound and the Old World for the last time. They had enjoyed kind hospitality in this Puritan town; but they would not see land again for sixty-six days. Their ocean voyage, not being a direct route, would cover some 3,500 miles, an average of about forty-six miles per day, or somewhat less than two miles per hour. Even after their arrival, the *Mayflower* would continue to be home for many families for several more months, while they cleared land and built their homes.

1. John Moore, another part owner of the *Mayflower*, was also from Rotherhithe.

2. First mate John Clarke had already made two trips to Jamestown, VA.

3. George Ernest Bowman, "The Division of the Land," *The Mayflower Descendant* 1, no. 4,(October 1899): 227f. (34 vols., compiled and published by George Ernest Bowman, from 1899 to 1937, Massachusetts Society of Mayflower Descendants), on "Mayflower Legacy," 43-vol. searchable CD edition, Wheat Ridge, CO: Search & Research Publishing Corporation, 1998, containing *The Mayflower Descendant With Other New England Town Records*.

4. Nathaniel Morton, *New England's Memorial* (1669; rpt. Boston: Congregational Board of Publications, 1855), 14, 20.

5. The best sources on the *Mayflower's* construction and actual navigation include Warren Sears Nickerson, *Land Ho! — 1620: A Seaman's Story of the Mayflower, Her Construction, Her Navigation, and Her First Landfall* (Boston: Houghton Mifflin Company, 1931); Captain Alan Villiers, "How We Sailed the New Mayflower to America," *The National Geographic Magazine* 112, no. 5 (November 1957): 627-72; and Crispin Gill, *Mayflower Remembered: A History of the Plymouth Pilgrims* (NY: Taplinger Publishing Co., 1970). Cargo ships of the period seem to have been built in similar styles for each size.

6. William Bradford, *Of Plymouth Plantation 1620-1647*, ed. Samuel Eliot Morison (1952; rpt. NY: Alfred A. Knopf, 1998), 47. This work is hereafter referred to as "Bradford, *Plymouth Plantation*."

7. Caleb Johnson, *A Brief History of the Mayflower* (*Mayflower* Web Pages: http://members.aol.com/calebj/mayflower.html).

8. Bradford, *Plymouth Plantation,* 367.

9. The good overview of Plymouth, England is R. A. J. Walling, *The Story of Plymouth* (NY: William Morrow & Company, 1950). The first "Plymouth Brethren" church was organized here at Plymouth in 1831.

10. Edward Arber, ed., *The Story of The Pilgrim Fathers, 1606-1623 A.D; as Told by Themselves, Their Friends, and Their Enemies* (London: Ward and Downey, Limited, 1897), 346.

CHAPTER 6

THE MAYFLOWER PASSENGERS, VOYAGE, AND COMPACT

It is often mistakenly assumed that the only reason for the difficulty in identifying and tracing the Pilgrims is that they were all of a humble stock, the yeomanry class, and that there was no "gentle blood" among them. In those days, however, those who were normally addressed as "Mr."—pronounced "master" at that time—were among the gentry. Generally, "Mr." was the same as "gentleman," which speaks of gentry, or a man of good birth, good breeding, or using the "coat-armor of right." The title "Mrs." was used in the same manner, indicating "gentlewoman." In those days, both married and unmarried women of quality were called "Mrs." or "Mistress." Edward Winslow is a noble example of the "Pilgrim gentry" who came over on the *Mayflower*. As mentioned previously, at the close of the First Dutch-English War, in 1654, Winslow was appointed by Oliver Cromwell and the Dutch States General as First Commissioner to arbitrate the differences between the two countries. As the first international diplomat from New England, he was acknowledged for his impartiality by both England and the Netherlands, where he had spent his years of exile. Twelve of the signers of the *Mayflower Compact* were in the gentry class. Bradford uses the title "Mr." for most of these throughout his history, including his listing of the passengers. They are John Carver, William Brewster, Edward Winslow, Isaac Allerton, Samuel Fuller, Christopher Martin, William Mullins, William White, Richard Warren, Stephen Hopkins, Myles Standish (also called "Captain"), and William Bradford (for sake of modesty he omits the title for himself). Throughout the literature of Plymouth Colony,

Bradford and certain of his family are repeatedly called "Mr.," "Gentleman," and even "Esq." or Esquire, which is the title above that of gentry and denotes nobility. Also, after the settlement at Plymouth, both John Alden and John Howland would regularly be addressed as "Mr." Such designations were often used arbitrarily, but were not given to those not entitled to them. Titles were earned by character, not inheritance. A gentleman's son, for example, would lose his title if he chose a lower occupation, or if convicted of a crime. Below the level of gentry came the great middle class of the population. The socially best of this group were termed "yeoman" or "goodman." England's yeomanry formed the well-to-do farming class who worked their own land. A yeoman farmer or artisan named John Brown might be addressed as "Goodman Brown." Below this division, the people had no further classifications. The term "servant," in the seventeenth century, was used in nearly the same way as the word employee is used today. It did not necessarily connote social inferiority or a menial position. When a *Mayflower* passenger is described as a servant, this merely means that he was an employee. On the other hand, an "indentured servant" was bound by contract to serve for a set amount of time; but there is no evidence of any *Mayflower* passengers who were "indentured" servants.

As in any normal society at large, the majority of the passengers were among the yeomanry, rather than the gentry. They were respectable farmers and artisans. For some of them, however, except for a line or two on parish parchments at birth, marriage, and burial, few records were made of them. Families oftentimes simply overlooked it, or had no secure place to keep records. Parish records were first required by law in 1538, but the law was often ignored. Many churches did not even have ministers. The earliest parish records in Gainsborough date from 1564, the oldest being illegible; Austerfield's records include William Bradford's baptism. Babworth's records start at 1623, and Scrooby's at 1695. This makes it difficult, especially after almost four hundred years, to identify all of the *Mayflower* passengers precisely. Another reason for the lack of complete records is that the Pilgrims had been fugitives, some of whom England had continued to hunt even while they were in Holland. Obviously, they would not be publishing much information on themselves. Most of them had quickly blended into the Dutch work force, taking whatever work the manufacturers offered them. Nevertheless, such sources as the Leiden Municipal Archives contain numerous documents about the Separatists, both those who left with the Pilgrims and those who stayed behind.[1] Civil marriage registration was a Dutch custom introduced into the English legal world. Betrothal records were also kept.[2] Recent research has produced an incredible amount of information about many of the passengers, and the search continues.

Once the Pilgrims boarded their ship, they were no longer an exclusive little group of church members. From this time on, they had to think also in terms of a civil society. Since Bradford uses the term Strangers, it has become traditional to think of all the Strangers as those who had not lived in Leiden or who were not Christians. Undoubtedly, both of those categories belong primarily to those termed *Strangers,*[3] but both categories might also be found among some of those linked with the Pilgrim "saints." The word was intended to suggest more of a general than an absolute division among the passengers. It should not even be assumed that every person in every Pilgrim household was a "saint," any more than it should be assumed that all of "Christendom" is "born again." Bradford and the Pilgrims never explained clearly and precisely what they meant by the word "Stranger." It is certain, however, that it does not always mean "unchristian" or "non-Separatist."

One of the Leiden Separatist leaders, Robert Cushman (Coachman), for example, twice uses the word "strangers" in his work, *The Cry of a Stone* (1642). First, he applies the actual biblical usage of the word as he writes that "we are all of us Pilgrims and strangers." Later, he uses the word to refer to "Churches in forraign nations, . . . not of our language."[4] In French, for example, the word *etranger* means "foreigner." Such was the normal meaning in use in sixteenth- and seventeenth-century England, which often had "Strangers' churches," Christian refugees who had fled from the religious wars on the Continent. One of the earliest was the "London Church of the Strangers," established by John à Lasco, the sixteenth-century Polish reformer. Other churches of Strangers were Flemish, Dutch, and Italian. Many were "Walloon," or French-speaking, congregations. This situation was the reason for England's "Strangers' Laws." At times there were thousands of such refugees living there, many of them only temporarily, along the eastern counties from Kent to Norfolk, from which many of the Pilgrims originated. A. H. Drysdale rightly calls it a "capricious inconsistency" that English refugees "were forced to flee *to* the Continent at the very time and for the very cause that French refugees and others were fleeing *from* the Continent and were being received and protected in England!"[5] In the city of Norwich, for example, "Strangers' Hall" stands as a reminder of those days. It is dangerous, therefore, to assume that William Bradford regarded every "Stranger," or passenger who was not a member of his church, as an unbeliever or totally unidentified with the Separatists.

While including all of the traditional "forty-one saints," the present study, using the categories "Separatists and Non-Separatists," adds sixteen people to the traditional forty-one.[6] This total of fifty-seven includes thirteen women, nineteen children (fourteen boys and five girls), and twenty-five men, one of whom (Giles Heale) is listed with the crew. Future research could eventually require further adjustments to the numbers.

The most recognizable addition to the list of Separatists in this chapter will be Myles Standish (d. 1656),[7] remembered as one of the triumvirate with William Bradford and Edward Winslow. William Hubbard (d. 1704), a Massachusetts Bay Colony Puritan writing near the end of the seventeenth century, said that Standish was outside "the school of our Saviour."[8] On the basis of Hubbard's remark, along with records of the Standish family going back to a thirteenth-century Roman Catholic family, there have been frequent references to Standish as a "Roman Catholic." This is definitely false information. His family roots can hardly be any proof of his own position. Bangs says, "The myth that Myles Standish was Catholic was created in Boston to inspire youthful Irish immigrants."[9] The following entry in the Plymouth Colony Records indicates that Myles Standish attended the Plymouth Church with his family and may have a been a member at the time the record was made: "Anno 1632 Aprell 2—the names of those which promise to remove their families to live in the town in the winter time that they may the better repaire to the worship of God— John Alden, Capt. Standish, Jonathan Brewster, Thomas Prence."[10] After arresting Thomas Morton for supplying guns to the Indians, Standish sent him back to England. To get back at the Pilgrims, Morton later wrote a caricature called *New English Canaan,* which refers to Myles Standish as "Captain Shrimp," because of his small statue.[11] That "little chimney [who] is quickly fired" has also been wrongly called a "soldier of fortune."

Perhaps the real Myles Standish will never be known, but there is more to him than popular descriptions imply. Already in Holland before the Pilgrims arrived, Standish was one of the thousands of British soldiers fighting in the Dutch army in the revolt against Spanish Hapsburg dominion. In Plymouth Colony, he knew what he needed to do in regard to defending the colony. It was sometimes a messy job. He was quiet about church matters, possibly because he wanted to avoid reflecting upon the testimony of the church. There is no way to determine Standish's personal spiritual condition. His four sons joined Separatist churches in the towns where they lived and there are numerous records of their serving in high places of spiritual leadership, such as deacons.[12] In addition to being the military captain, Myles Standish served for six years as Treasurer of the Colony. In 1649, he was made commander-in-chief for all the Colony. He was faithful to the end in giving his life for the Separatists of Plymouth. William Bradford mentions people who, during the starving time, were special examples of sacrifice and loyalty, "showing herein their true love unto their friends and brethren; a rare example and worthy to be remembered. Two of these seven were Mr. William Brewster, their reverend Elder, and Myles Standish, their captain and military commander."[13]

William Bradford's nephew, Nathaniel Morton, arrived in Plymouth in 1623, grew up in the Bradford home, and earned a reputation of being strict, orthodox, and Separatist. In his *New England's Memorial* (1669), Morton wrote this of Myles Standish at his death in 1656:

> This year Captain Miles Standish expired his mortal life. . . . In his younger time he went over into the low countries, and was a soldier there, and came acquainted with the church at Leyden, and came over into New England, with such of them as at the first set out for the planting of the plantation of New Plimouth, and bare a deep share of their first difficulties, and was always very faithful to their interest. He growing ancient, became sick of the stone, or stranguary, whereof, after his suffering of much dolorous pain, he fell asleep in the Lord, and was honourably buried at Duxbury.[14]

On one occasion, during a skirmish with the Indians, seven Indians were killed. Upon receiving reports of the killing of these "poore Indeans," John Robinson, in one of his last letters from Leiden, rebuked the Pilgrims, saying, "Oh, how happy a thing had it been, if you had converted some before you had killed any!" Yet in the same letter Robinson refers to Myles

Standish as the "Captain, whom I love, and am persuaded the Lord in great mercy and for much good hath sent. . . , if you use him aright. He is a man humble and meek amongst you, and towards all in ordinary course."[15] Standish left a legacy to John Robinson's granddaughter, Mercy. He refers to her in his will as "marcye Robenson[,] whome I tenderly love for her Grandfathers sacke." Most of the books listed in Standish's library were sermons and theological works of some of the greatest of the Puritans, especially by Jeremiah Burroughs, but also John Preston and a couple of others. Standish also owned three "old Bibles," plus "a Testament," and "one Psalme booke."[16] It should not be surprising, therefore, that the Pilgrims themselves regarded Myles Standish as one of the most beloved of all the passengers on the *Mayflower.* Isaac de Rasière, Secretary of the West India Company's Government at Manhattan, visited Plymouth in March 1627. He penned the following description of the Pilgrims' place of worship and order of assembling:

> Upon the hill they had a large square house, with a flat roof, made of thick sawn planks, stayed with oak beams, upon the top of which they have six cannons, which shoot iron balls of four and five pounds, and command the surrounding country. The lower part they use for their church, where they preach on Sundays and the usual holidays. They assemble by beat of drum, each with his musket or firelock, in front of the captain's door; they have their cloaks on, and place themselves in order, three abreast, and are led by a sergeant without beat of drum. Behind comes the Governor, in a long robe; beside him on the right hand comes the preacher with his cloak on, and on the left hand the captain with his side-arms and cloak on, and with a small cane in his hand; and so they march in good order, and each sets his arms down near him. Thus they enter their place of worship, constantly on their guard night and day.[17]

Originally, there were 120 passengers—thirty on the *Speedwell* and ninety on the *Mayflower.* When the *Speedwell* dropped out of the voyage, eighteen of her passengers remained behind, while the other twelve boarded the *Mayflower.* So the *Mayflower* set sail with 102 passengers (fifty men; twenty women; twenty-two boys; and ten girls).[18] This traditional number,

"102 passengers," actually includes three crew members who were hired to remain permanently in Plymouth and two crew members hired to remain for one year. Not included in the number are Oceanus Hopkins (a boy born at sea) and Peregrine White (a boy born on the ship while it was anchored off Provincetown, Cape Cod)—making the actual number of "passengers" to be 104, all included in the list below. William Butten died at sea and four more,[19] including Dorothy Bradford, died on board after arrival at Cape Cod, making ninety-nine the total of those who actually reached Plymouth "rock." The average age of a passenger was about thirty-two. The oldest passenger, James Chilton, was sixty-four. As closely as we can determine, only fourteen of the passengers were over forty, only five of whom were over fifty. About sixty passengers were between twenty and forty years of age and at least thirty were under the age of seventeen.

Including the five who died on board, forty-five died before the *Mayflower* sailed for home on April 5, 1621. Five or six additional deaths[20] occurred before the *Fortune* arrived on November 9, 1621. Some fifty[21] of the total number of passengers, therefore, had died by the time of the *Fortune*'s arrival, including twenty-seven adult males, fourteen adult females, and nine children (seven boys and two girls). By 1635, some sixty-seven more Leiden Separatists would arrive: the ship *Fortune* brought twelve on November 9, 1621; the *Anne* and the *Little James* brought thirty-two in July 1623; a second *Mayflower* ship brought nine in 1629; and by 1635, some fourteen others from Leiden had arrived independently at various times. By 1635, the "Pilgrim ships" had brought approximately 120 Separatists.

THE MAYFLOWER PASSENGERS (104):

The number 104 includes the two who were born on board the vessel. Those who died before the arrival of the *Fortune* on November 9, 1621, are marked by asterisks.* (See Appendix J for the best sources on tracing genealogies.)

SEPARATISTS (56):

Giles Heale, the Separatist listed with the crew, makes 57 Separatists.

Allerton (5):

Isaac, from London, was a tailor. He was one of Plymouth's earliest assistant governors, but moved away from Plymouth in the 1630s.

*Mary (Norris), his wife, was from Newbury. She gave birth to a stillborn son on board the *Mayflower,* just as the first houses were being built at Plymouth. When Mary died, Isaac married Fear Brewster. The three surviving children of Mary and Isaac were on the *Mayflower.* They were:

Bartholomew (son); born in Leiden;

Remember (daughter); born in Leiden;

Mary (daughter); born in Leiden. She married Thomas Cushman, son of Robert Cushman who, with John Carver, had negotiated for the Pilgrims' first patent to come to America. Thomas Cushman succeeded William Brewster as ruling elder of the Plymouth Church. When Mary died in 1699, she was the last survivor of the *Mayflower* passengers who actually made the voyage. (Peregrine White died in 1704, but he was born on board the ship while it was anchored at Provincetown.)

Allerton: (1):

*John, from London; brother of Isaac Allerton, John was a crew member hired to return for the others at Leiden.[22]

Bradford (2):

William, from Austerfield (Yorkshire); second governor and historian.

*Dorothy (May), his wife, was from Wisbech (Cambridgeshire). She drowned from the *Mayflower* off Cape Cod; their one son, John, came to America later.[23] William Bradford's second wife, Alice (Carpenter), bore him two sons (William and Joseph)[24] and a daughter (Mercy)[25]. William Bradford's Bible can be seen at Pilgrim Hall Museum, in Plymouth, Massachusetts.

Brewster (4):

William, from Scrooby (Nottinghamshire), was the organizer and ruling elder of Scrooby church. A chair belonging to him is at Pilgrim Hall Museum, in Plymouth, Massachusetts.

Mary, his wife; from Scrooby area; known for her virtue and meekness, died in 1627. In addition to a child who was born and died in Leiden, the Brewsters had five other children. The elder son, Jonathan, came over on the *Fortune* (1621);[26] two daughters, Patience[27] and Fear,[28] came over on the *Anne* (1623). Two sons came on the *Mayflower:*

Love (son);[29] born in Leiden;

Wrestling (son);[30] born in Leiden.

Carver (2):

*John, from Doncaster (Yorkshire); first governor of Plymouth Plantation;

*Catherine, his wife, was from Sturton-le-Steeple (Nottinghamshire). She died within six weeks of her husband, "being overcome with excessive grief for the loss of so gracious an husband" (Morton's *New England's Memorial*, p. 47.)

Chilton (3):[31]

*James, a Canterbury tailor; he was the oldest passenger on board the *Mayflower;* he died while the ship was still at Provincetown;

*Susanna (?); his wife, from Canterbury;[32]

Mary (teenage daughter); born in Canterbury; claimed by tradition to be the "first female to step on Plymouth rock." (Her sister Isabella came over later.) Mary's life is like a fairyland story of a suffering little orphan finding romance with royalty. Mary did not remain with the Separatists. She married Edward Winslow's brother, John Winslow, who came over on the *Fortune;* they later moved to Boston where she lived in luxury for the remainder of her life. Mary is buried under the Winslow Coat-of-Arms at the front of Kings Chapel Burial Ground in Boston.[33]

Cook(e) (2):

Francis; from Blythe (Notthinghamshire); a wool comber who had already moved to Leiden and started a family before the Separatists arrived. His wife, Hester, along with two children (Jane and Jacob), arrived on the *Anne* in 1623. Francis brought with him one son:

John (about thirteen years old); born in Leiden.

Cooper (1):

Humility; an infant female relative of either Edward or Ann Tillie (Separatists); Humility was likely under their care. Mrs. Tillie could have been Humility's aunt.[34]

Crackston (2):

*John Sr. was from Colchester (Essex);

John, his young son; born in Leiden; died of exposure and frostbite while lost in the forest.

English: (1):

*Thomas was hired to be the master of the shallop at Plymouth Plantation and to remain there permanently.

Fletcher (1):

*Moses, from Sandwich (Kent), was a blacksmith.[35]

Fuller (3):[36]

*Edward, from Redenhall (Norfolk);

*Ann (his wife); from Redenhall (Norfolk);

Samuel (their young son); born in Leiden. In 1635, in Scituate (Plymouth Colony), he married Jane, a daughter of the Rev. John Lathrop (Lothrop), the pastor who had arrived with members of London's first independent, congregationalist Church.

Fuller (1):

Samuel, from London, was a "say" (silk or satin) maker and the physician (surgeon).[37] His third wife, Bridget, arrived 1623 on the *Anne*.

Goodman (Codmore) (1):

John, a linen weaver. Bradford seems mistaken to say that he died the first winter; "John Goodman" is listed with the sharers of the land division of 1623. Incidentally, there are some interesting references to two dogs that he brought along.

Hooke (1):

*John (age 14); born in Leiden; servant in the Isaac Allerton home.

Howland (1):

John, who fell overboard and was rescued on the *Mayflower;* he came over with the household of John Carver and soon rose to high positions of leadership in church and community. He married Elizabeth Tillie. On his tombstone is a citation from the *Plymouth Records:* "Hee was a godly man and an ancient professor in the wayes of Christ. . . . [and] was the last man that was left of those that came over in the shipp called the *Mayflower.*" He died in 1673.

Minter (1):

Desire; a woman (about twenty years old), probably from Norwich, who came as a servant to the Carvers; she returned to England about 1625.

Priest (1):

*Degory, a London hat maker; his wife (Sarah) and two daughters (Mary and Sarah) came over to Plymouth on the *Anne* in 1623.

Rogers (2):

*Thomas was a camlet merchant in Leiden;

Joseph (his young son); probably born in Leiden. Other children came over later.

Samson (1):

Henry; a child cousin of either Edward or Ann Tillie (Separatists); Henry was quite possibly under their care.[38]

Standish (2):

Myles, from Ellenbane (Isle of Man) (and Lancashire ?); captain of the military defenses.

*Rose (his wife). Standish's second wife was named Barbara. There is no evidence to suggest that Myles pursued Priscilla Mullins, as in Henry Wadsworth Longfellow's fictional poem, "The Courtship of Myles Standish."

Tillie [Tilley] (2):

*Edward was a London cloth maker, living in Leiden before the Separatists arrived there.

*Ann, or Agnes (née Cooper), his wife.

Tillie [Tilley] (3):

*John was a London silk worker; brother of Edward.

*Joan (?) (Hurst), his wife;

Elizabeth, their daughter, married John Howland. She was about thirteen or fourteen when she arrived in Plymouth.

Tinker (3):

*Thomas;

*Wife (name unknown);

*Son (name unknown); probably born in Leiden.

Turner (3):

*John was a merchant. (His daughter came later and lived in Salem.)

*Son (name unknown);

*Son (name unknown).

117

White (4):

*William, a wool comber;

Suzanna [Ann] (his wife); she later married Edward Winslow, the diplomat. This was the first wedding in Plymouth, and the first civil wedding ceremony "in the English legal world."[39]

Resolved (their son); born in Leiden;

Peregrine, a son, born on the *Mayflower* after arrival at Cape Cod. He died in 1704, at age eighty-three, as the last surviving *Mayflower* "passenger." His name means "one who journeys to foreign lands." The cradle in which his mother rocked him is at Pilgrim Hall Museum at Plymouth, Massachusetts.

Williams (1):

*Thomas; from Yarmouth (Norfolk).

Winslow (2):

Edward, from Careswell, near Droitwich (Worcestershire), was a printer, a diplomat, and historian. His portrait, painted from life, is the only true picture that exists of any of the Pilgrims; it is at the Pilgrim Hall Museum, in Plymouth, Massachusetts.

*Elizabeth (née Barker), his wife; from Chattisham (Norfolk); Edward's second wife was Suzanna White, widow of William White.

NON-SEPARATISTS (48):

Alden: (1):

John, from Harwich (Essex), was the ship's cooper, hired at Southampton. Family tradition insisted that he was "the first man to step on Plymouth rock." He remained permanently in Plymouth and later married Priscilla Mullins.

Billington (4):

John, from London; the first to be hanged in Plymouth; he murdered John Newcomen.

Eleanor (Ellen), his wife;

Francis (son);

John (son).

Britteridge (1):

*Richard; he was the first person to die after the *Mayflower* reached Plymouth.

Browne (1):

Peter, from Great Burstead (Essex).

Butten (1):

*William, a youth from Austerfield (Yorkshire) who died at sea. He came with the household of Samuel Fuller.

Carter (1):

*Robert; arrived with household of William Mullins.

Clarke (1):

*Richard.

Doty (1):

Edward (from London); arrived with household of Stephen Hopkins.

Eaton (3):

Francis, from Bristol, was a carpenter.

*Sarah (his wife); probably from Bristol;

Samuel (their infant son).

Ely (or Ellis?) (1):

_____; first name of this seaman is unknown. He was hired to remain for one year in Plymouth. Future research could establish that he was among the Leiden Separatists.[40] He is included in the number of 102 "passengers."

Gardiner (1):

Richard, from Harwich (Essex).

Holbeck (1):

*William (from Norwich); arrived with household of William White.

Hopkins (6):

Stephen; from Wotton-under-Edge (Gloucestershire); the only passenger who had been to the New World previously; he had spent two years in Jamestown, Virginia.

Elizabeth (his wife). They brought three children:

Giles (a son, by Stephen's first wife);

Constance (a daughter, by Stephen's first wife);

Damaris (a daughter, about three years old); she died during the early years; a later daughter was also named Damaris.

Oceanus was born at sea on the *Mayflower;* he died prior to 1627.

Langmore (1):

*John; arrived with household of Christopher Martin.

Latham (1):

William (a boy); he arrived with the household of John Carver.

Leister (1):

Edward (from London); arrived with household of Stephen Hopkins.

Margeson (1):

*Edmund (or Edmond).

Martin (2):

*Christopher, from Great Burnstead (Essex); was treasurer to the Merchant Adventurers and created financial problems for the Pilgrims.

*Marie (Mary) (née Prower); his wife.

More (children)—siblings (4):

Richard, from London; arrived with household of William Brewster. Although he was healthiest of the four More children, he was only six or seven years old when he arrived. He was the only one of the More children to survive the first winter. Richard later moved to Salem and became a sea captain;

*Ellen (Elinor), eight years old; arrived with the household of Edward Winslow;

*Jasper, age seven; arrived with the household of John Carver; he died on board the *Mayflower* in Provincetown.

*_____, (name unknown); four years old; arrived with the household of William Brewster. Bradford refers to this child as "a brother," but this could possibly have been a girl called Mary. Bradford did rely at times on memory for some of his entries; he seldom makes a mistake, though![41]

Mullins (4):

*William, from Dorking (Surrey), was a shopkeeper.

*Alice (his wife);

*Joseph (son).

Priscilla (daughter); married John Alden.

Prower (1):

   *Solomon, from Essex, was stepson of Christopher Martin. He arrived with household of Christopher Martin.

Rigdale (2):

   *John (from London);

   *Alice (his wife).

Soule (1):

   George [from Eckington (Worcestershire)]; arrived with the household of Edward Winslow.

Story (1):

   *Elias (from London); arrived with the household of Edward Winslow.

Thompson (1):

   *Edward (died on board the *Mayflower* at Provincetown). He came over with the household of William White.

Trevore: (1):

   William was a seaman, hired to remain for a year in Plymouth. He is included in the 102 "passengers."

Warren (1):

   Richard was a London merchant; his wife, Elizabeth, and five daughters came over on the *Anne* in 1623.

Wilder (1):

   *Roger; he arrived with the household of John Carver.

Winslow (1):

   Gilbert, who was brother to Edward and returned to England in 1626.

Unknown last name (1):

   Dorothy (a maidservant); arrived with the household of John Carver.

THE REST OF THE SHIP'S CREW:

Besides the five crew members mentioned above—John Alden (the cooper); John Allerton; Ely (Ellis?); Thomas English; and William Trevore—sources mention the following seven:[42]

   Christopher Jones—Captain

John Clarke—Master's Mate and Pilot

Robert Coppin—Second Master's Mate and Pilot

Giles Heale—ship's surgeon; identified with the Separatists[43]. He is not counted as one of the 102 "passengers."

Andrew Williamson—Seaman

John Parker—Seaman

Master Leaver—Seaman

While no one knows precisely how many additional crew members there were, there is little doubt that the *Mayflower*'s crew suffered as its passengers did, perhaps nearly half of them dying that first winter. The ship set sail for her English home on April 5, 1621, arrived on May 6, then made trading runs to Spain, Ireland, and France. Captain Christopher Jones died on March 5, 1622, however; and the ship lay dormant for some two years, when it was appraised for probate. It was described as in poor condition. Such ships were more valuable as wood (a rare commodity); so the *Mayflower* was probably sold as scrap.[44] There is no confirmation, though, for the various claims that the *Mayflower*'s timber ended up as a barn in rural Jordans (north of London), or as a church in Walpole, or that one of her masts ended up on a Berkshire maypole!

THE VOYAGE

On September 16, 1620, the *Mayflower* departed from Plymouth, England. A seaman who had delighted in harassing the Separatists died on October 3 and was buried at sea. After this a severe westerly gale arose and fierce storms were encountered. The *Mayflower* was tossed about like a floating toy. A main beam in midships bowed and cracked. For a time Captain Jones feared serious disaster and was tempted to turn back. He consulted with the leaders of the voyage, and it was decided to continue on; someone had found a "great screw," which the passengers had brought from Holland, to meet the damaged beam. In a series of storms, the ship drifted under "bare poles. " In one of the fiercest of these, John Howland was washed overboard and would have been lost if he had not caught hold of a "topsail halyard" trailing in the ocean, as the ship was leaning in the waves. After holding on "sundry fathoms under water," Howland was hauled back on board with a hook. There was another cause to celebrate at mid-ocean, with the arrival of a new passenger, Oceanus Hopkins. On November 16, a servant named William Button died and was buried at sea. Two days later, floating objects were observed, which indicated that land was not far away. On November 19, the long-awaited cry of "Land Ho!" was heard from the crow's nest. Cape Cod had been sighted and the historic voyage was at its end. The Pilgrims "fell upon their knees and blessed the God of Heaven who had brought them over the vast and furious ocean."[45] While the *Mayflower* rode anchor off Provincetown on Saturday, November 21, forty-one men placed their signatures on the historic *Mayflower Compact*. That day, some of them waded ashore and became the first to step upon the shores of Cape Cod. *Mourt's Relation* records that the cold water brought "colds and coughs"[46] as they carefully walked along the shoreline, every man with "his musket, sword, and corslet."

Today, a memorial plaque marks the site where the men first stepped ashore. Nearby, one can walk to the top of "Pilgrim Monument," standing just over 252 feet tall, for a superb view of the Cape. The monument was dedicated in 1910 to commemorate that first landfall of the Pilgrims at Provincetown, on November 21, 1620 (N.S.). William Bradford's classic narration of the Pilgrims' voyage is provided below.

Bradford's Entry Sept. 16 (N.S.)—the Day the *Mayflower* Sailed out Alone from Plymouth, England:

These troubles being blown over, and now all being compact together in one ship, they put to sea again with a prosperous wind, which continued divers days together, which was some encouragement unto them; yet according to the usual manner many were afflicted with sea sickness. And I may not omit here a special work of God's providence. There was a proud and very profane young man, one of the sea-men, of a lusty, able body, which made him the more haughty; he would always be condemning the poor people in their sickness, and cursing them daily with grievous execrations, and did not let to tell them, that he hoped to help to cast half of them overboard before they came to their journey's end, and to make merry with what they had; and if he were by any gently reproved, he would curse and swear most bitterly. But it pleased God before they came half seas over, to smite this young man with a grievous disease, of which he died in a desperate manner, and so was himself the first that was thrown overboard. Thus his curses light on his own head; and it was an astonishment to all his fellows, for they noted it to be the just hand of God upon him.

After they had enjoyed fair winds and weather for a season, they were encountered many times with cross winds, and met with many fierce storms, with which the ship was shroudly shaken, and her upper works made very leaky; and one of the main beams in the mid ships was bowed and cracked, which put them in some fear that the ship could not be able to perform the voyage. So some of the chief of the company, perceiving the mariners to fear the sufficiency of the ship, as appeared by their mutterings, they entered into serious consultation with the master and other officers of the ship, to consider in time of the danger; and rather to return then to cast themselves into a desperate and inevitable peril. And truly there was great distraction and difference of opinion among the mariners themselves; fain would they do what could be done for their wages sake, (being now half the seas over,) and on the other hand they were loath to hazard their lives too desperately. But in examining of all opinions, the master and others affirmed they knew the ship to be strong and firm under water; and for the buckling of the main beam, there was a great iron screw the passengers brought out of Holland, which would raise the beam into his place; the which being done, the carpenter and master affirmed that with a post put under it, set firm in the lower deck, and other-ways bound, he would make it sufficient. And as for the decks and upper works they would caulk them as well as they could, and though with the working of the ship they would not long keep staunch, yet there would otherwise be no great danger, if they did not overpress her with sails. So they committed themselves to the will of God, and resolved to proceed.

In sundry of these storms the winds were so fierce, and the seas so high, as they could not bear a knot of sail, but were forced to hull, for divers days together. And in one of them, as they thus lay at hull, in a mighty storm, a lusty young man (called John Howland) coming upon some occasion above the gratings, was, with a seele of the ship thrown into the sea; but it pleased God that he caught hold of the topsail halyards, which hung overboard, and ran out at length; yet he held his hold (though he was sundry fathoms under water) till he was hauled up by the same rope to the brim of the water, and then with a boat hook and other means got into the ship again, and his life saved; and though he was something ill with it, yet he lived many years after, and became a profitable member both in church and commonwealth. In all this voyage there died but one of the passengers, which was William Butten, a youth, servant to Samuel Fuller, when they drew near the coast.

But to omit other things, (that I may be brief,) after long beating at sea they fell with that land which is called Cape Cod; the which being made and certainly known to be it, they were not a little joyful. After some deliberation had amongst themselves and with the master of the ship, they tacked about and resolved to stand for the southward (the wind and weather being fair) to find some place about Hudson's River for their habitation. But after they had sailed that course about half a day, they fell amongst dangerous shoals and roaring breakers, and they were so far entangled therewith as they conceived themselves in great danger; and the wind shrinking upon them withal, they resolved to bear up again for the Cape, and thought themselves happy to get out of those dangers before night overtook them, as by God's providence they did. And the next day they got into the Cape-harbor where they rid in safety.

A word or two by the way of this cape; it was thus first named by Captain Gosnold and his company, Anno. 1602, and after by Captain Smith was called Cape James; but it retains the former name amongst seamen. Also that point which first showed these dangerous shoals unto them, they called Point Care, and Tucker's Terror; but the French and Dutch to this day call it Malabar, by reason of those perilous shoals, and the losses they have suffered there.

Being thus arrived in a good harbor and brought safe to land, they fell upon their knees and blessed the God of heaven, who had brought them over the vast and furious ocean, and delivered them from all the perils and miseries thereof, again to set their feet on the firm and stable earth, their proper element. And no marvel if they were thus joyful, seeing wise Seneca was so affected with sailing a few miles on the coast of his own Italy; as he affirmed, that he had rather remain twenty years on his way by land, then pass by sea to any place in a short time; so tedious and dreadful was the same unto him.[47]

In his *New England Memorial* (1669), Nathaniel Morton records the belief of some that the Dutch bribed Captain Jones into taking them to New England rather than the Hudson River, since they were making their own plans for a settlement there.[48] Neither Bradford nor Winslow mentions such a conspiracy. Morton adds that God in His Providence had brought them to Plymouth in own mysterious ways. Although he mentions the winds, perilous shoals, and breakers, perhaps Morton was establishing, "just for the record," one more explanation for the "unauthorized" settlement at Plymouth.

THE MAYFLOWER COMPACT

While still in Provincetown Harbor, some of the nonseparatist strangers began to grow restless, insisting that since they had not landed within the Virginia territory, they had a right to be as independent as they wished, and to take orders from no one. Thus, Bradford explains that the *Mayflower Compact* was "the first foundation of their government in this place," and that it was "occasioned partly by the discontented and mutinous speeches that some of the strangers amongst them had let fall from them in the ship."[49] *Mourt's Relation,* another first-hand account, adds that "some [were] not well affected to unity and concord, but gave some appearance of faction [and thus] it was thought good . . . that we should combine together in one body, and to submit to such government and governors as we should by common consent agree to make and choose."[50] John Robinson, in his farewell address, had suggested the idea of a compact:

Lastly, whereas you are become a body politic, using amongst yourselves civil government, and are not furnished with any persons of special eminence above the rest, to be chosen by you into office of government; let your wisdom and godliness appear, not only in choosing such persons as do entirely love and will promote the common good, but also in yielding unto them all due honour and obedience in their lawful administrations.[51]

The term "*Mayflower* Compact" was not assigned to the document until 1793, when it first appeared in Alden Bradford's *Topographical Description of Duxborough.* Previous descriptions of it include "association and agreement" (William Bradford); "combination" (*Plymouth Colony Records*); "solemn contract" (Thomas Prince, 1738); and "covenant" (Charles Turner, 1774). Although the original document does not survive, the text which Bradford transcribed into his *Plymouth Plantation* was first printed in *Mourt's Relation* (1622). The earliest known list of the signers appears in Nathaniel Morton's *New England's Memorial* (1669).[52] Forty-one men signed the *Compact,* which states essentially that each person would submit to majority rule. After the signing, they "confirmed" John Carver, "a man godly and well approved amongst them," as their governor for the first year. Carver is sometimes called the first colonial governor chosen by "free election." After Carver's death in the spring of 1621, William Bradford was chosen to succeed him, governing first with one assistant, Isaac Allerton, and later with as many as seven assistants, acting as magistrates who collectively constituted the Council, that is, the executive and judicial body of the plantation colony. From the beginning, all important positions were elective, even Myles Standish being officially chosen by the people as military leader of the citizens' militia.

The Mayflower Compact

In the Name of God, Amen. We whose names are underwritten, the loyal subjects of our dread sovereign Lord, King James, by the grace of God, of Great Britain, France and Ireland, King, Defender of the Faith, etc.,

Having undertaken, for the glory of God, and advancement of the Christian faith and honor of our King and Country, a voyage to plant the first colony in the northern parts of Virginia, do by these presents solemnly and mutually in the presence of God, and one of another, covenant and combine ourselves together into a civil body politic, for our better ordering and preservation and furtherance of the ends aforesaid; and by virtue hereof to enact, constitute and frame such just and equal laws, ordinances, acts, constitutions and offices, from time to time, as shall be thought most meet and convenient for the general good of the Colony: unto which we promise all due submission and obedience. *In witness whereof:* we have hereunder subscribed our names at Cape Cod the 11 of November, in the year of the reign of our sovereign Lord, King James of England, France and Ireland the eighteenth, and of Scotland the fifty-fourth. *Ano. Dom.* 1620.

John Carver	William White	Edward Fuller	Gilbert Winslow
William Bradford	Richard Warren	John Turner	Edmond Margeson
Edward Winslow	John Howland	Francis Eaton	Peter Brown
William Brewster	Stephen Hopkins	James Chilton	Richard Britteridge
Isaac Allerton	Edward Tilly	John Crackston	George Soule
Myles Standish	John Tilly	John Billington	Richard Clarke
John Alden	Francis Cooke	Moses Fletcher	Richard Gardiner
Samuel Fuller	Thomas Rogers	John Goodman	John Allerton
Christopher Martin	Thomas Tinker	Degory Priest	Thomas English
William Mullins	John Rigdale	Thomas Williams	Edward Doty
			Edward Leister

1. For a list of all transcriptions and summaries of the Leiden documents, see Caleb Johnson's *Mayflower* Web Pages: http://members.aol.com/calebj/mayflower.html

2. Often, the records give only the betrothal date, and fail to reveal the marriage date. Dexter says, "Betrothals had more prominence than marriages, the latter merely being regarded as consummating the former;" Henry Martyn Dexter and Morton Dexter, *The England and Holland of the Pilgrims* (1906; rpt. Baltimore: Genealogical Publishing Co., Inc., 1978), 502.

3. For example, as Robinson was praying prior to the Pilgrims' departure from Delfshaven, amidst the tears of farewell, there were "Strangers" watching from the dock, who apparently felt much in common with the Christians: "The Dutch strangers that stood on the quay as spectators could not refrain from tears." Regrettably, Bradford did not identify these tender-hearted "Strangers." William Bradford, *Of Plymouth Plantation 1620-1647*, ed. Samuel Eliot Morison (1952; rpt. NY: Alfred A. Knopf, 1998), 48.

4. *The Cry of a Stone, or, A Treatise Shewing What is the Right Matter, Forme, and Government of the Visible Church of Christ* (London: R. Oulton and G. Dexter, 1642), 23, cited in Jeremy D. Bangs, *Strangers on the Mayflower* (Leiden: unpublished paper, 1999), 5. I am endebted to Dr. Bangs for sharing this paper with me.

5. A. H. Drysdale, *History of the Presbyterians in England: Their Rise, Decline, and Revival* (London: Publication Committee of the Presbyterian Church of England, 1889), 107; see also Drysdale's chapter on the London Church of the Strangers, pp. 40-51.

6. Both the number forty-one and the narrow use of the word "strangers" have become traditional, largely from the sometimes misleading, but of course still valuable and delightful, study by George F. Willison, *Saints and Strangers* (NY: Reynal & Hitchcock, 1945), 437ff. and *passim*. Obviously, even Willison's title suggests an arbitrary division. Much additional research, however, has been done since 1945.

7. For a valuable and recent study see G. V. C. Young, "Pilgrim Myles Standish: His European Background," in *The Pilgrims in the Netherlands: Recent Research,* ed. Jeremy D. Bangs, (1985; rpt. Leiden, The Netherlands: Leiden American Pilgrim Museum, 1998), 35-43.

8. William Hubbard, *General History of New England* (Cambridge: Massachusetts Historical Society, 1815), 63. Hubbard is critical of the Pilgrims' relations with the Indians; this no doubt influenced his personal opinion of Standish.

9. Jeremy D. Bangs, *Pilgrim Life in Leiden* (Leiden: Leiden American Pilgrim Museum, 1997), 45.

10. Nathaniel B. Shurtleff and David Pulsifer, ed., *Records of the Colony of New Plymouth in New England (1620-1691)* (Boston, 1855-61; rpt., 12 vols. in 6, NY: AMS Press 1968), I:1632-33.

11. See Bradford, *Plymouth Plantation,* 204-10.

12. For example, one of the Standish sons, Alexander, was a deacon and the town clerk at Duxbury, MA. The *Plymouth Church Records* contain numerous miscellaneous statistics as well. Myles Standish Jr. married Sarah, the daughter of John and Mary Winslow. Not a lean legacy for a fiery old "Shrimp!"

13. Bradford, *Plymouth Plantation,* 77.

14. Nathaniel Morton, *New England's Memorial* (1669; rpt. Boston: Congregational Board of Publications, 1855), 170.

15. Bradford, *Plymouth Plantation,* 374-75.

16. "Myles Standish's Will and Inventory," *The Mayflower Descendant* 3, no. 3 (July, 1901): 154 (34 vols., compiled and published by George Ernest Bowman, from 1899 to 1937, Massachusetts Society of Mayflower Descendants), on "Mayflower Legacy," 43-vol. searchable CD edition, Wheat Ridge, CO: Search & Research Publishing Corporation, 1998, containing *The Mayflower Descendant With Other New England Town Records.*

17. Lyman Denison Brewster, "William Brewster," *The Mayflower Descendant* 4, no. 2 (April 1902): 103; see also Nathaniel Morton, *New England's Memorial* (1669; rpt. Boston: Congregational Board of Publications, 1855), 497.

18. This present study includes everyone under twenty in the "boys and girls" category.

19. Those who died on board the *Mayflower*, after its arrival at Cape Cod but before its arrival at Plymouth, included Dorothy Bradford, James Chilton, Jasper More, and Edward Thompson.

20. Those who died after the *Mayflower* set sail for England on April 5, 1621 but before the arrival of the *Fortune* on November 9, 1621 include Alice Mullins, her son Joseph Mullins, John and Katherine Carver, and Robert Carter.

21. Included in these fifty deaths are two crew members, John Allerton and Thomas English, who were hired to become a permanent part of the settlement. The names and numbers of other crew members who died are not known. At Coles Hill in Plymouth, Massachusetts, a sarcophagus lists those "of the one hundred and four passengers" who died the first winter. Based upon William Bradford's listing, it includes the name "John Goodman." Although Bradford is normally astoundingly accurate, the present study will not include Goodman among those who died that winter, since he is listed as one of the sharers of the land division of 1623. That is one of only two places in which the present study contradicts Bradford; the other one regards one of the More children. Also, unlike the sarcophagus, the present study will include the five who died on board the *Mayflower* before it reached Plymouth. They should be listed because they were actually a part of those 104 passengers; they are William Butten, Dorothy Bradford, James Chilton, Jasper More, and Edward Thompson.

22. John Allerton lived in Leiden's *Pieterskerkhof* and buried a child there on May 21, 1616; see Henry Martyn Dexter and Morton Dexter, *The England and Holland of the Pilgrims*, 601. Of course, Separatists Isaac and Mary Allerton lived in the *Pieterskerkhof* as well; John was the brother of Isaac. It was a natural thing for him to join them on the *Mayflower*, since people tended to travel in family groups.

23. John Bradford married twice but left no children.

24. William Jr. and Joseph Bradford both left descendants; William Jr. became a prominent leader of Plymouth.

25. Mercy Bradford married Benjamin Vermayes, but there is no record of any surviving children.

26. Jonathan Brewster became successful in various business endeavors in New England; he married Lucretia Oldham at Plymouth in 1624; they had three sons and five daughters.

27. In 1624 Patience Brewster married Thomas Prence, who had come over on the *Fortune*. They had a son and three daughters, but Patience died within ten years. Prence, would outlive several other wives. He served as governor in 1634 and was elected assistant governor in 1635. He served in one of those offices every year for the remainder of his life. After William Bradford's death, Prence became the most influential person in Plymouth.

28. Fear Brewster married the *Mayflower* passenger Isaac Allerton whose first wife, Mary Norris, had died. Fear died at an early age.

29. Love Brewster married Sarah Collier and they had four children.

30. Wrestling Brewster died without issue at a young age.

31. Although previous works on the Pilgrims have excluded the three Chiltons from the Leiden Separatists, there is now more than ample evidence for placing them here, as we have shown previously. See Jan van Dorsten, "Why the Pilgrims Left Leiden," in *The Pilgrims in the Netherlands: Recent Research*, ed. Jeremy D. Bangs, (1985; rpt. Leiden: Leiden American Pilgrim Museum, 1998), 34.; and Eugene A. Stratton, *Plymouth Colony: Its History & People 1620-1691* (Salt Lake City, UT: Ancestry Publishing, 1986), 262.

32. There is a May 8, 1609, record, in St. Peter's Parish Church in Sandwich, England, of the wife of James Chilton being excommunicated, along with some others, for participating in an unlawful funeral of an infant. Mrs. Chilton's excommunication may be the first record of

the prosecution of a female *Mayflower* Pilgrim for Separatist acts. See the "New England Historical and Genealogical Register," (volume 153, Number 612). The group apparently buried a young child without following the proper ceremonies prescribed by the Church of England. Separatist dissenters opposed such ceremonies, since they resembled the rites of the Roman Catholic Church and were not based on the Scriptures. See the valuable discussion in Horton Davies, *The Worship of the American Puritans, 1629-1730* (Morgan, PA: Soli Deo Gloria Publishers, 1999), 229-45. The parish churches of England likewise deeply resented Separatists who refused to bring their children to them for baptism and for the placing of their names into the registries.

33. Mary Chilton's will mentions such things as "my Best Gowne and Pettecoat and my silver beare bowl," a "silver cup with a handle," and "my Pretty Coate with the silver Lace."

34. Previous studies have placed Humility Cooper with the "strangers"; however, see the discussion by Jeremy D. Bangs, Director of the Leiden American Pilgrim Museum in the *Mayflower Quarterly* 52:9; see also Eugene A. Stratton, *Plymouth Colony: Its History & People 1620-1691*, 273.

35. The May 8, 1609, excommunication record in St. Peter's, in Sandwich, includes Moses Fletcher for participating in the unlawful burial of a baby. See the *New England Historical and Genealogical Register,* (vol. 153, No. 612); see note above on Mrs. James Chilton.

36. Although previous works on the Pilgrims have excuded Edward Fuller, his wife, and their son from the Leiden Separatists, there is now more than ample evidence for placing them here. See Jeremy D. Bangs, *Mayflower Quarterly* 51:58; and Eugene A. Stratton, *Plymouth Colony*, 294-95.

37. Samuel Fuller died in the 1633 epidemic at Plymouth. William Bradford wrote, "And in the end, after he had much helped others, Samuel Fuller who was their surgeon and physician and had been a great help and comfort unto them. As in his faculty, so otherwise being a deacon of the church, a man godly and forward to do good, being much missed after his death. And he and the rest of their brethren much lamented by them and caused much sadness and mourning amongst them, which caused them to humble themselves and seek the Lord; and towards winter it pleased the Lord the sickness ceased" (Bradford, 260).

38. Previous studies have placed Henry Samson with the "strangers;" however, see Eugene A. Stratton, *Plymouth Colony*, 347-48.

39. Jeremy D. Bangs, *Strangers on the Mayflower* (Leiden: unpublished paper, 1999), 2. Bangs points out that the Pilgrims acquired the custom of civil marriage from the Dutch, whose government had started the practice to accommodate refugees who were outside the official Dutch Reformed Church. Governor William Bradford officiated the Winslow wedding.

40. Ely could possibly be either John or Christopher Ely (Ellis) of Leiden, according to Jeremy D. Bangs (*Mayflower Quarterly* 51:59); see Eugene A. Stratton, *Plymouth Colony*, 289; and D. Plooij, *The Pilgrim Fathers from a Dutch Point of View* (1932; rpt. NY: AMS Press, Inc., 1969), 85.

41. Eugene A. Stratton, *Plymouth Colony*, 328-29; see also George Ernest Bowman, "The Date of Governor Bradford's Passenger List," *The Mayflower Descendant* 1, no. 3 (July 1899): 161f.

42. Caleb Johnson, *Crew of the Mayflower* (*Mayflower* Web Pages: http://members.aol.com/calebj/mayflower.html).

43. The surgeon Giles Heale was a great benefit to the Pilgrims while the *Mayflower* remained in Plymouth. Heale's personal hymn book, a second edition of Henry Ainsworth's *Annotations Upon the Book of Psalmes*, published in 1617, contains an inscription, dated February 10, 1620, written by Pilgrim Separatist Isaac Allerton, stating that he was giving it as a gift to Giles Heale. Allerton served as one of Plymouth's earliest assistant governors. See Henry Martyn Dexter and Morton Dexter, *The England and Holland of the Pilgrims*, 589; and Francis R. Stoddard, *The Truth About the Pilgrims* (NY: Society of Mayflower Descendants, 1952), 19.

44. Caleb Johnson, *A Brief History of the Mayflower.*
Mayflower Web Pages: (http://members.aol.com/calebj/mayflower.html).

45. Bradford, *Plymouth Plantation,* 61.

46. G. Mourt (Edward Winslow and William Bradford), *Mourt's Relation: A Journal of the Pilgrims at Plymouth* (1622; rpt. edited, with an introduction and notes, by Dwight B. Heath. Bedford, MA: Applewood Books, 1986), 17.

47. Bradford, *Plymouth Plantation,* 58-61.

48. Nathaniel Morton, *New England's Memorial* (1669; rpt. Boston: Congregational Board of Publications, 1855), 22. The whole idea of the Dutch bribing Captain Jones is strongly opposed by Edward Arber, ed., *The Story of The Pilgrim Fathers, 1606-1623 A.D; as Told by Themselves, Their Friends, and Their Enemies* (London: Ward and Downey, Limited, 1897), 389-91.

49. Bradford, *Plymouth Plantation,* 75.

50. G. Mourt (Edward Winslow and William Bradford), *Mourt's Relation: A Journal of the Pilgrims at Plymouth* (1622; rpt. Bedford, MA: Applewood Books, 1986), 17.

51. Bradford, *Plymouth Plantation,* 370.

52. Morton, *New England's Memorial,* 26. A list of the signers of the *Mayflower Compact* later appears in Thomas Prince's *Chronological History of New England in the form of Annals* (1736), and in Thomas Hutchinson's *History of the Providence of Massachusetts Bay* (1767). Incidentally, both Prince and Hutchinson had made use of Bradford's manuscript while it was in Boston's Old South Church. One wonders if perhaps the original *Mayflower Compact* was lost from there as well. Of course, the Pilgrims might possibly have sent the original copy of the Compact back to England with Christopher Jones.

CHAPTER 7

THE OUTCOME:
FROM THE LANDING AT CAPE COD TO 1800

On the day following the November 21 signing of the *Compact,* the weather was mild and it was Sunday; the Pilgrims spent the day in quiet worship. Bradford marvels at "this poor people's present condition":

> No friends to welcome them, nor inns to entertain or refresh their weather-beaten bodies, no houses . . . to repair to. . . . Whichever way they turned their eyes (save upward to the heavens) they could have little solace. . . . For summer being done, all things stand upon them . . . and the whole country, full of woods and thickets, represented a wild and savage hue. If they looked behind them, there was the mighty ocean. . . . What could now sustain them but the Spirit of God and His grace?

Beautifully weaving into his narrative portions of Deuteronomy 26:7 and Psalm 107:1-8, Bradford now makes an eloquent comparison of the Pilgrims with the Hebrews coming up out of Egyptian bondage:

> May not and ought not the children of these fathers rightly say: "Our fathers were Englishmen which came over this great ocean, and were ready to perish in this wilderness; but they cried unto the Lord, and He heard their voice, and looked on their adversity," etc. "Let them therefore praise the Lord, because He is good: and His mercies endure forever." Yea, let them which have been redeemed of the Lord, shew how He hath delivered them from the hand of the oppressor. When they wandered in the desert wilderness out of

the way, and found no city to dwell in, both hungry, and thirsty, their soul was overwhelmed in them. Let them confess before the Lord His loving kindness, and His wonderful works before the sons of men."[1]

On Monday, the men took the small boat, called a shallop, to the beach for repair and caulking, while the women went ashore to do the much-needed laundry. Francis Eaton, the carpenter, had his hands full with the shallop, which was "bruised and shattered" from being used for sleeping quarters.[2] It would take the men two weeks to complete the repairs. With the *Mayflower* riding at anchor off the cape, families would continue living in it, as the men formed exploring parties and made three "discoveries," searching the coastline for a suitable place to settle. There were times when as many as three-fourths of the men would be gone, as the women and children waited and wondered what would become of them. On Wednesday, November 25, the first exploring party of sixteen men set out by land and soon "espied five or six [Indians] with a dog." The following day, they discovered Truro Springs, Pamet River, and the long-awaited "fresh water." A memorial plaque at the location quotes the lines from *Mourt's Relation:*

About ten o'clock we came into a deep valley, full of brush, wood-gaile, and long grass, through which we found little paths or tracks, and there we saw a deer, and found springs of fresh water, of which we were heartily glad, and sat us down and drunk our first New England water with as much delight as ever we drunk drink in all our lives.[3]

They made a fire to signal the ship, then continued on, discovering a fresh water pond. They soon found Indian corn buried in the sand. Today, on the beach at "Cornhill," a memorial plaque cites the account in *Mourt's Relation*[4] and notes Bradford's conviction that this was "a special providence of God, and a great mercy to this poor people, that here they got seed to plant them corn next year, or else they might have starved."[5] They also found an old fort and saw two canoes. The party then returned to their campsite for the night. The next day, William Bradford caught his leg in a deer trap made by the Indians. They returned to the ship.

At last the shallop was repaired and on December 7, a large body of thirty-four men, making up the second expedition started out, some in the shallop and others in the longboat. At the beginning of their four-day trip, "it blowed and did snow all that day and night, and froze withal."[6] Many of the later deaths were attributed to this exposure to the severe weather. They did get "three fat geese and six ducks" for their supper one night. They revisited the Cornhill. Captain Jones and some others returned to the ship after the third day. The rest continued on, finding wigwams and Indian graves. That night they returned to the ship, to find that Peregrine White had been born. On December 14, Edward Thomson died. The next day, fourteen-year-old Francis Billington almost blew up the *Mayflower!* The adventuresome Francis, in the absence of his father, "had got gun powder and had shot off a piece or two, and made squibs, and there being a fowling-piece charged in his father's cabin, shot her off in the cabin; there being a little barrel of powder half full, scattered in and about the cabin, the fire being four foot of the bed between the decks, . . . and many people about the fire; and yet, by God's mercy, no harm done."[7]

On Wednesday, December 16, a party of eighteen men set out in the shallop for the third expedition. It was so cold "the water froze on our clothes." The party reached Eastham in the evening. The next day, they explored up toward Wellfleet Bay. They passed the night at Great Meadow Creek. On Friday, December 18, the party had its "First Encounter" with the Indians. There is a memorial plaque marking the site on "Encounter Beach." On future military expeditions, the men would start wearing protective armor consisting of a helmet and sometimes a metal corslet (vest). They would carry swords, knifes, and daggers attached to the belt. They had two basic types of muskets—the matchlock and the flintlock. The matchlock was more common because it was cheaper; but loading and firing a matchlock was a slow process. The flintlock was faster because it did not require a match for lighting the firing mechanism. Both types were usually fired with the heavy, cumbersome muzzle resting in a stand.[8] Following the First Encounter, the party coasted along the cape and ran in under the lee of Clark's Island in Plymouth Harbor and spent the night. They would not realize that it was an island until the next day. Here on Clark's Island, the Pilgrims held their first actual thanksgiving. Bradford explains, "They found themselves to be on an island secure from the Indians, where they might dry their stuff, fix their pieces and rest themselves; and gave God thanks for His mercies in their manifold deliverances. And this being the last day of the week, they prepared there to keep the Sabbath."[9]

On December 21, they made their historic landing at Plymouth, exactly a month after making landfall at Provincetown. It was a pleasant day, as the party "sounded the Harbor" and came into the land. The exploring party found that the land had been already cleared at "Plymouth," which had been named that on Captain John Smith's map. The Pilgrims kept the name, because Plymouth, England, was the last town they left in their native land and where the people had expressed much kindness to them. Now it seemed as if some unseen friend had prepared this very spot in anticipation of their arrival. Seeing that it was "a very good harbor," they returned to the *Mayflower,* probably by taking the shorter twenty-six-mile route directly across Cape Cod Bay. So they arrived back "with good news to the rest of our people, which did much comfort their hearts." To William Bradford, however, it was a sad day; his young wife, Dorothy, had fallen overboard and drowned shortly after the exploring party had left. On December 25 the *Mayflower* set sail from Cape Cod for Plymouth, but was driven back by a change in the wind. The next day, she crossed the Bay and dropped anchor in Plymouth harbor. The *Mayflower* would be the only winter home for many, and the scene of great sickness and death during the next three months. The company spent their first Lord's Day in Plymouth, December 27, on board their ship. Early Monday morning, a party left to explore the vicinity by land. The following day, one party explored by land, and another in the shallop. They discovered the Jones River, and soon decided to settle near what is now Burial Hill, along Town Brook. On Thursday, Richard Britteridge became the first death after reaching Plymouth. On Saturday, Solomon Prower died. The women could hear the Indian cries in the distance, as the men assembled their material for building a Common House, which would also serve as their first church building. During January, Degory Priest and Christopher Martin would be among those who died. On January 4, 1621, more Indian cries were heard. Fresh water was brought to the ship, and it was recorded that those on the *Mayflower* first began to " drink water on board." The women spent another day doing the general washing of clothes. Governor Bradford describes the scene:

The Mayflower II

The Mayflower Pub:
Home of Mayflower in
Rotherhithe (London)

Jetty at Mayflower Pub

London's Tower Bridge

River Thames

City of Oxford-Coat of Arms

Big Ben

Cambridge University (England)

*St. Helena's Church, Austerfield
(England)*

*William Bradford was baptized in
St. Helena's Church, Austerfield*

Cottage thought to be birthplace of William Bradford

Gainsborough Old Hall (England)

Great Hall in
Gainsborough's Old Hall

*Hampton Court Palace
(England)*

*Parish Church in Babworth,
England*

Parish Church in Babworth (England)

St. Botolph's Church, Boston
(England)

John Cotton's Pulpit,
St. Botolph's Church

Remnant of Scrooby Manor House

Boston's Guildhall, where the cells are located

Cells in which Pilgrims were imprisoned (Boston)

St. Wilfred's Parish Church in Scrooby (England)

English Reformed Church in the Begijnhof (Amsterdam)

Amsterdam's Dam Square

*Pieterskerk in
Leiden, Holland*

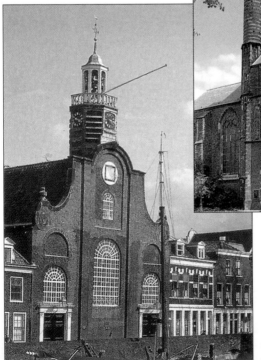

*Pieterskerk in
Leiden, Holland*

*Pilgrim Fathers' Church
Delfshaven (Netherlands)*

West Gate at Southampton, England

*Mayflower Memorial
(Southampton, England)*

*Mayflower Stone,
Dartmouth, England*

Dartmouth, England

Mayflower Memorial (Plymouth England)

Closeup of plaque on the Mayflower Memorial (Plymouth, England)

Plymouth Rock

Statue of Massasoit

First Fort (Plymouth, Massachusetts)

Harlow house, built with wood from dismantled fort.

Feeding sheep at Plimoth Plantation

Burial Hill (Plymouth, MA)
where William Bradford's tomb stands above the two churches

Statue of William Bradford

Forefathers' Monument (Plymouth, Massachusetts)

Liberty   *Law*   *Education*   *Morality*

They fetched them wood, made them fires, dressed them meat, made their beds, washed their loathsome clothes[,] . . . in a word, did all the homely and necessary offices . . . which dainty and queasy stomachs cannot endure . . . and all this willingly and cheerfully, without any grudging in the least, showing herein their true love unto their friends and brethren; a rare example and worthy to be remembered.[10]

The Pilgrims buried their dead in shallow unmarked graves, so that the Indians could not know their losses. By November 1621, the Plantation would lose fifty-one people, half their original number of passengers. In Plymouth, a sarcophagus lists the names of those who died during the "starving time" of the first winter. On the west side of this monument, in enduring bronze letters, these lines soberly appeal to future generations:

> This monument marks the First Burying Ground of the Passengers of the Mayflower. Here, under cover of darkness, the fast dwindling company laid their dead, levelling the earth above them lest the Indians should know how many were graves. Reader, History records no nobler venture for faith and freedom than that of the Pilgrim band. In weariness and painfulness, in watching, often in hunger and cold, they laid the foundations of a state wherein every man, through countless ages, should have liberty to worship God in his own way. May their example inspire thee to do thy part in perpetuating and spreading the Holy ideals of our republic throughout the world.

Especially sad is the story of the More children—Richard, Jasper, Ellen, and a fourth child described by Bradford as a boy, but who may have been a four-year-old girl named Mary. These children were without their parents, Samuel and Catherine More, who had recently gone through a bitter divorce. Finding strong evidence which led him to believe that Catherine had for some time been involved in an adulterous affair with Jacob Blakeway, Samuel More observed in the four children a close resemblance to Mr. Blakeway. Documents suggest that Catherine and Jacob admitted to the affair. Paying a sum of money for their passage, temporary support, and fifty acres of land for each of them, Samuel arranged for the children to be turned over to John Carver and Robert Cushman and taken away on the *Mayflower*. There are no records to indicate that any adult family members ever made an attempt to contact these children again. It is not surprising that little seven-year-old Jasper died while the *Mayflower* was still anchored off Provincetown. The four-year-old, along with eight-year-old Ellen, died in the epidemic of the first winter. Richard, the only More child to survive, was six or seven years old upon arrival, lived in the Brewster home, and eventually moved to Salem and became a sea captain. The life and adventures of Richard More could make an intriguing novel.[11]

One day in January, young Francis Billington climbed a tree and saw what appeared to him to be a "great sea." His discovery turned out to be a shallow pond, which was later called "Billington Sea." The Billingtons, however, turned out to be "one of the profanest families amongst them."[12] Francis' father, John, would later be hanged for murder, after shooting John Newcomen; Francis's mother Ellen would be fined for slander and be made to "sit in the stocks and be publickly whipt;"[13] and his older brother, John Jr., wandered off into the woods and was captured five days later by the Nauset Indians, the same hostile Indians the Pilgrims had encountered during their initial exploration around Cape Cod. At the familiar sight of the Pilgrims' muskets, the Nausets gladly turned the young Billington over to the ten men who had come to rescue him! That same month, John Goodman and Peter Brown were lost in the woods. Before the end of January, the thatch on the Common House burned, and the men began to build the storehouse. In February, Captain Myles Standish's wife Rose died. Sickness and death seemed to prevail. The men erected several shelters, which soon caught fire mysteriously. One day, Captain Standish and Francis Cooke inadvertently left some tools in the woods, where they had been cutting thatch and felling timber for the houses. The tools were carried off by Indians. Following some serious encounters with the Indians, an important meeting was held for formulating a military policy; Myles Standish was chosen captain of the militia company and, within a few weeks, the "great guns were mounted on the hill." These mounted cannons were strategically important for the struggling Plantation. The brass minion could fire a three-pound ball approximately a third of a mile. The saker could fire a slightly smaller ball about the same distance.

On March 3, two influential members of the company died, William Mullins and William White. It is recorded that two others also died, making four in one day. Although the weather was still "wintry", there were distinct signs of an early spring, and snow was fast disappearing. Sickness and death still stalked among the Pilgrims, however, and on March 7, Mary (Norris) Allerton died. The birds were chirping merrily on March 13, and during the day a short thunderstorm arose. Those who were fortunate enough to have garden seed proceeded to plant it on March 17. There was a desperate need for green vegetables, the lack of which probably caused most of the sickness, which was a type of scurvy. Captain Standish called another meeting on March 26 to discuss military strategy. Suddenly, Chief Samoset walked right into Plymouth, speaking English. He was an Algonquin and had learned English from various fishing captains. The story he told gave the Pilgrims cause to thank God once again for His Providence. According to Samoset, this area had been the territory of the Patuxets, a large hostile tribe that killed every white man who landed on these shores. Less than four years prior to the Pilgrims' landing, a mysterious plague had devastated the tribe. Convinced that some great spirit had destroyed the Patuxets, neighboring tribes had shunned the entire area. So the cleared land on which the Pilgrims had settled apparently belonged to no one. Their nearest neighbors, explained Samoset, were the Wampanoags, some fifty miles to the southwest. These Indians numbered about sixty warriors and Massasoit, their chief, also ruled over several other tribes.

On March 31, it was recorded that the "carpenter fitted the shallop" to "fetch all from aboard." Apparently, this meant that the *Mayflower* was now empty. For many, it had been a home and headquarters from the departure from Southampton, England, until now (August 15 to March 31), a period of seven and a half months. In the earliest days, the settlement consisted of the First (now Leyden) Street with twelve houses, a common storehouse, and the governor's house. These structures were surrounded by a palisade, with the fort dominating the scene from the nearby hill. The fort was connected with the village by a palisade. The New England spring was now in delightful evidence. On April 1, a meeting was interrupted by the return of Samoset with another Indian named

Tisquantum (Squanto), who also spoke English and who, according to Bradford, was to become "a special instrument sent of God for their good, beyond their expectation."

Squanto was the last of the Patuxets. His story begins in 1605 when Captain George Weymouth bribed and kidnapped him and four other Indians and took them to England for the purpose of impressing his financial backers. In England Squanto lived with Sir Ferdinando Gorges of the Plymouth Company. Gorges taught Squanto and the other Indians the English language so that he could question them in much detail about their native land. In 1614 Captain John Smith, working for Gorges, brought Squanto as an interpreter on a mapping expedition back to New England. When Smith departed, he turned the project and Squanto over to Captain Thomas Hunt. Hunt soon sailed into Patuxet (Plymouth). Through the promise of trading, Hunt lured twenty-seven Indians, some from the Nauset tribe and some from the Patuxet tribe, on board his ship, then kidnapped and bound them. Squanto was among them. Hunt took these Indians to Malaga, Spain, and sold them, along with Squanto, as slaves. Local friars brought Squanto to live with them.

Somehow managing to escape, Squanto boarded an English ship to Newfoundland, where he was recognized by Captain Thomas Dermer, who worked for Gorges. Dermer took Squanto back to England and to Gorges, who in 1619 sent the two of them back to Cape Cod on a trading and exploration voyage, arriving at Patuxet (Plymouth harbor) just six months before the Pilgrims arrived. Squanto discovered that the entire Patuxet tribe had been exterminated by a "Great Plague" in 1616-1617. In despair, Squanto went to Pokanoket, the home of Wampanoag sachem Massasoit, where he found a welcome home. (Captain Dermer eventually died from wounds inflicted by hostile Indians.) Squanto lived out the rest of his life in the Plymouth Colony. Without Squanto's help, the Pilgrims would have suffered even more severely over the next year. He taught them how to plant and manure their fields and how to catch fish, including the trapping of herrings in the Town Brook. They would soon learn such things as waiting in the spring until the white oak bud had reached the size of a mouse's ear before they planted their corn. Squanto served as their guide and interpreter among Indian neighbors who had been angered by cruel and evil treatment received from such English captains as

Thomas Hunt. Squanto and Samoset arranged a meeting between Massasoit and the Pilgrims. From this meeting came a peace treaty that would last for forty years.

THE PEACE TREATY WITH MASSASOIT (1621)

1. That neither he nor any of his should injure or do hurt to any of our people.
2. And if any of his did hurt to any of ours, he should send the offender, that we might punish him.
3. That if any of our tools were taken away when our people were at work, he should cause them to be restored; and if ours did any harm to any of his, we would do the like to them.
4. If any did unjustly war against him, we would aid him; if any did war against us, he should aid us.
5. He should send to his neighbor confederates, to certify them of this, that they might not wrong us, but might be likewise comprised in the conditions of peace.
6. That when their men came to us, they should leave their bows and arrows behind them, as we should do our pieces when we came to them.

    Lastly, that doing thus, King James would esteem of him as his friend and ally.[14]

Indian tribes in the whole area looked upon Squanto with awe, since he knew the white man and his language and had even crossed the "great sea." Within a year, however, Squanto was using his position with the Pilgrims for his own gain—threatening other Indians that if they did not do as he told them, he would have the Pilgrims "release the plague" against them. He said that the Pilgrims kept the plague buried under their storehouse and could release it at will against anyone.[15] When Massasoit learned that Squanto was abusing his position, he demanded that the Pilgrims turn Squanto over to him for execution, in accordance with the peace treaty they had signed together. The Pilgrims stalled indefinitely, hoping that the problem would somehow go away. The problem did indeed go away, but not the way any human planned it. In November 1622, while on a trading expedition to the Massachusetts Indians, Squanto came down

141

with Indian fever and died. Governor Bradford, possibly Squanto's closest friend, was with him when he died. Bradford wrote the following about the sudden death:

> In this place Squanto fell sick of an Indian fever, bleeding much at the nose (which the Indians take for a symptom of death) and within a few days died there; desiring the Governor to pray for him that he might go to the Englishmen's God in Heaven; and bequeathed sundry of his things to sundry of his English friends as remembrances of his love; of whom they had great loss.[16]

On April 2, 1621, John Carver was chosen governor for the ensuing year. The next day, Elizabeth (Barker) Winslow, wife of Edward Winslow, died. Two days later, the *Mayflower* sailed for England. Sometime within a month, during planting time, Governor Carver "came out of the field very sick, it being a hot day. He complained greatly of his head and lay down, and within a few hours his senses failed, so he never spake more till he died, which was within a few days after." It was probably a stroke. Governor Carver's funeral included "volleys of shot by all that bore arms."[17] Mrs. Carver, "being overcome with excessive grief for the loss of so gracious an husband," died within a short time.[18] William Bradford, still recovering from a sickness, succeeded Carver as Governor; Isaac Allerton became his assistant. Between this time and his death in 1657, William Bradford would be elected annually to this highest office thirty times and lead the Colony through its most difficult years. In May, a happy event occurred when Edward Winslow was married to the widow Suzanna White. It was the first marriage in the colony. In July 1621, Stephen Hopkins and Edward Winslow visited Massasoit and renewed their friendships. The summer months of 1621 provided the Pilgrims opportunity to adjust themselves to their new home, especially with the coming of the garden produce. By this time, sickness had practically ceased, a suitable shelter had been built, although of a temporary nature, and the outlook was more encouraging.

THE ORIGIN OF THANKSGIVING

The Pilgrims adopted the observance of thanksgiving days from the Dutch, who had adopted them from the thank offerings of the Old Testament. During their Eighty-Year War with Roman Catholic Spain, the

Dutch observed thanksgiving days to show their thanks to the Creator for His aid in the repelling of the invaders. Finally, on October 3, 1574, at the end of the Spanish siege, Leiden's citizens poured into the Pieterskerk for a great "Thanksgiving Day" celebration for their miraculous relief. That date immediately became Leiden's Thanksgiving Day, which the Pilgrims observed while there, and which continues to be observed today. The hymn "The Prayer of Thanksgiving" was of Dutch origin and was first sung in the sixteenth century. The ideas for many of the traditional Thanksgiving Day customs in America, therefore, were first introduced to the Pilgrims from Holland.

Although the exact date is nowhere provided, it was probably sometime in October of 1621 when Governor Bradford declared a three-day thanksgiving harvest celebration. They invited Massasoit who arrived, not only with ninety hungry Indians, but also with five dressed deer and wild turkeys. All enjoyed the games that followed. A joyous occasion indeed! The oldest *Mayflower* passenger still alive at that first Thanksgiving was "the man of prayer," William Brewster, about fifty-five years old at the time. The earliest account of the first Thanksgiving is *Mourt's Relation: A Journal of the Pilgrims at Plymouth* (1622), the first published account of Plymouth. After explaining that, "according to the manner of the Indians, we manured our ground with herrings, or rather shad, which we have in great abundance," the author tells of the harvest and thanksgiving:

> Our corn did prove well, and, God be praised, we had a good increase of Indian corn, and our barley indifferent good, but our pease not worth the gathering, for we feared they were too late sown. They came up very well, and blossomed, but the sun parched them in the blossom. Our harvest being gotten in, our governor sent four men on fowling, that so we might after a special manner rejoice together after we had gathered the fruit of our labors. They four in one day killed as much fowl as, with a little help beside, served the company almost a week. At which time, amongst other recreations, we exercised our arms, many of the Indians coming amongst us, and among the rest their greatest king Massasoit, with some ninety men, whom for three days we entertained and feasted, and they went out and killed five deer, which they brought to the plantation and bestowed on our governor, and upon the captain and

others. And although it be not always so plentiful as it was at this time with us, yet by the goodness of God, we are so far from want that we often wish you partakers of our plenty.[19]

The second account is Bradford's *History Of Plymouth Plantation,* which includes the traditional "turkey meal:"

They began now to gather in the small harvest they had, and to fit up their houses and dwellings against winter, being all well recovered in health and strength and had all things in good plenty. For as some were thus employed in affairs abroad, others were exercising in fishing, about cod and bass and other fish, of which they took good store, of which every family had their portion. All the summer there was no want; and now began to come in store of fowl, as winter approached, of which this place did abound when they came first (but afterward decreased by degrees). And besides waterfowl there was great store of wild turkeys, of which they took many, besides venison, etc. Besides they had about a peck of meal a week to a person, or now since harvest, Indian corn to that proportion.[20]

It was in 1623 that no rain fell between the third week in May and the middle of July. All of their fields began to dry and wither, and it seemed that all crops would be lost and famine would be their lot. The Pilgrims called on God, in a special day of humiliation and prayer. Bradford describes what took place:

They set apart a solemn day of humiliation, to seek the Lord by humble and fervent prayer, in this great distress. And He was pleased to give them a gracious and speedy answer, both to their own and the Indians' admiration that lived amongst them. For all the morning, and greatest part of the day, it was clear weather and very hot, and not a cloud or any sign of rain to be seen; yet toward evening it began to overcast, and shortly after to rain, with such sweet and gentle showers as gave them cause of rejoicing and blessing God. It came without either wind or thunder or any violence, and by degrees in that abundance as that the earth was thoroughly wet and soaked and therewith. Which did so apparently revive and quicken the decayed corn and other fruits, as was wonderful to see, and the Indians astonished to behold. And afterwards the Lord sent them such seasonable showers, with interchange of fair warm weather as, through His blessing, caused a fruitful and liberal harvest, to their no small comfort and rejoicing. For which mercy, in time convenient, they also set apart a day of thanksgiving.[21]

Although the Pilgrims never observed a set "thanksgiving day," on November 15, 1636, an ordinance was passed "that it be in the power of the governor and assistants to command solemn days of humiliation by fasting, etc., and also for thanksgiving, as occasion shall be offered."[22] Other New England colonies likewise fixed certain days of thanksgiving by formal proclamation.[23]

Around the Pilgrim Table at Mealtime[24]

For special occasions, and even every day for some, the Pilgrims had white linen cloths and napkins for their tables. An inventory list, for example, of a woman who died in 1631, includes twenty-four napkins; a man who died in 1633 had owned two table "carpets." This was the norm. Except for one large fork used for cooking, forks were not used in the seventeenth century. At their tables, they used spoons, knives and fingers. (It was not unusual for people to carry their own spoons and knives with them when they ate at other homes.) Their small plates were made of wood, pewter, or the blue glazed pottery of delft. Lobed dishes from the Netherlands were used as fruit bowls and dessert dishes, and also as finger bowls for washing the hands. The food was served on large pewter platters (called chargers), placed in the center of the table.

There was quite a variety of available food. Main dishes could have included turkey, goose, duck, and partridge, as well as various other waterfowl such as crane and swan. According to *Mourt's Relation,* they also apparently ate eagles, which "tasted like mutton."[25] There is no mention of pork during this earliest period. Venison was very plentiful. Other main courses could have included an abundance of seafood—once they learned how to catch it—such as cod, herring, shad, bluefish, bass, and eel. Sometimes, six-foot lobsters could be found on the beaches after a storm.[26] By this time, the Pilgrims would have also discovered clams, mussels, and possibly oysters. Olive oil and butter were scarce, because these were among the items they had to sell before they left England.[27] Herbs and seasonings may have included onions, leeks, currants, sorrel, liverwort, flax, watercress, and strawberry leaves.

From seeds that they brought over, they could have had radishes, lettuce, carrots, beans, cabbage, squash, and peas, though the crop of peas was poor the first year. There were no sweet potatoes in New England at this time. They did have plenty of corn meal (the only way Indian corn could be used). They may have still had some wheat flour which they brought over. Barley was reserved mainly for beer-making. Eggs would have been fairly plentiful. They may have still had some Dutch cheese, but most of that would be too hard for most people to eat.

Most of their foods, so rich in fats and carbohydrates, would have created a thirst for substantial amounts of fluid. The Pilgrims discovered that the safest places to obtain drinking water were spring heads, but even then it was often fatal. The colonists usually avoided the water, for fear of waterborne diseases now known as cholera, typhoid, amebic dysentery, and so on. Words like "bacteria" and "parasites" were unknown in the seventeenth century, and the idea of boiling water for health reasons would never have occurred to anyone. They did know, however, that they could drink alcoholic beverages without getting sick. Indeed, wine and beer would have been the basic staple beverages, watered down to one-half to one percent alcoholic content[28]. This made beer and wine not only safe but suitable even for children and infants. Liquors such as whiskey were available, especially for medicine, but abuse was punishable by law. Coffee was not introduced into England until after 1620. The British discovered tea sometime after 1650, and quickly became the only Europeans to reject coffee for tea as their favorite beverage. Perhaps their love for it led to the Boston Tea Party!

The Pilgrims' dried fruits could have included grapes, plums, strawberries, raspberries, cherries, blueberries, and gooseberries. Cranberries were available (but since there was no sugar they would not have had cranberry sauce). They did have pumpkins, which mixed well with maple syrup and honey. When the honeybees were brought over later, the Indians would referred to them as "English flies." Also generally plentiful at this time would be walnuts, chestnuts, acorns, and hickory nuts. All of this sounds like an abundance of food, but obviously most of these items were seasonal. The Pilgrim women usually had to "scrape" to create an appetizing meal, especially in the early years.

THE NATIONAL DAY OF THANKSGIVING

Thanksgiving became a national day of observance when the Continental Congress, on November 7, 1777, by formal proclamation, recommended that Thursday, December 18, 1777, be recognized as such. This was probably motivated by the defeat of British General Burgoyne at the Battle of Saratoga. This practice was continued annually by the Continental Congress until and including the year 1783. No day was thereafter set aside until, on October 3, 1789, President George Washington, at the request of Congress, issued his first National Thanksgiving proclamation, recommending and appointing Thursday, November 26, 1789 (the last Thursday of the month), as the Day of Thanksgiving. Thereafter other dates were sometimes selected by proclamation as follows: President George Washington himself selected Thursday February 19, 1795; President John Adams selected May 5, 1798, and Thursday, April 25, 1799; President James Madison selected Thursday, January 12, 1815 and Thursday, April 13, 1815; and thereafter the practice was discontinued for forty-seven years. On his own initiative, President Abraham Lincoln issued a formal proclamation dated April 10, 1862, selecting Sunday, April 13, 1862, as a Day of National Thanksgiving. In 1863 and 1864, President Lincoln followed the example of Washington and selected the last Thursday in November. In 1865, President Andrew Johnson selected Thursday, December 7, 1865; and in 1869, President Ulysses S. Grant selected Thursday, November 18, 1869. In 1870, President Grant changed back to the last Thursday in November, which was followed by all succeeding presidents, except for the times that President Franklin D. Roosevelt tried to move the day forward a week, causing two days frequently to be celebrated.[29] In 1939 he reverted to the fourth Thursday in November, and so it has remained to the present time.

WHAT THE PILGRIMS WORE[30]

The Pilgrim man wore baggy breeches which buttoned in the front and extended to the knee. His stockings were knee-length tights. He wore a long, off-white linen shirt with short-sleeves and collar. Over that, he wore a rather close-fitting jacket (doublet), with long sleeves and broad padded shoulders. The jacket buttoned down the front and had tabs at the waist. A lace collar and cuffs were worn, as was a felt cap or hat, of which there were many varieties. The hair was usually worn short, but sometimes down to the collar and straight. He often draped a cloak over his shoulders. Colors for men's clothing might include whites, beige, earthy greens, and browns. Only on Sundays and formal occasions was black the generally-dominant color. Myles Standish sported a red cape! Public figures and older men often wore an outer, full-length wool gown. Governor Bradford's will reveals that he had a two hats (a black one and a colored one), a lead-colored suit with silver buttons, a red waistcoat, and a violet cloak. Elder Brewster's inventory list included "a red cap, a violet coat, a blue suit, and green drawers." Men's shoes were generally made of leather, low-cut and low-heeled; leather boots were often preferred. Most footwear was made to fit either foot and could be switched to equalize wear and allow for longer life. Buckles were not worn on anything during this period.

The Pilgrim woman's undergarments consisted of a shift, a corset, stockings, and a petticoat. The shift was a long, off-white linen gown. Over this she wore the close-fitting, vestlike corset, which laced up the front and was ribbon-tied at the collar and cuffs. An ankle-length, sometimes colorful, petticoat tied at the waist. The outer dresses (gowns) were actually three-pieced, consisting of bodice, skirt, and sleeves. The bodice and skirt were each made of wool, sometimes of different colors. The bodice buttoned down the front. The sleeves were attached to the bodice. (Sometimes sleeves were actually a part of the bodice.) The skirt, about ankle-length, gathered at the waist. Often, a long-sleeved, fitted jacket (waistcoat) was worn over the top. A lace collar, cuffs, and a cloak completed the outfit, except for the apron which was worn during work. Colors included much more than simple blacks and whites. Dresses, aprons, cloaks, and even stockings appeared in greens, browns, blues, violets, grays, and even reds. The Pilgrim woman always wore her hair up, pulled tightly back, and usually worn under a linen cap. When outdoors a woman would often wear a coif (bonnet) over her cap.

Girls and boys both wore ankle-length gowns or dresses (called shifts, or shirts), usually made of wool or linen and fastened in the back. Over this was worn the long-sleeved, high-necklined bodice, which laced in the back. An apron, often with bib, was also worn. Then a close-fitting cap (biggin) tied under the chin. Popular colors included blue, gray, red, earthy greens, yellows, and browns. Girls and boys both wore stockings and leather shoes. Girls' hair was long, pulled tightly back, and always under a bonnet or hat. Women and girls never appeared in public with their heads uncovered. During their early teens, girls were allowed to begin the change from a child's gown to a young woman's clothing. Boys were "breeched," that is, allowed to dress as young men, usually between the ages of six and nine.

THE ARRIVAL OF MORE PILGRIM SHIPS

In November 1621, the Colony welcomed to its shores the unexpected arrival of the ship *Fortune* from London. Aboard were twelve Pilgrims from Leiden, including Robert Cushman, his son Thomas, and Jonathan Brewster. They also brought a letter from John Robinson, expressing his hopes of joining them as soon as he could. In the summer of 1623, a second group arrived in the *Anne* and the *Little James*. On board were some thirty-two Separatists from Leiden, including the Brewster children, Patience and Fear. Also joining them was George Morton, the last of the original Scrooby group to reach the New World. Along with his family, Morton had brought along his sister-in-law, Alice Southworth, widow of Edward Southworth of John Robinson's Church. Alice soon married William Bradford and they would bring three children into the world—William, Mercy (a girl), and Joseph. They had hoped that John Robinson would be on this ship. They longed for his presence, to preach and to administer the sacraments, which they sorely missed. In April 1626, they received news of Pastor Robinson's death, which had occurred more than a year earlier. Robinson was only forty-nine years old when he died. The loss was a shattering blow, and it would take the Pilgrims years to find another man of his qualities. A second ship called the *Mayflower* brought nine more Separatists in 1629; and by 1635 some fourteen others from Leiden arrived independently at various times. By 1635, the "Pilgrim ships" had brought approximately 120 Separatists. John Robinson's widow, Bridget, and three of the children were booked on that second *Mayflower,* but at the last minute, they changed their plans for making a voyage to the New World.

THE TWO PEIRCE PATENTS

Since Cape Cod was far north of latitude forty-one, the original Peirce Patent with the Virginia Company of London (February 2, 1620) was useless. The *Mayflower Compact* was the solution to an immediate threat of mutiny from some of the sailors. The document was instrumental in establishing a bond of unity in a critical time. The *Mayflower Compact* was the superb solution to an immediate problem, but it lacked one important thing—authorization by the English government. The Pilgrims knew they would need the authority of the English government behind them if they wanted to continue living at Plymouth. When the *Mayflower* arrived back in England in May 1621 with the news that the Pilgrims had settled north of the Virginia grant, the Merchant Adventurers (stockholders in the Plymouth Plantation), led by John Peirce and Thomas Weston, went to the Council of New England to obtain a valid patent giving the Pilgrims the rights to live and establish a government of their own at Plymouth. King James had granted to the Council of New England (a group of noblemen) all the land in North America between forty and forty-eight degrees latitude north. (roughly Philadelphia to Canada's Bay de Chaleur). A second patent, dated June 1, 1621, was secured in the name of John Peirce and his associates. The basic policies of Plymouth Plantation's independent operation from 1621 to 1630 are outlined in this Second Peirce Patent (June 1, 1621), which confirmed and superseded the *Mayflower Compact*. (See Appendix I for the complete Second Peirce Patent.) Written to promote the growth of the new plantation and to attract capital, this Patent actually favored the financial investor more than the planter, as Langdon explains:

> For every person transported to America, it granted 100 acres to John Peirce and Associates; to men who came to the Plantation at their own expense, it also gave 100 acres; and to each of the Adventurers went a direct grant of an additional 1500 acres. For the planters, it held out the promise that after seven years, if the settlement succeeded, the Council would issue a new patent more suitable to the needs of an established plantation.[31]

Under the Patent, the Pilgrims were required to work for seven years in an economic communal agreement, which was not "communism" *per se* but rather an exploiting capitalism which forwarded the profits to overseas

Adventurers. Bradford complained that locally the system promoted laziness and discouraged production. By 1623, upon the planters request, Governor Bradford assigned to each family, according to its size, a temporary plot of land, whereby they could at least work for themselves and pay a special tax towards the plantation's debt. Under the Patent, they still had to hold all assets in common until the seven years expired. In 1626, however, the Adventurers sold all shares and all debts of Plymouth Plantation to fifty-eight planters (called Purchasers), for the sum of £1,800. In 1627, these Purchasers granted one "share" of company properties to each adult male settler who was "of ability and free." Each single man received the one share, while each family head received one share for each member of his household. The number of shares a settler owned would determine the extent of his property and the amount of his taxes, at the 1628 division of land.

Bradford and eleven associates feared that the plantation's debts would never be paid if divided directly among the settlers themselves. The twelve men sacrificially took upon themselves the personal responsibility for the Plantation's finances. They decided to liquidate the plantation's debts, including the £1,800. The fifty-eight Purchasers then turned over the responsibility of all shares and all debts to the twelve associates, called "Undertakers," eight from Plymouth and four from London.[32] The Undertakers were now responsible for collecting taxes from the settlers and fulfilling the plantation's financial obligations. The settlers themselves, in 1627, consisted of just under forty families, totaling 156 people. For the division of livestock and land, the settlers were grouped into twelve companies or lots, consisting of thirteen people each. Each company received a cow and two goats. The following year, they divided the land.

THE BRADFORD PATENT (1630)

On January 23, 1630 (N.S.), the Council of New England granted to Governor William Bradford and his associates a new patent, replacing the Peirce Patent. Signed by the Earl of Warwick, this third patent—sometimes called the Bradford Charter or the Warwick Charter—granted to Bradford and associates the rights to make laws for Plymouth Colony, so long as such laws did not conflict with the laws of England.[33] The Bradford Patent remained the basic law of the colony for almost the remainder of its independent existence to 1691, when it was swallowed up by Massachusetts

Bay Colony. By 1642, after episodes of financial discouragement, Plymouth Colony finally paid her early debts, with the help of negotiators from the Bay Colony and with Bradford and other associates selling portions of their own properties. On March 12, 1641 (N.S.), when Plymouth's debts were virtually paid, Governor Bradford officially surrendered the Bradford Patent to a General Court of Freemen. Meanwhile, Massachusetts Bay Colony had grown to nearly 17,000 people by 1641.

DISAPPEARANCE OF THE OLD COLONY AND THE OLD SEPARATISTS

By now, the Old Colony was steadily developing other towns, and many of the members of the original Plymouth Congregational Church were leaving. "And thus was this poor church," says Bradford, "left like an ancient mother[,] grown old and forsaken of her children, . . . her ancient members being most of them worn away by death, and these of later times being like children translated into other families, and she like a widow left only to trust in God. Thus she that had made many rich became herself poor."[34]

With Boston's fine harbor, the Bay Colony would soon become the center of New England. Only about 120 Separatists ever reached Plymouth Colony. By 1630, the colony's population had grown only to about three hundred, but over three thousand by 1660, and five thousand by 1675. When it merged into Massachusetts Bay Colony in 1691, its population was well over seven thousand-five hundred.

By then, the Plymouth Separatists, like the Leiden Separatists who remained behind, would have become totally absorbed into their worldly surroundings and culture. Ironically, it had been the fear of such loss of identity that had caused the original Pilgrims to leave Holland. Moreover, by the time the larger Colony swallowed up Plymouth, Puritanism itself had ceased to exist as a movement. As Puritanism in England had divided into two major branches—Presbyterianism and Independent Congregationalism—so likewise, Puritanism in America divided into two major branches—Presbyterianism and Congregationalism. The most vibrant life that was to emerge from the ashes of the Puritan movement was the great Scotch-Irish Presbyterian movement that began to emerge in America at the turn of the eighteenth century. A brief survey of each movement is necessary for an accurate picture of the turmoil of change that occurred in the eighteenth century, changing the very structure of Plymouth Church.

PRESBYTERIAN BEGINNINGS IN AMERICA

The background of American Presbyterianism begins in Great Britain, with the death of Oliver Cromwell and the Restoration of the Stuart dynasty to England's throne. Kings Charles II and James II attempted to eradicate Presbyterianism from Northern Ireland. It was during these dreadful years of persecution that many Scotch-Irish Presbyterians fled to the New World. (Francis Makemie, "the Father of American Presbyterianism," came to America from Ireland in 1683.) When King James II sent his pro-Roman Catholic troops to take possession of the Protestant city of Londonderry, in Ulster, a Presbyterian minister named James Gordon led the citizens to close the city gates. A one-hundred-day siege of the city resulted in the eating of rats for survival. Relief finally came in 1688-1689, when the English Parliament dethroned James II in a Glorious Revolution, bringing William and Mary to England's throne and resulting in a Bill of Rights to protect Protestants from further royal attacks. This was followed by the English Act of Toleration (1690). However, the Woolens Act of 1699 created trade restrictions and great economic stress in Northern Ireland. This caused many Presbyterians to immigrate to America. A great transplant of Scotch-Irish Presbyterians came to the New World during the reign of Queen Anne (1702-1714), when severe measures were taken against Presbyterians in Ireland. During her reign, the Test Act of 1704 stripped Irish Presbyterian churches of legal recognition. No Presbyterian could hold an office in the Army or Navy. They were forbidden from performing legal marriages. All citizens of Northern Ireland were assessed for the support of the established Anglican clergy. Civil office holding was allowed only to those who received the sacraments of the Church of England. By 1710, therefore, large numbers of these Presbyterians were coming to America.

In Scotland, the strict enforcement of lay patronage, in 1711-1712, caused many Presbyterians to transplant directly from there to the New World. Under enforced "lay patronage," the Scottish Presbyterian churches could not choose their own pastors. Powerful landowners usurped that right. Those who opposed lay patronage were called "Covenanters," because they regarded two covenants as sacred and foundational to Scotland's basic government: the National Covenant (1638) and the Solemn League and Covenant (1643). The Covenanters charged that the English monarchs were usurping and violating these covenants. Thus, by the opening of the eighteenth century, a large Presbyterian element was scattered throughout the American colonies. These churches and pastors would help to infuse spiritual life back into the soul of America.

EIGHTEENTH-CENTURY AMERICAN CONGREGATIONALISM:
HISTORICAL BACKGROUND TO THE UNITARIANISM AT PLYMOUTH CHURCH

The second major remnant of American Puritanism was the Congregationalist movement. When the Puritans had first arrived and began establishing Salem and Boston, the Pilgrims were in near perfect agreement with their doctrines and practices; and there was no Church of England from which to separate in a wilderness. So the two groups were quite compatible. They were both congregationalists and covenantal Calvinists. Both believed that true churches were formed by "voluntary covenant" among individuals who had, through faith and repentance, experienced the new birth, by personal faith in the shed blood of Jesus Christ, the second Person of the Trinity. Many former Puritan churches became a part of this movement, which played a large role in America's Great Awakenings and religious education. On the other hand, the larger segment of eighteenth-century Congregationalism experienced gradual but gargantuan changes, from orthodoxy to Unitarianism, in most of its original New England churches. Major innovations would steadily bring most of New England's original Puritan, Pilgrim, and Congregational churches into Unitarianism.

First, there was a shift in emphasis from preaching to ritual. Second, there was the insistence of many in practicing the Half-Way Covenant. The first generation of Puritans had taught that the necessary prerequisites to the Lord's Supper and full membership in the local church were baptism and public profession of faith in Christ as Lord and Savior. The second generation had been baptized as infants, but most had never made public professions of faith. A serious question naturally arose. Can these baptized but unregenerate parents present their own children for baptism? The leaders addressed this question in 1662 and presented their decisions in the document known as the Half-Way Covenant. The Covenant stated that as long as the parents were not living in some open sin in the community, they could present their children for baptism. Thus, the churches of New England continued to be filled with half-way members who eventually became full members by virtue of their increasing majority status. Solomon Stoddard, Congregationalist pastor in Northampton, Massachusetts, insisted in admitting moral unregenerates to the Lord's Supper. The basis for his argument was that the Old Testament instructs all Israel to partake of the Passover. The church, he insisted, is Israel and the Lord's Supper is the Passover. The rules and qualifications did not change with the cross. (Stoddard's grandson and successor, Jonathan Edwards, did not follow him in these matters.)

The third innovation was the gradual abolishing of the required personal public profession of faith. The old Puritans called it the "Conversion Narrative,"[35] and they considered it foundational to the churches. Now, those who were calling themselves the "broad and catholic" were encouraging the churches to replace this personal testimony with a churchwide communal chant. This would not only keep the unregenerate members in the churches, but it would also keep them feeling good about themselves. Soon, in many churches, the congregational chant, called "owning the covenant," replaced the individual public profession of faith in Christ as Lord and Savior. This spared the ministers the embarrassment of having so few in the churches who could make a personal public profession. Their "church marketing" techniques focused on the need to instill life in churches where people had "simply lost interest." Preaching was no longer popular and could no longer hold the focus of the church service. The old Puritans, reacting to Anglican ceremonialism, had insisted that when ministers read the Bible in public, they should expound it. Simple reading, without comment, they regarded as "dumb reading." Those old Puritans knew that even in their day some ministers had not only lost their bite but also their bark. Preachers, they insisted, are supposed to have a call and a passion to communicate God's Word to a lost and dying people. The second generation would lose the convictions; the third generation lost the churches—and the school! Doctrine was no longer important.

When a liberal board of trustees, at Harvard College, appointed Henry Ware,[36] a Unitarian, to the Hollis Chair of Divinity to replace the orthodox David Tappan in 1805, the battle was over; Harvard was lost to Unitarianism. Samuel Webber immediately became the first Unitarian president (1806-1810) of a Harvard whose typical student now possessed an atheistic mindset.[37] Under John T. Kirkland, president from 1810 to 1828, Harvard

155

added a Unitarian Divinity School (seminary) in 1812. The story of Puritanism's and Harvard's drift into Unitarianism runs exactly parallel to and sets the stage for the drift of Plymouth Church into the same movement. The calling of Unitarian Henry Ware to Harvard in 1805 and the calling of Unitarian James Kendall to the pastorate of Plymouth's Pilgrim Church in 1801 are monumental and terminal events.

PLYMOUTH CHURCH FROM BREWSTER TO UNITARIANISM

During the first year in Plymouth, the church services were held in the Common House, which was the first structure erected in the colony. Subsequently, services were held in the lower part of the fort, the blockhouse, erected during the spring or summer of 1622, at the top of Burial Hill. Four cannons from the *Mayflower* stood in place on the flat roof. Inside, on rough-hewn log benches, the men sat on the left, the women on the right as Elder Brewster preached "powerfully and profitably." There was no one, in those days, to administer baptism and the Lord's Supper, because Brewster was not ordained. When Brewster resigned from his pulpit ministry in 1629, an ordained man, Ralph Smith, succeeded him. Roger Williams assisted as teacher during 1631-1633. In 1636, John Reyner (Rayner)[38] became the next pastor. During his pastorate, the church erected its first official Meeting House, sometime between 1637 and 1648, on the north side of Town Square. When Elder Brewster died in 1644, William Bradford said of him, "He would labour with his hands in the fields as long as he was able. Yet when the church had no other minister, he taught twice every Sabbath, and that both powerfully and profitably, to the great contentment of the hearers and their comfortable edification; yea, many were brought to God by his ministry."[39] He adds that Brewster was careful to preserve purity of doctrine "and to suppress any error or contention that might begin to arise."[40]

Following Brewster's death, spiritual stagnation set in. A deeply discouraged pastor, John Reyner resigned in 1654, and the church went without any pastor, or any regular preaching of the Word, for the next fifteen years. Meanwhile, William Bradford died in 1657. About 1669, John Cotton, son of the celebrated John Cotton of Boston, began his ministry at Plymouth Church. Cotton was gifted for his successful labors among the Indians. In 1676, he had the whole Plymouth Church stand and renew their covenant with the Lord;[41] in 1683, he led them to construct a new Meeting House, this one located at the head of Town Square. Finally, his critics, along with the town gossips, spread around an alleged scandal concerning Cotton and young women. This led him to resign in 1698 in the midst of controversy and bitterness among members of the congregation. Cotton moved to Charleston, South Carolina, gathered a new and prosperous congregation, and died there the following year.[42] In 1699, Ephraim Little began his long pastorate at Plymouth. Upon his resignation, however, the church was without a pastor for five more years, during which time the church fell into a state of spiritual decay.

In 1724, they installed Nathaniel Leonard as pastor and, by 1731, he persuaded the congregation to adopt the Half-Way Covenant. When Great Awakening evangelists, George Whitefield, Gilbert Tennent, and Andrew Croswell preached in the town, it appeared to some that "at least three-quarters of Plymouth's church members were actually unconverted."[43] The local revivals resulted in a temporary split in Plymouth Church. During Leonard's ministry, the Meeting House was replaced on its same site, with a new building, in 1744. In 1760, the church installed Chandler Robbins[44] as pastor. Robbins was quite conservative and, in a last-ditch effort to stop the church's spiritual drift, he tried unsuccessfully to persuade the church to drop the Half-Way Covenant. The Covenant itself, however, had allowed the church to become largely unregenerate. Robbins then brought in a strong conservative, Jedidiah Morse, to preach a series of "revival" services. Morse did see several conversions, and he even convinced the congregation to draw up a statement of faith. This was all temporary, however, for Chandler Robbins died in 1799, and the next year the congregation installed James Kendall, a Unitarian, as their pastor.[45]

Immediately, fifty-three people (one fewer than half the membership) withdrew and gathered a new church, which is now called the Church of the Pilgrimage. When this church was officially organized in 1802, it had 154 members who believed that, while "the other church kept the furniture, we kept the faith." They installed Adoniram Judson Sr. as their first pastor. His son and future missionary, Adoniram Judson Jr., who was then fourteen years old, listened attentively as his father preached from the text, II Corinthians 6:17, "Wherefore, come out from among them, and be ye separate, saith the Lord." In 1840, they dedicated the present building, located on almost the exact site of the Pilgrims' original (1637) Meeting House, on the north side of Town Square. On the front of this white-painted Church of the Pilgrimage, with its pillared and domed belfry, a tablet reads:

> This tablet is inscribed in grateful memory of the Pilgrims and their successors who, at the time of the Unitarian controversy in 1801, adhered to the belief of the Fathers and on the basis of the original Creed and Covenant perpetuated at great sacrifice in the Church of the Pilgrimage the evangelical faith and fellowship of the Church of Scrooby, Leyden, and the Mayflower organized in England in 1606.

Since the 1950s, this Church of the Pilgrimage (Congregational UCC) has been a member of a denomination widely recognized as one of the most liberal in America, the United Church of Christ. This denomination began officially in 1957, as an ecumenical amalgamation of several liberal groups.

On the east side of Town Square, a stone's throw away, still occupying its place at the head of the square, the First Church in Plymouth (Unitarian) erected its fourth building in 1831, and its fifth (the present, heavy stone) building in 1897 (dedicated 1899). Its tablet reads:

> The church of Scrooby - Leiden - and the Mayflower
> Gathered on this Hillside in 1620
> Has ever since preserved unbroken records
> and maintained a continuous ministry
> Its first covenant being still the basis of its fellowship
> In reverent memory of its Pilgrim Founders
> This Fifth Meeting House was
> Erected A.D. MDCCCXCVII.

Standing tall on the brow of Burial Hill, in full sight, above both of the contending "Pilgrim" churches, a monument marks the site of William

Bradford's grave. It carries a significant message of warning, inscribed in Latin, from the Pilgrim Governor: "What your fathers with such difficulty attained, do not basely relinquish:"

Qua patres difficillime
adeptisunt nolite
turpiter relinquere

WILLIAM BRADFORD'S FORESIGHT OF SPIRITUAL AND DOCTRINAL DECLINE

In his record *Of Plymouth Plantation,* Bradford speaks of the young Pilgrim church as now "weaned from the delicate milk of our mother country," and ready to face "the difficulties of a strange and hard land." He says, "We are knit together as a body in a most strict and sacred bond and covenant of the Lord, of the violation whereof we make great conscience, and by virtue whereof we do hold ourselves straitly tied to all care of each other's good." Near the end of his life, William Bradford was rereading his manuscript, and came to the passage cited above. With his aged hand, he picked up his pen once again and, on the blank page opposite, wrote the following paragraph for future generations:

O sacred bond, whilst inviolable preserved! How sweet and precious were the fruits that flowed from the same! But when this fidelity decayed, then their ruin approached. O that these ancient members had not died or been dissipated (if it had been the will of God) or else that this holy care and constant faithfulness had still lived, and remained with those that survived, and were in times afterwards added unto them. But (alas) that subtle serpent hath slyly wound in himself under fair pretenses of necessity and the like, to untwist these sacred bonds and tied, and as it were insensibly by degrees to dissolve, or in a great measure to weaken, the same. I have been happy, in my first times, to see, and with much comfort to enjoy, the blessed fruits of this sweet communion, but it is now a part of my misery in old age, to find and feel the decay and want thereof (in a great measure) and with grief and sorrow of heart to lament and bewail the same. And for others' warning and admonition, and my own humiliation, do I here note the same.[46]

CONCLUDING THOUGHTS

One could create a fair-sized list of Pilgrim contributions, some originating in England, some in the Netherlands, many in the New England wilderness. Without categorizing or prioritizing, a general overview might include their stress upon character as a supreme requisite of true religion; their acceptance of civil marriages and private funerals; their simplicity in the administration of law and the enforcing of basic criminal codes; their measures designed to prevent "officialdom," such as electing officers for a term of no more than one year; their methods of recording deeds and mortgages, conveying land, probating wills, and recording births, marriages, and deaths by towns; their system of administering estates by permitting the inclusion of any children—male or female, not simply the oldest son; their emphasis on the laity, as an integral part of the church; their general practice of the autonomy and independence of the local church and freedom of religious worship, which led eventually to disestablishment, and often prompted observers of later generations to exclaim, "We are all Separatists now." But these things are not the real Pilgrim story. These are peripheral.

The real Pilgrim story is not one of governments and institutions. The Pilgrims never set out to build worldly enterprises. They did not write the *Mayflower Compact* for a national constitution or government. They wrote it as a measure for survival. The Pilgrim story is essentially a story of conviction and survival. It is a story of personal and ecclesiastical conviction, born in persecution, developed in exile, and based upon the Bible. It is a story illustrating the importance of sound doctrine. It is a story, not founded upon the tradition of Plymouth rock, but upon the truth of Providence. It is a story of faith, hope, charity, sacrifice, loyalty, and working together. America would be honored and blessed if those things alone were the Pilgrims' contributions. Their story reveals that Christianity is not perpetuated by the faith of the fathers; it is perpetuated by personal and present conviction, each individual and each local assembly finding the depth of biblical conviction and divine awareness which moved Pilgrim fathers and mothers to forsake all, for a cause whose purpose and reward looks beyond this present existence. It is a story of the believer's struggle against the world, the flesh, and the Devil. Its earthly conclusion is not with the "good guys winning." The Pilgrim story does not end on earth. Looking "not so much on these things," they saw with the eye of faith that there is a place where life is fair, and where every person will give an account for his own pilgrimage.

An accurate illustration of the Pilgrims' most significant contributions might be Forefathers' Monument, dedicated in 1899, standing on the summit of a hill behind Plymouth, Massachusetts. Surmounted atop its forty-five-foot-high pedestal is a heroic lady whose name is Faith, weighing 180 tons, and measuring thirty-six feet tall. From the ground to the top of her head, the monument measures eighty-one feet—its gigantic proportions illustrating gigantic principles. With her outstretched arm, measuring nineteen feet, ten and a half inches, her right forefinger, over two feet long, points to heaven. When, on August 23, 1912, a bolt of lightning ran down the finger and arm, causing damage, she kept pointing.

The massive granite pedestal on which she stands is octagonal, with four large and four small faces; from the latter project four buttresses, or wing pedestals. On each of these four pedestals is seated a figure, and the four figures are symbolic of the most important principles which the Pilgrims brought to New England. The first seated figure is *Liberty* (something the Pilgrims longed for in England), with "Tyranny" overthrown on one side, and "Peace" resting under its protection on the other side. The second figure is *Law* (holding liberty in proper check). On one side of its throne is "Justice," and on the other, "Mercy." The third seated figure is *Education* (which the Pilgrims rested with parents), with "Wisdom" ripe with years on one side, and "Youth" led by experience on the other. The fourth seated figure is *Morality* (holding education in proper check, something the Pilgrims struggled to maintain in Holland). She holds the decalogue of God's "Law" in her left hand and the scroll of His "Revelation" in the right one. She looks upwards, her eyes drawn towards Faith. In a niche on one side of Morality's throne is a "Prophet," and in the niche on the other side is an "Evangelist" (Gospel writer). Below the four seated figures are four marble bas-reliefs, representing scenes from the Pilgrims' history—the departure from Delfshaven, the signing of the *Compact,* the landing at Plymouth, and the treaty with the Indians. On each of the four large faces of the main pedestal is an arched panel—for the records—three of which are already inscribed, two with the names of the *Mayflower* passengers, and one with an expression of gratitude to the forefathers. The fourth is blank, reminding each individual that his or her record is yet incomplete, but will one day also be revealed.

"As one small candle may light a thousand, so the light here kindled hath shone unto many, yea in some sort to our whole nation; let the glorious name of Jehovah have all the praise." (Bradford, *Plymouth Plantation,* 236).

1. William Bradford, *Of Plymouth Plantation 1620-1647,* ed. Samuel Eliot Morison (1952; rpt. NY: Alfred A. Knopf, 1998), 61-63. This work is hereafter referred to as "Bradford, *Plymouth Plantation.*"

2. G. Mourt (Edward Winslow and William Bradford), *Mourt's Relation: A Journal of the Pilgrims at Plymouth,* ed. Dwight B. Heath (1622; rpt. Bedford, MA: Applewood Books, 1986), 19. This work is hereafter referred to as *Mourt's Relation.*

3. *Mourt's Relation,* 20-21.

4. Ibid., 22-23.

5. Bradford, *Plymouth Plantation,* 66.

6. *Mourt's Relation,* 25.

7. Ibid., 31. Actually, the citation confuses Francis with his father John.

8. Harold L. Peterson, *Arms and Armor of the Pilgrims 1620—1692* (Plymouth, MA: Plimoth Plantation, Inc. and the Pilgrim Society, 1957), 13f.

9. Bradford, *Plymouth Plantation,* 72.

10. Ibid., 77.

11. Some good places to begin researching Richard More are Eugene A. Stratton, *Plymouth Colony: Its History & People 1620-1691* (Salt Lake City, UT: Ancestry Publishing, 1986), 328-29; Leon Clark Hills, *History and Genealogy of the Mayflower Planters and First Comers to Ye Olde Colonie* (1936, 1941; rpt., 2 vols. in 1, Baltimore: Genealogical Publishing Co., Inc., 1977), 188; and Dorothy Brewster, *William Brewster of the Mayflower: Portrait of a Pilgrim* (NY: New York University Press, 1970), 96-101.

12. Bradford, 234.

13. *Plymouth Church Records 1620-1859* (1920-23; rpt. Baltimore, MD: Genealogical Publishing Company, 1975), I:40-42.

14. The Treaty is recorded in *Mourt's Relation,* 56-57.

15. Edward Winslow, *Good Newes from New England* (1623-24; rpt. Bedford, MA: Applewood Books, 1996), 16.

16. Bradford, *Plymouth Plantation,* 114.

17. Ibid., 86.

18. Nathaniel Morton, *New England's Memorial* (1669; rpt. Boston: Congregational Board of Publications, 1855), 47.

19. *Mourt's Relation,* 82.

20. Bradford, *Plymouth Plantation,* 90.

21. Ibid., 131-32.

22. Ibid., 132, n.1.

23. Morton, *New England's Memorial,* 113. This is a record of Governor Winthrop's Thanksgiving at the Bay Colony.

24. The best sources on the Pilgrims' food, dress, and customs include Pilgrim Hall Museum, http://www.pilgrimhall.org; Plimoth Plantation, http://www.plimoth.org; and Caleb Johnson, *Mayflower* Web Pages, http://members.aol.com/calebj/mayflower.html; These sources have been helpful for covering these three topics here. Their careful research in these areas is greatly appreciated.

25. *Mourt's Relation,* 43.

26. Dale Taylor, *The Writer's Guide to Everyday Life in Colonial America* (Cincinnati: Writer's Digest Books, 1997), 78. Taylor also mentions oysters up to fourteen inches, but it is not absolutely certain that the Pilgrims had discovered them at this time.

27. Bradford, *Plymouth Plantation,* 49. According to Bradford, they sold as much as four thousand pounds of butter before they ever got underway.

28. Taylor, 87-88.

29. Franklin D. Roosevelt had tried to move Thanksgiving Day forward in order to lengthen the Christmas shopping season and spur the economy. Many responded by referring to it as "Franks-giving day."

30. The best sources on Pilgrim costumes include Margot Lister, *Costume: An Illustrated Survey from Ancient Times to the 20th Century* (London: Herbert Jenkins Ltd., 1967); Charles Simmons, ed., *Plymouth Colony Records: Wills & Inventories, 1633-69* (Camden, ME: Picton Press, 1996); Blanche Payne, *History of Costume: From the Ancient Egyptians to the Twentieth Century* (NY: Harper, 1965); Caleb Johnson, *Mayflower* Web Pages, http://members.aol.com/calebj/mayflower.html; Pilgrim Hall Museum, http://www.pilgrimhall.org; and Plimoth Plantation, http://www.plimoth.org

31. George D. Langdon Jr., *Pilgrim Colony: A History of New Plymouth 1620 - 1691* (New Haven: Yale University Press, 1966), 17.

32. The eight Plymouth Undertakers were William Bradford, Miles Standish, Isaac Allerton, Edward Winslow, William Brewster, John Howland, John Alden, and Thomas Prince. The four from England were James Sherley, John Beauchamp, Richard Andrews, and Timothy Hatherly.

33. The complete text of the Bradford Patent of 1630 can be found in Eugene A. Stratton, *Plymouth Colony: Its History & People 1620-1691* (Salt Lake City, UT: Ancestry Publishing, 1986), 399-403.

34. Bradford, *Plymouth Plantation,* 334.

35. See Patricia Caldwell, *The Puritan Conversion Narrative: The Beginnings of American Expression* (New York: Cambridge University Press, 1983). See also the helpful definition in Daniel Reid et al., ed., *Dictionary of Christianity in America* (Downers Grove, IL: InterVarsity Press, 1990), 317.

36. Compare with the article by C. C. Wright, "The Election of Henry Ware: Two Contemporary Accounts Edited with Commentary," *Harvard Library Bulletin* 17 (July 1969): 245-78.

37. Samuel E. Morison, *Three Centuries of Harvard 1636-1936* (Cambridge: The Belknap Press of Harvard University Press, 1964), 185; see also David Beale, "The Rise and Fall of Harvard," *Detroit Baptist Seminary Journal* 3 (Fall 1998): 89-101.

38. There are various spellings of the name; the one used here is found in the *Plymouth Church Records 1620-1859,* I:107; see also *Mourt's Relation,* 432. The latter work has it "Rayner."

39. Bradford, *Plymouth Plantation,* 327.

40. William Bradford, *Memoir of Elder William Brewster,* in Alexander Young, ed., *Chronicles of the Pilgrim Fathers of the Colony of Plymouth, from 1602 to 1625* (1844; rpt. Baltimore: Genealogical Publishing Co., Inc., 1974), 469.

41. *Plymouth Church Records 1620-1859,* I:148-52. The record includes a copy of the covenant; see also I:182.

42. Robert Merrill Bartlett, *The Faith of the Pilgrims* (New York: United Church Press, 1978), 249; see also William B. Sprague, *Annals of the American Pulpit; or Commemorative Notices of Distinguished American Clergymen of Various Denominations, From the Early Settlement of the Country to the Close of the Year Eighteen Hundred and Fifty-Five* (NY: Robert Carter & Brothers, 1857-69), I:29.

43. Harold Field Worthley, "Doctrinal Divisions in the Church of Christ at Plymouth 1744-1801," in *They Knew They Were Pilgrims: Essays in Plymouth History,* ed. L. D. Geller (NY: Poseidon Books, Inc., 1971), 106.

44. John Cuckson, *A Brief History of the First Church in Plymouth* (Boston: Geo. H. Ellis Co., 1902), 70-76.

45. *Plymouth Church Records 1620-1859,* II:538-49.

46. Bradford, *Plymouth Plantation,* 33.

CHAPTER 8

How the Earliest English Baptists Originated from the Pilgrim Separatists

There are two strands of English Baptist beginnings: General Baptists and Particular Baptists. The name "General" refers to the group's belief in Christ's general atonement, i.e., that Christ died for all men. The name "Particular," on the other hand, refers to that group's belief that Christ died only for the elect (a particular number of people). The latter position is often called "limited atonement." The years of origin for the English General Baptists are 1611-1612, while the Particular Baptists organized their first church in 1638 (or perhaps 1633). Both groups of Baptists emerged from Separatist groups and are historically indebted to those groups for their congregational and independent type of church government.

General Baptist Beginnings

A Separatist church was established in the English town of Gainsborough, on the River Trent, in 1602. The Lord of the Manor, Sir William Hickman, befriended the group and allowed these sixty to seventy Separatists to hold their services in the "Old Hall" of the stately Manor House. John Smyth (c. 1570-1612)[1] soon became their minister and the people who attended the services included such well-known Separatists as Richard Clyfton, John Robinson, William Bradford, and William Brewster.

Harassed by ecclesiastical authorities, John Smyth formed his Manor House group into a Separatist church. With the Bible as their guide, they read how King Josiah had assembled "all the people, great and small: and . . . read in their ears all the words of the book of the covenant, . . . and made a

covenant before the Lord, to walk after the Lord, and to keep his commandments, and his testimonies, and his statutes, with all his heart, and with all his
soul, to perform the words of the covenant which are written in this book.
And he caused all that were present in Jerusalem and Benjamin to stand to it"
(II Chronicles 34:30-32). Likewise, the Gainsborough Church made its
covenant and stood to it: "We covenant with God and with one another, to
walk in His ways made known or to be made known unto us, according to our
best endeavors, whatsoever it shall cost us, the Lord assisting us."[2]

For their safety, the Gainsborough church divided in 1606, when a
number of them began worshipping at the Scrooby Manor house, which
was Brewster's home. Due to persecution, in late 1607 or early 1608,
Smyth and at least forty members of his Gainsborough congregation settled in Amsterdam. Upon arrival, they worshipped jointly with the Ancient
Church led by Pastor Francis Johnson and teacher Henry Ainsworth.
Smyth had studied with Johnson at Christ's College, Cambridge. He found
work as a physician in Amsterdam and was probably successful, since the
Low Countries were suffering greatly from many diseases at that time and
there was a great demand for medical doctors. It was during this time that
John Smyth began to reveal a growing propensity to drift away from other
English Separatists. Embracing a more rigid Separatist position than the
Pilgrims of Scrooby would ever take, Smyth now maintained that the
Church of England was totally apostate, that none of its churches were true
churches, and that "God's people" must shun all such churches and minis-
ters as the plague. Smyth led his people, in 1608, to withdraw from the
Ancient Church,[3] because he thought that its pastors were wrong to use
Bible translations in public worship.

Smyth's congregation moved into a former bakehouse (bakery), sometimes called the "Great Cake House,"[4] which they rented from the Mennonite Jan Munter. Until 1603, the building had served as the Dutch East
India Company's bakery for ships' biscuits. With its attached buildings, the
bakehouse seems to have provided both living quarters and a meeting hall
for the Smyth congregation and served to bring Smyth into close contact
with Mennonite influence. Here, Smyth preached directly from the original Greek and Hebrew and prohibited all speakers from using written or
printed helps. Having a well educated congregation, Smyth did not object
to the private use of such helps. He only opposed the use of them in public

166

worship. Reacting to the use of the *Book of Common Prayer* in the Church of England, Smyth insisted that not only prayer but preaching and even the singing of Psalms must be totally spontaneous. Disgustingly abhorrent to him were the "read and dead services" of the Church of England. On a typical Sunday, Smyth held two four-hour services. Two of the original members of his church, Hugh and Anne Bromhead, wrote a letter about 1609 describing a regular service in Smyth's church. They make no mention of any type of music:

> The order of the worship and government of our church is:— We begin with prayer, after[wards] read some one or two chapters of the Bible; give the sense thereof and confer upon the same; that done, we lay aside our books, and after a solemn prayer made by the first speaker, he propoundeth some text out of the Scripture, and prophesieth out of the same by the space of one hour, or three quarters of an hour. After him standeth up the second speaker and prophesieth out of the [same, or said] text the like time and [way],[5] sometime[s] more, sometime[s] less. After him the third, the fourth, the fifth, so many as the time will give leave. Then the first speaker concludeth with prayer as he began with prayer; with an exhortation to contribute to the poor, which collection being made is also concluded with prayer. This Morning exercise begins at eight of the clock and continueth unto twelve of the clock; the like course of exercise is observed in the afternoon from two of the clock unto five or six of the clock. Last of all the execution of the government of the Church is handled.[6]

John Smyth soon began to entertain doubts concerning a practice which other English Separatists considered an important covenant symbol between God and His people. It was infant baptism. Probably due to the influence of Dutch Mennonites, Smyth came to completely reject infant baptism and to adopt believer's baptism. In late 1608 or early in 1609, Smyth re-baptized himself (se-baptism) and his congregation "out of a basin"[7] by affusion (pouring), thus establishing yet another Separatist church, described simply as "brethren." Dexter describes them gathered around "a three-legged stool, which held a basin of water." Smyth then "dipped up the water in his hand and poured it over his own forehead in the name of the Father, Son and Holy Ghost. Then he repeated the ceremony in the case of each of the others." After this, "worship was held, ending with the Lord's Supper; and at last they felt themselves a genuine church of Christ; if the only one upon the earth."[8] This constituted Smyth's break from the English Separatist movement represented by such men as Francis Johnson, John Robinson, William Bradford, and William Brewster.

By 1610, however, Smyth doubted the validity of his own baptism and began seeking for a church that might have some type of successionist line back to the first century. He quickly disbanded his church and persuaded most of the flock to repent of their error and seek acceptance and membership with the Dutch Mennonites. Immediately, Thomas Helwys (d. 1616)[9] and some eight to ten others of Smyth's group, convinced that they were still a true church, excommunicated Smyth and the thirty or more members who stood by him.[10] Their strong opposition to Smyth in this matter had a deep theological basis. Some Dutch Mennonites at the time were teaching that Christ's body came from heaven and was not completely human. The first-century church had condemned a similar view as gnostic heresy. In addition, some Dutch Mennonites were teaching the doctrine of Pelagianism, which denies that any person is born a sinner. This had been officially condemned as heresy by the Christian Church at the Council of Ephesus (A.D. 431). John Smyth was now willing, however, to abandon the Puritan doctrines embraced by the *Mayflower* Pilgrims and to embrace doctrines declared by Christianity as heretical, in order to satisfy his temporary longing for a successionist connection with the apostolic church, which he hoped to find in the Mennonites' history. With Helwys' group maintaining their own separate existence, Smyth and his followers sent a *Short Confession of Faith in XX Articles* (1609), along with a letter of application, to the Mennonites for their perusal and consideration. The original was in Latin, since English Separatists were not yet fluent in Dutch. The fifth article declares that "there is no original sin [lit., *no sin of origin or descent*], but all sin is actual and voluntary, viz., a word, a deed, or a design against the law of God; and therefore, infants are without sin."[11] Thomas Helwys sent a letter and a copy of some nineteen propositions to the Mennonites, opposing Smyth's application. The Mennonites, however, sent to the Smyth congregation, in thirty-eight articles, *A Short Confession of Faith* (1610), for their own perusal. The fourth article asserts that "none of [Adam's] posterity are guilty, sinful, or born in original sin."[12]

Meanwhile, during 1611 and 1612, Helwys' small group returned to London in the face of persecution and established, in the Newgate area, the first English Baptist church. This church's twenty-seven article *Declaration of Faith,* written by Helwys himself in 1611, "is rightly judged the first English Baptist Confession."[13] It was the true beginning of what became the General Baptist movement, and it represents another departure from Puritanism. Helwys had been trained in Puritan doctrine and had taught the same. It is unknown precisely when he had made the transition into Arminian doctrine; nonetheless, some have thought that perhaps Helwys had Smyth himself in mind when he emphasized in Article 7 "that men may fall from the grace of God" and that "a righteous man may forsake his righteousness and perish."[14]

John Smyth died of tuberculosis in August 1612, never seeing the merger of his congregation with the Mennonites. In 1615 Smyth's congregation issued a confession of some one hundred articles called *Propositions and Conclusions Concerning True Christian Religion* (1612-1614), which was instrumental in accomplishing the union. Meeting in Jan Munter's bakehouse, on January 21, 1615, Smyth's followers officially united with the Mennonites, thus disappearing from history as a distinct group. Although the bakehouse complex was removed long ago, the location of the area, just outside the former city walls, was along the River Amstel, in the neighborhood of the *Blauwe Brug* and the *Rembrantsplein.* A tiny lane called *Engelse-Pelgrimsteeg* (English Pilgrim Lane) led to the bakehouse area, which is still remembered by the name of the street, *Bakkersstraat,* named after the East India Company's familiar bakery. The houses which are now in this area are from a later date. Eventually, the local Mennonite church which absorbed Smyth's group merged with another nearby Mennonite church, whose building still stands by the water of the Singel. Interestingly, as Keith Sprunger shows, "although Smyth's baptisms of his followers were accepted as true baptisms, his own baptism of himself, his se-baptism, was not considered adequate; and had he lived until 1615, when the union took place, the Mennonites would have demanded from him a new, lawful baptism."[15] At any rate, "ending his days without membership in any organized church,"[16] John Smyth was buried in Amsterdam's *Nieuwe Kerk* (New Church), which in the nineteenth century became the prestigious coronation site for the House of Orange. Situated in Dam Square, next to the Royal Palace, New Church is now used only as a museum and civic center.[17] The magnificent Palace was not there in Smyth's day.

Thomas Helwys and his General Baptist group, meanwhile, agreed with the Mennonite/Anabaptist rejection of infant baptism, but emphatically repudiated any assumed historic connection with Anabaptists. Following the Particular Baptists' precedent, General Baptists seem to have begun practicing immersion sometime in the 1640s and Helwys' church became recognized as the mother of all General Baptist churches of England. Thomas Helwys and the earliest English Baptists saw no need for historic successionism. They were convinced that any church founded on the Bible has no need for any successionism outside the Bible. To them, church successionism was one of the false claims of Romanism. Helwys's wife, Joan, was in a prison in England in 1608 for her Separatist views. It is likely that she was still there and the children were with friends or relatives when Thomas fled to Amsterdam with John Smyth's group. They had probably planned for Thomas to establish a home in Amsterdam, then bring the family over at the time of Joan's release. Some have questioned why this man returned to the very place of persecution from which the Separatists had fled. If Joan and the children were still there, however, Thomas certainly had a powerful motive for taking his tiny church to London in 1611-1612. He had, in fact, come to the conviction that it is often necessary for the church to remain in the midst of persecution in order to maintain a witness for Christ. Indeed, the little church immediately came under severe persecution. Thomas Helwys was himself incarcerated in Newgate Prison for writing a book called *A Short Declaration of the Mystery of Iniquity* (1612), sometimes described as the first defense of freedom of worship ever published in the English language. Expressing a growing Separatist conviction, it identifies the first beast of Revelation as the Church of Rome and the second beast as the Church of England. Helwys wrote a note inside the cover of one copy. It is addressed to King James:

> Hear, O king, and despise not the counsel of the poor, and let their complaints come before thee.

> The king is a mortal man and not God, therefore has no power over the immortal souls of his subjects, to make laws and ordinances for them, and to set spiritual lords over them.

If the king has authority to make spiritual lords and laws, then he is an immortal God and not a mortal man.

O king, be not seduced by deceivers to sin against God whom you ought to obey, nor against your poor subjects who ought and will obey you in all things with body, life, and goods, or else let their lives be taken from the earth.

God save the king.[18]

Helwys apparently died in Newgate Prison in 1616. John Murton (or Morton), from Gainsborough, England, succeeded him to the pastorate and was often incarcerated for his preaching. From Newgate Prison, even in 1615, Murton wrote a treatise called *Persecution for Religion Judg'd and Condemn'd.* From the same prison in 1620, Murton secretly wrote his *Humble Supplication.* Deprived of his ink, Murton used milk, carefully inscribing his words on the paper stoppers of the daily jugs of prison milk and smuggling the crumpled stoppers to Baptists who browned them over candles to make the words visible. Upon Murton's death, his wife Jane returned to Amsterdam about 1630 and joined the same Mennonite church which had absorbed the John Smyth congregation. This was a rare exception to the typical seventeenth-century Baptist attitude towards Anabaptists.[19]

Baptists have differed from Anabaptists over several major areas: pacifism, forbidding all oath taking, and forbidding Christians from holding public office. Since the 1640s, Baptists have also differed with Anabaptists on the mode of baptism. Except for a small number of them, the Mennonites never adopted immersion. The Baptists opposed also the heretical, mystical view of Christ's body, as well as the Pelagianism which some Mennonites were teaching. Mainstream Mennonites themselves eventually discarded those heresies.

By 1644 there were forty-seven General Baptist churches. Some of these Baptists, agreeing with Helwys, were Arminian in theology, believing that true believers can lose their salvation. Not all General Baptists, however, have held to strict Arminianism. Over the years, many moved closer to Calvinism and maintained remarkable balance in emphasis. Meeting in members' homes and other hiding places, these earliest Baptist churches left behind virtually no buildings or other physical monuments.

London's Newgate Prison, where both Helwys and Murton probably died, stood as a reminder of the price paid by these pioneers.

OVERVIEW OF GENERAL BAPTIST DEVELOPMENT:

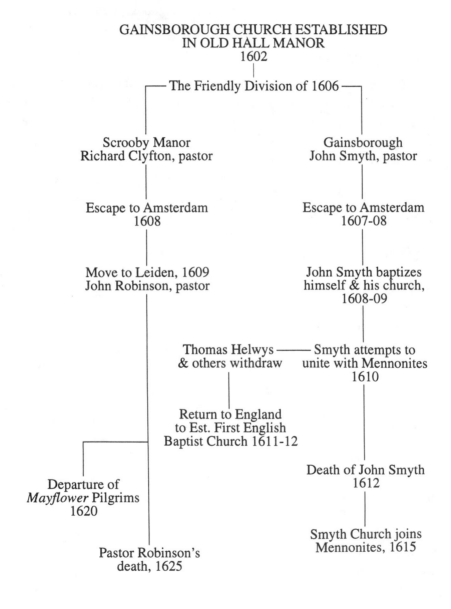

GAINSBOROUGH CHURCH ESTABLISHED
IN OLD HALL MANOR
1602

The Friendly Division of 1606

Scrooby Manor
Richard Clyfton, pastor

Gainsborough
John Smyth, pastor

Escape to Amsterdam
1608

Escape to Amsterdam
1607-08

Move to Leiden, 1609
John Robinson, pastor

John Smyth baptizes
himself & his church,
1608-09

Thomas Helwys ———— Smyth attempts to
& others withdraw   unite with Mennonites
                      1610

Return to England
to Est. First English
Baptist Church 1611-12

Death of John Smyth
1612

Departure of
Mayflower Pilgrims
1620

Smyth Church joins
Mennonites, 1615

Pastor Robinson's
death, 1625

PARTICULAR BAPTIST BEGINNINGS

Particular Baptists originated in 1638 (or 1633) as an entirely distinct movement from the General Baptists by withdrawing from an Independent Congregational church called the "J-L-J" Church, so named for its first three pastors—Jacob, Lathrop, and Jessey. Henry Jacob (1563-1624)[20] established it in the Southwark area of London in 1616. Jacob had grown up at Cheriton (Kent), then received his Bachelor of Arts and his Master of Arts from Oxford University during the 1580s. The Church of England had ordained him pastor of the parish church near Cheriton, his birthplace. Although the time and circumstances are not known, Jacob was converted under Francis Johnson.[21] However, upon his conversion he became a semi-Separatist Puritan, in disagreement with full separatism.[22] In 1591 he resigned his church; although, he was still not a full Separatist. By 1606 he had made two visits to Holland, promoted the Puritans' Millenary Petition (calling for reform within the Church of England), and suffered imprisonment in London's Clink Prison for writing a treatise of *Reasons Taken Out of Gods Word, and the Best Humane Testimonies Proving a Necessitie of Reforming Our Churches in England* (1603-1604). This was in spite of the fact that this early treatise stopped short of advocating separation from the national Church of England. Jacob fled to Holland, probably in 1605-1606, and ministered to the English Merchant Adventurers Church in Middelburg, in Zeeland, where Francis Johnson had once served before becoming a Separatist. Jacob followed closely England's political and spiritual climate. In the wake of the Hampton Court Conference, where James I threatened dissenters, Jacob "was gained to the side of truth"[23] and moved to Leiden, Holland, in 1610 to confer with and sit under the ministry of Pilgrim pastor John Robinson.[24] Here he became "the intimate friend and companion of Robinson." Jacob's writings from this time on are no longer semi-Separatist in nature; Jacob was now a Separatist. Such was the conclusion of Nathaniel Morton, author of *New England's Memorial* (1669). Morton had grown up in the home of his uncle, William Bradford, who knew Henry Jacob personally. Morton, therefore, would likely have known and recorded accurately these basic facts concerning Jacob. It was while Jacob was attending the Pilgrim services at Bell Alley that he made the transition from semi-Separatist to Separatist.[25] While "in close conference with Robinson," he wrote his *Declaration and Plainer Opening of Certaine Pointes in the*

173

Divine Beginning of Christes True Church (1611). In his treatise, Jacob "agrees entirely with Robinson"[26] concerning basic doctrine, the practice of ecclesiastical separation, and church polity.

In 1616 Jacob returned to Southwark, near London Bridge and, in a private home, gathered the J-L-J Church, "the first Independent or Congregational church in England."[27] The term *Congregationalist,* coined by Jacob himself, indicates their preferred way of church government, i.e., a local church polity based upon congregationalism, with authority resting with the members of the congregation rather than with the national church, or any other human authority outside the local church. It had become "the conviction of Henry Jacob that the time was come to take a firm and decided, though quiet, stand, and plant a church in Southwark on the model of the New Testament."[28] Like John Robinson and the *Mayflower* Pilgrims, Henry Jacob refused the "Brownist" mindset of labeling as "apostate" every church or individual identified with the national Church of England. No one in their day, however, referred to them as "semi-Separatists." As independents, Jacob and Robinson were consistent Separatists. Jacob is likely the earliest to use the term "Independent" to describe the local church, when he says, "Each congregation is an entire and *Independent* body politic, and endowed with power immediately under and from Christ, as every proper Church is and ought to be."[29] While a clear implication in that sentence is that the Churches of England were not "proper" churches, Jacob was not repudiating the validity of every individual church and pastor within the national church. He was arguing simply that independent congregations should be allowed to exist as Separatists and outside of state control. The J-L-J Church, therefore, was Puritan (Calvinist, covenant, and Reformed) in doctrine, and Independent-Separatist in organization. In his *Catechism* (1605), Jacob teaches that the officers of the local church should consist of "a pastor or bishop, with Elders, & Deacons."[30] Jacob remained with the J-L-J Church until sometime between 1622 and 1624, when he moved to Jamestown, Virginia, reportedly planted a small independent settlement,[31] and died within two years, before his wife Sara and their children were able to join him.

John Lathrop (Lothrop) (d. 1653),[32] a Cambridge graduate, became the second pastor of the J-L-J Church, in 1624. The sixty members worshipped secretly in private homes and in nearby sandpits. On April 29, 1632, Lathrop and about forty-two members of his congregation were meeting for worship in the home of Humphrey Barnet in Blackfriars. Officers of King Charles discovered them, surrounded the house, seized them, and imprisoned them—some in London's Clink Prison, some in New Prison, and some in the Gatehouse. One of the prisoners with Lathrop was Praise-God Barebone, who would serve as a member of Oliver Cromwell's Long Parliament, then as pastor of the J-L-J Church, and eventually as a Baptist pastor. The crime committed by Lathrop and his church was their refusal to support the Church of England. Eventually, eighteen escaped and all the others except Lathrop were released. Lathrop remained in the Clink for a full two years, while his wife died from illness. It is believed that the oldest of the nine orphaned children begged the Bishop of Lambeth to intercede with the king for their father. In 1634 John Lathrop was released on condition that he go into exile. On September 18 of that year, Lathrop and about thirty-two of his members arrived in Boston on the ship *Griffin* and settled at Scituate, in Plymouth Colony. The following year one of Lathrop's daughters, Jane, married Samuel Fuller[33], who had arrived on the *Mayflower* in 1620 and whose late uncle was Samuel Fuller (d.1633), the physician of the *Mayflower* and of Plymouth Colony. In 1639, the colony offered land to Lathrop and his group at the town of Barnstable, on Cape Cod. Thus, they made Barnstable their permanent settlement, erecting a church building there in 1646. Immediately upon arrival in Barnstable, they celebrated communion at a site now known as Sacrament Rock, now located on Route 6A, about a half mile from the site of the original meetinghouse. A historical sign marks the location, and the church still possesses the ancient pewter communion tankard and baptismal bowl that Lathrop brought over from London in 1634. Lathrop described that first Barnstable communion service as "another day of humiliation for the grace of our God to settle us here in church estate, and to unite us together in holy walking, and to make us faithful in keeping the covenant with God and one another."[34]

Most interestingly, one who joined with Lathrop in Scituate was Isaac Robinson, son of Pastor John Robinson, who had fled with the Scrooby Pilgrims to Leiden, Holland, and remained there with his large Separatist flock. Isaac, the only member of John Robinson's family to come to the New World, arrived in Plymouth in 1631 when Roger Williams was there. Isaac Robinson changed his membership from the Plymouth Church to the

175

Scituate church on November 7, 1636, then moved with that church in 1639 when it went to Barnstable.[35] Robinson served in Barnstable in a variety of positions, including tax collector and deputy. For his opposition to persecution against dissenters, he suffered disfranchisement from 1659 to 1672. He lived for a while in Falmouth (Cape Cod) and in Tisbury (Martha's Vineyard). In April 1702 Judge Samuel Sewall, of Boston's Old South Church, traveled to Martha's Vineyard as Commissioner of the Society for the Propagation of the Gospel among the Indians. During this journey, he noted a special visit that he had with an aged Isaac Robinson:

> [April 4] . . .Visit Mr. [Isaac] Robinson, who saith he is 92 years old, is the son of Mr. [John] Robinson pastor of the church of Leyden, part of which came to Plimoth. But to my disappointment he came not to New England, till the year [1631] in which Mr. [John] Wilson was returning to England after the settlement of Boston. I told him I was very desirous to see him for his Father's sake, and his own. Gave him an Arabian piece of gold to buy a book for some of his grandchildren.[36]

During all these years, Isaac Robinson had kept his church membership at Barnstable and returned there in his last years to live with a daughter. He died there in 1704, at the age of ninety-four, leaving behind ten children who would realize to some degree the dream of their grandfather—the Pilgrim pastor who wanted so desperately to see New England and religious liberty for all people. During his first twenty years in New England, Isaac Robinson would have doubtless spent many hours with his friend and pastor, John Lathrop, whose house (built in 1644) still stands as part of the Sturgis Library in Barnstable village. Lathrop ministered there for fourteen years, until his death in 1653. The church records describe Lathrop as "endowed with a competent measure of gifts and earnestly endowed with a great measure of brokenness of heart and humility of spirit."[37] Lathrop's successor was Thomas Walley, who refused an invitation to become pastor of Boston's First Church, in order to accept the pastorate of the church in Barnstable. Today, that West Barnstable church is the only existing remnant of London's J-L-J (Jacob-Lathrop-Jessey) Church.

With Henry Jacob in Jamestown and John Lathrop in Barnstable, London's Separatist J-L-J Church found a worthy successor in Henry Jessey, who in 1637 became its third pastor. By 1645 Jessey would be a Particular Baptist. When Jessey became the pastor at the J-L-J Church, he faced an unusual problem. Since 1630, some of the members had been leaving the Church. One of these former members, John Spilsbury, in 1638 became pastor of a London church which eventually became recognized as the first Particular Baptist church in history (possibly founded in 1633). Spilsbury's Particular Baptist church began by rejecting infant baptism and embracing believers' baptism only. In 1640 Spilsbury's church came to the additional conviction that immersion is the only Scriptural mode of baptism. The following year, they received immersion.[38]

By 1644, when John Spilsbury and William Kiffin authored the First London Confession,[39] there were seven Particular Baptist churches in London. They were first called "Baptists" in that year. From their origin to 1644, Baptist churches had been called "Brethren," or "Baptized Churches," or "Churches of the Baptized Way."[40] The original Spilsbury church met in secret places, including a home on Old Gravel Lane, in London's Wapping section. The church later moved to Prescot Street, then to Commercial Street, and finally to Walthamstow, where it remains to this day as the historic continuation of Spilsbury's church. Today it is called the Church Hill Baptist Chapel and is London's oldest Baptist church.[41]

At the J-L-J Church, Pastor Henry Jessey followed Spilsbury in 1645 by becoming a Particular Baptist. In fact, the J-L-J Church eventually spawned several other independent Particular Baptist churches before discontinuing its own British existence. All that remains today of the original, Puritan, Congregational J-L-J Church—the matrix of the first Particular Baptist churches—is the Parish Church of West Barnstable, Massachusetts, still known as "one of the seven 'Pilgrim churches' of New Plimoth Plantation."[42] Its present meetinghouse was erected in 1717. Hanging from its tall spire is a Paul Revere bell, bequested from the estate of Colonel James Otis, father of James Otis II, the Patriot known as the "Firebrand of the Revolution." Watching high above the bell is a 1732 gilded weathercock, made in England and measuring over four feet from its bill to the tip of its tail. New England churches often chose the symbolism of the rooster to warn the people of the "winds" of doctrinal apostasy, and of the words of Jesus to Peter, "Verily I say unto thee, That this night, before the cock crow, thou shalt deny me thrice" (Matthew 26:34). The present Congregational Christian

Church (UCC) which gathers beneath that symbol long ago repudiated the original separatist position. Nevertheless, by 1689 there were 107 separated, independent, Particular Baptist churches in the London area alone and a growing number in the American colonies. America's earliest Baptist churches, founded in Rhode Island by Roger Williams and John Clarke, were Particular in doctrine and Separatist in practice. Today, Calvinistic Baptists still claim the heritage initiated by those Particular Baptists of the seventeenth century. Although some do not necessarily insist on a limited atonement or a strict covenant theology which rigidly equates Israel with the church, many Separatist Baptists continue to appreciate their heritage and to honor these historic roots.

ROGER WILLIAMS AND PLYMOUTH COLONY

Roger Williams[43] (c. 1600-1683) was born in England and educated at Pembroke College, Cambridge. Receiving the B.A. degree in 1627, Williams continued for two years of graduate training, after which he received ordination as a Puritan minister. Abandoning a promising future in the Church of England, Williams became a dissenter, and immediately came under the persecuting hand of Bishop William Laud of London. To avoid arrest, he immigrated to New England in February 1631. In Boston, Williams declined an invitation to become teacher at the Puritans' First Church, because he considered it "an unseparated church." After a brief and unsatisfactory visit to Salem, Williams went down to Plymouth Colony where he served for a short time as teacher of the Pilgrims' First Church (1631-1633). During that time, Plymouth's minister was Ralph Smith. While there, Williams took his separatist views to a rigid and extreme level. H. Leon McBeth notes that Williams "insisted that Christians should not only withdraw from the Church of England but also from everyone who failed to withdraw from that church, even if a member of one's own family."[44] Williams was confusing personal separation with ecclesiastical separation. William Bradford describes the stormy relationship that developed between Roger Williams and the Plymouth Church:

> Mr. Roger Williams, a man godly and zealous, having many precious parts but very unsettled in judgment, came over first to the Massachusetts; but upon some discontent left that place and came hither, where he was friendly entertained according to their poor

ability, and exercised his gifts amongst them and after some time was admitted a member of the church. And his teaching well approved, for the benefit whereof I still bless God and am thankful to him even for his sharpest admonitions and reproofs so far as they agreed with truth. He this year began to fall into some strange opinions, and from opinion to practice, which caused some controversy between the church and him. And in the end some discontent on his part, by occasion whereof he left them something abruptly. . . . But he is to be pitied and prayed for; and so I shall leave the matter and desire the Lord to show him his errors and reduce him into the way of truth and give him a settled judgment and constancy in the same, for I hope he belongs to the Lord, and that He will show him mercy.[45]

At this time, it was the Pilgrim Church, not Roger Williams, that was maintaining the consistent separatist position set forth by Pastor John Robinson back in Leiden. In the summer of 1633, Williams returned to Salem and served unofficially as Pastor Samuel Skelton's assistant. The Salem church was Puritan, but its early pastors were sometimes sympathetic to independent practices. When Skelton died, within a few weeks, Williams served as their pastor for a short while. His extreme separatist rhetoric, however, finally resulted in his banishment from the colony. On land which he purchased from the Indians along Narragansett Bay, Williams then established the settlement which he called "Providence," around which Rhode Island Colony emerged.

At Providence Plantation, in 1639, Williams established the church which many consider to be the first Baptist church in America. Williams, however, did not remain with the church which he founded. Four months after the church's establishment, Williams broke all denominational ties, believing that, since Emperor Constantine's day (fourth century), all churches have remained in various degrees of apostasy. Williams did maintain a friendly relationship with the Baptists, but from that time he devoted his entire life to teaching the Indians. He had a rare gift for languages. At Cambridge University, he had learned Latin, Greek, Hebrew, French, and Dutch. In Salem, New England, he had remarkably mastered the Narragansett Indian tongue. Finally, in 1643, Roger Williams published his *Key into the Language of America*, the first of his numerous

179

works. The *Key* includes abundant first-hand knowledge of the Indians' religion and customs. Williams spent much time preaching to the Indians, learning their language, and even translating portions of Scripture into their tongue. "God was pleased," testified Williams, "to give me a painful, patient spirit, to lodge with them in their filthy, smoky holes . . . to gain their tongue." His "soul's desire" was "to do the natives good." Roger Williams's major contributions to posterity were his pioneer missionary work among the Indians, his insistence that the Indians were the rightful owners of the land, and his advancement of the basic principle of separation of church and state.

---

1. The best sources on John Smyth include Walter H. Burgess, *John Smyth the Se-Baptist, Thomas Helwys, and the First Baptist Church in England with Fresh Light upon the Pilgrim Fathers' Church* (London: James Clarke & Co., 1911); John Smyth, *The Works of John Smyth Fellow of Christ's College, 1594-8*, ed. W. T. Whitley, 2 vols. (Cambridge: Cambridge University Press, 1915); E. Catherine Anwyl, *John Smyth: The Se-Baptist at Gainsborough* (Gainsborough, England: G. W. Belton Ltd., 1991); James R. Coggins, *John Smyth's Congregation: English Separatism, Mennonite Influence, and the Elect Nation* (Scottdale, PA: Herald Press, 1991); B. R. White, *The English Separatist Tradition: From the Marian Martyrs to the Pilgrim Fathers* (London: Oxford University Press, Ely House, 1971), 116-41; and Keith L. Sprunger, *Dutch Puritanism: A History of English and Scottish Churches of the Netherlands in the Sixteenth and Seventeenth Centuries* (Leiden: E. J. Brill, 1982), 76-90.

2. E. Catherine Anwyl, *John Smyth: The Se-Baptist at Gainsborough,* pages unnumbered; see also William Bradford, *Of Plymouth Plantation 1620-1647,* ed. Samuel Eliot Morison (1952; rpt. NY: Alfred A. Knopf, 1998), 9.

3. Smyth outlined their disagreements in his work *The Differences of the Churches of the Separation* (1608).

4. Edward Arber, ed., *The Story of The Pilgrim Fathers, 1606-1623 A.D; as Told by Themselves, Their Friends, and Their Enemies* (London: Ward and Downey, Limited, 1897), 131-40.

5. The word is not legible in the manuscript.

6. *Letter of the Bromheads to Sir William Hammerton* (n.d.). The original manuscript is in the British Museum (Harleian MS 360, folio 71); I have slightly modernized some of the punctuation and spelling in order to preserve the meaning of the damaged text, which is cited verbatim in Horton Davies, *Worship and Theology in England,* vol. I, *From Cranmer to Hooker, 1534-1603,* vol. II, *From Andrewes to Baxter and Fox, 1603-1690* (1970, 1975; rpt. Grand Rapids, MI: William B. Eerdmans Publishing Co., 1996 combined edition), I:338-39; it is cited with various modernization by Anwyl; and by Champlin Burrage, *The Early English Dissenters in the Light of Recent Research* (1550-1641) (Cambridge: Cambridge University Press, 1912), II:176-77; B. R. White, 126-27; and Henry Martyn Dexter and Morton Dexter, *The England and Holland of the Pilgrims* (1906; rpt. Baltimore: Genealogical Publishing Co., Inc., 1978), 384-85.

7. B. R. White, *The English Separatist Tradition,* 133.

8. Henry Martyn Dexter and Morton Dexter, *The England and Holland of the Pilgrims,* 456.

9. The best sources on Thomas Helwys include Ernest A. Payne, *Thomas Helwys and the First Baptist Church in England* (London: The Baptist Union of Great Britain and Ireland, 1966);

and Walter H. Burgess, *John Smyth the Se-Baptist, Thomas Helwys, and the First Baptist Church in England with Fresh Light upon the Pilgrim Fathers' Church.*

10. Henry Martyn Dexter and Morton Dexter, *The England and Holland of the Pilgrims,* 520-21.

11. William L. Lumpkin, *Baptist Confessions of Faith* (Valley Forge: The Judson Press, 1969), 100.

12. Ibid., 103.

13. Ibid., 115; see also Burrage, II:167-68.

14. Lumpkin, 118-19. Helwys also wrote *A Short and Plain Proof, by the Word and Works of God, that God's Decree is Not the Cause of Any Man's Sin or Condemnation: and that All Men are Redeemed by Christ; as Also that No Infants Are Condemned,* a twenty-four-page treatise dedicated, on June 2, 1611, to Lady Bowes, wife of Sir William Bowes in whose Coventry home Helwys had attended the 1606 meeting of concerned Separatists, including Richard Clyfton and John Robinson.

15. Keith L. Sprunger, *Dutch Puritanism,* 85.

16. Leon McBeth, *The Baptist Heritage* (Nashville: Broadman Press, 1987), 38.

17. Amsterdam's New Church suffered a major fire and has had several renovations since Smyth's day.

18. Thomas Helwys, *A Short Declaration of the Mystery of Iniquity,* ed. Richard Groves (Macon, GA: Mercer University Press, 1998), xxiv.

19. Jane Murton's close relative, Alexander Hodgkin, was a member of this Mennonite church; in fact, he had been a member of Smyth's own church at the time of the merger. He was probably Jane's brother (possibly her father). This, of course, explains her action in joining this church at the death of her husband.

20. The best sources for Henry Jacob and the J-L-J Church include David Waite Yohn, *The Gist of Jacob: Being an Investigation of the Thought of the Rev. Henry Jacob Who Coined the Designation "Congregational" and Gathered the Most Ancient Church Still Called by that Name* (West Barnstable, MA: West Parish Memorial Foundation, Inc., 1982). Yohn wrote as "Pastor/Teacher of the West Parish Congregational Church." The book contains numerous quotations from Jacob; see also Walter R. Goehring, "Henry Jacob (1563-1624) and the Separatists," Ph.D. dissertation, New York University, 1975. For a discussion of the first three J-L-J pastors, see Henry Martyn Dexter, *The Congregationalism of the Last Three Hundred Years, as Seen in Its Literature* (NY: Harper and Brothers, Publishers, 1880), 635ff.; Burrage, I:281-356; II:146-66 and *passim;* Benjamin Brook, *The Lives of the Puritans* (Pittsburgh, PA: Soli Deo Gloria, 1994), II:330-34; and Sir Leslie Stephen and Sir Sidney Lee, ed., *Dictionary of National Biography* (1917; rpt. London: Oxford University Press, 1921-22), X:554-55. Henry Jacob's works consist of thirteen volumes; some of the titles themselves reveal his thought: *A Treatise of the Sufferings and Victory of Christ* (1598); *A Defence of the Churches and Ministery of Englande* (1599); *A Defence of a Treatise Touching the Sufferings and Victorie of Christ* (1600); *Principles and Foundations of the Christian Religion; A Third Humble Supplication of Many Faithful Subjects in England Falsely called Puritans Directed to the King's Majesty* (1605); *A Christian and Modest Offer of a Most Indifferent Conference* (1606); *An Humble Supplication for Toleration and Libertie to Enjoy and Observe the Ordinances of Christ Jesus in th'Administration of His Churches in Lieu of Human Constitutions* (1609); *The Divine Beginning of Christs Church* (1610); *A Plaine and Cleere Exposition of the Second Commandement* (1610); *A Declaration and Plainer Opening of Certaine Pointes in the Divine Beginning of Christes True Church* (1611); *An Attestation of Many Divines that the Church-government Ought to bee Alwayes with the Peoples Free Consent* (1613); and *A Confession and Protestation of the Faith of Certaine Christians in England* (1616).

21. See Nathaniel Morton, *New England's Memorial* (1669; rpt. Boston: Congregational Board of Publications, 1855), 446.

22. That Jacob was not a full Separatist at this time is confirmed in Francis Johnson's *Answere to Maister H. Iacob* [and] *His Defence of the Churches* (1600).

23. Morton, *New England's Memorial,* 444.

24. Ibid., 446.

25. This is contrary to the oft-repeated view expressed in H. Shelton Smith et al., ed., *American Christianity: An Interpretation with Representative Documents* (NY: Charles Scribner's Sons, 1960), I:82-89.

26. Morton, *New England's Memorial,* 444.

27. Ibid.

28. Ibid., 446.

29. Jacob, *A Declaration and Plainer Opening of Certaine Pointes in the Divine Beginning of Christes True Church* (1611), cited in A. H. Drysdale, *History of the Presbyterians in England: Their Rise, Decline, and Revival* (London: Publication Committee of the Presbyterian Church of England, 1889), 5 n. 2.

30. Cited in Burrage, II:160.

31. Perhaps in derision, some referred to Henry Jacob's Jamestown, VA settlement as "Jacobopolis;" see Brook, *The Lives of the Puritans,* III:163-65.

32. He spelled his name "Lothropp." Some of his New England descendants later changed the spelling to "Lathrop." Occasionally, it appeared as "Laythrop," representing the New England pronunciation of Lathrop. See *Dictionary of National Biography,* XII:147-48.

33. Eugene A. Stratton, *Plymouth Colony: Its History & People 1620-1691* (Salt Lake City, UT: Ancestry Publishing, 1986), 60-64.

34. Ibid., 7. Although John Lathrop's diary is now lost, Ezra Stiles, later president of Yale College, borrowed it and copied parts of it in 1769; Stiles' citations are the only extant remains of Lathrop's diary. Fortunately, some of these quotations are rather lengthy. They are published in volumes nine and ten of *The New England Historical and Genealogical Register* (101 Newbury Street, Boston, Massachusetts). See also Jeremy D. Bangs, ed., *The Seventeenth-Century Town Records of Scituate, Massachusetts* (Boston, MA: New England Historic Genealogical Society, 1997), I:26-31 and *passim.*

35. See George F. Willison, *Saints and Strangers* (NY: Reynal & Hitchcock, 1945), 452; see also Stratton, 344-45.

36. Judge Samuel Sewall (1652-1730) was one of the best known members of Old South Church. Remembered for his public repentance for his part in the witchcraft trials, Sewall became Chief Justice of the Superior Court of Judicature of Massachusetts. His diary has become a classic. Sewall introduces the reference to Isaac Robinson by mentioning his seeing John Lathrop's widow, as well as John Howland Jr., son of the *Mayflower* Pilgrim who was rescued after falling overboard: "Before which time one [Thomas] Crocker comes up, who married the widow of young Mr. [John] Lothrop, and becomes our Pilot. Saw Lieut. [John] Howland upon the Rode, who tells us he was born Febr. 24. 1626, at our Plimoth." See Samuel Sewall, *The Diary of Samuel Sewall: 1674-1729,* ed. M. Halsey Thomas (NY: Farrar, Straus and Giroux 1973), I:463-64.

37. Walter R. Goehring, *The West Parish Church of Barnstable: An Historical Sketch—Being an Account of the Gathering of the Church Body in London in 1616 with Henry Jacob and its Early History in the New World and Particularly of the West Parish Meetinghouse Built in 1717 in West Barnstable, Massachusetts* (West Barnstable, MA: The West Parish Memorial Foundation, 1959), 9. Nathaniel Morton, a contemporary in Plymouth, said that Lathrop was "a man of a humble and broken heart and spirit." See Nathaniel Morton, *New England's Memorial,* 446.

38. See the full discussion in William H. Whitsitt, *A Question in Baptist History* (rpt. NY: Arno Press, 1980), *passim.*

39. For an excellent coverage of these Particular Baptists and their confessions of faith, see Michael A. G. Haykin, *Kiffin, Knollys and Keach: Rediscovering Our English Baptist Heritage* (Leeds, England: Reformation Today Trust, 1996); Michael A. G. Haykin, ed., *The British Particular Baptists: 1638-1910* (Springfield, MO: Particular Baptist Press, 1998); B. R. White, ed., *Association Records of the Particular Baptists of England, Wales and Ireland to 1660* (London: Baptist Historical Society, 1974); and B. R. White and Roger Haydon, ed., *English Baptists of the Seventeenth Century* (London: Baptist Historical Society, 1996).

40. H. Leon McBeth, *The Baptist Heritage,* 48-49.

41. A good source on the original Particular Baptist Church is Robert W. Oliver, *From John Spilsbury to Ernest Kevan: The Literary Contribution of London's Oldest Baptist Church* (London: Grace Publications Trust, 1985).

42. Yohn, 4.

43. The best sources include Roger Williams, *The Complete Writings of Roger Williams,* ed. Perry Miller, 7 vols. (NY: Russell and Russell, Inc., 1963); Ola Elizabeth Winslow, *Master Roger Williams* (NY: Octagon Books, 1973); and James Emanuel Ernst, *Roger Williams: New England Firebrand* (NY: AMS Press, 1969); see also Edmund Sears Morgan, *Roger Williams: The Church and the State* (NY: Harcourt, Brace & World, 1967); and Emily Easton, *Roger Williams: Prophet and Pioneer* (Boston: Houghton Mifflin, 1930).

44. H. Leon McBeth, *The Baptist Heritage,* 129.

45. Bradford, *Plymouth Plantation,* 257.

About the Author

Dr. Beale regularly conducts "Mayflower Tours" to the British Isles and Holland, tracing the Old World footsteps of the Pilgrims. He has authored several books, including *A Pictorial History of Our English Bible* and *In Pursuit of Purity: American Fundamentalism Since 1850,* the most complete narrative history of fundamentalism ever written. He conducts Bible and history conferences each year. His favorite hobbies include photographing American, European and Middle Eastern sites of religious and historical significance. His slide collection numbers around 10,000, and he often uses them in classes and conferences.

David Beale (born 1944) grew up near Franklin, Virginia. He attended Eastern Baptist College in Virginia and Baptist Bible College (Seminary) in Clarks Summit, Pennsylvania, before going to Bob Jones University and Seminary to complete his education. He received his Ph. D. in church histroy, and his dissertation was entitled "Ante-Nicene Eschatology: An Historical and Theological Analysis." Dr. Beale has taught at Bob Jones University and Seminary since 1973. Courses that he teaches include Colonial American Church History, Baptist History, Presbyterian History, History of Doctrine, and Church Fathers. He is listed in the Directory of American Scholars.

His wife, Mary, serves in the BJU Museum and Gallery. The Beales have a daughter, two sons, and three grandchildren.

MAYFLOWER TOUR
ENGLAND, WALES & HOLLAND
Great gift idea for students, pastors, or retirees
Host, David Beale

Join Dr. Beale on the next unique and unforgettable two-week adventure in England, Wales, and Holland, tracing the footsteps of the Puritans, Presbyterians, Pilgrims, early Baptists, and Wesleys (as well as the usual sites). Enjoy the services of a multi-lingual European tour director. Stroll along quaint streets, visit ancient churches, and chat with locals in the villages and hamlets of England's "Holy Triangle" where the English Separatist movement originated. Enjoy Amsterdam, an evening in a Welsh castle, the excitement of London, and the picturesque English countryside, with its thatched roofs and grazing sheep. Travel with experts to explore the Christian heritage; experience wholesome fellowship, fine foods and accommodations and, if desired, earn three hours undergraduate, graduate, or seminary credit. Dr. Beale developed and customized this tour by repeated visits throughout the United Kingdom and Holland. For more information, contact Dr. Beale at Bob Jones Seminary, Greenville, SC 29614.

APPENDIX A

CHRONOLOGY OF THE ENGLISH MONARCHS

PLANTAGENET MONARCHS 1377-1485

  I. Richard II 1377-1399; marries Anne of Bohemia 1383; John Wyclif (c. 1320-1384), "Morning Star of the Reformation," translates all of the N. T. and most, if not all, of the O. T. from the Latin Vulgate into the English vernacular (c. 1382). Wyclif's works are sent to Bohemia, where they influence reformer John Huss (c. 1374-1415).

  II. Henry IV 1399-1413

  III. Henry V 1413-1422; John Huss of Bohemia is martyred in 1415. Hussites increase in Bohemia

  IV. Henry VI 1422-1461; Gutenberg Bible published in Mainz, Germany about 1456.

  V. Edward IV 1461-1483; Hussites organize the Unitas Fratrum or Moravian Church in 1467.

  VI. Edward V 1483 (two months).

  VII. Richard III 1483-1485; lodged in Gainsborough Old Hall one night in 1483.

TUDOR MONARCHS 1485-1603

  I. Henry VII 1485-1509; Reformers Ulrich Zwingli (1484-1531) and Martin Luther (1483-1546); discovery of America (1492).

  II. Henry VIII 1509-1547; became king the same year that John Calvin (1509-1564) was born in Noyon, in Northern France. Although

Henry established the Church of England in 1534, when Calvin was only twenty-five years old, by the time of Henry's death, Calvin would be well established as the reformer of Geneva, Switzerland. Martin Luther's Ninety-five Theses were nailed to the door of the Castle Church in Wittenberg, Germany in 1517, just eight years after Henry came to England's throne; and Luther died in 1546, just a year before Henry died. So Henry was very much aware of the continental reformers. Although Henry broke with the pope and made himself the Supreme Head of the national Church of England for political purposes, he eventually permitted English Bibles to be placed in the churches, where all could hear them read. By 1539 there were six Bibles in London's St. Paul's Cathedral, where illiterate common people flocked to hear the reading of them.

1525   The *Tyndale New Testament* is surreptitiously printed in Antwerp and Worms and begins to be secretly distributed throughout England.

1527   Henry VIII desires to divorce Catherine of Aragon and marry Anne Boleyn. Papal legate, Thomas Cardinal Wolsey, Archbishop of York, was in charge of the English clergy at this time. Wolsey, failing to obtain papal sanction from Pope Clement VII, is stripped of power, accused of treason, and sentenced to death.

1533   Thomas Cranmer is appointed Archbishop of Canterbury.

1534   Act of Supremacy declares the king "Supreme Head of the Church of England Under Christ."

1535   The *Coverdale Bible* is printed as the first complete Bible in English.

1536   10 Articles of Religion published (same year in which Calvin published the first edition of his *Institutes*).

1537   The *Matthew Bible* is published.

1539 - Six Articles of Religion published;Complete liquidation of English monasteries; *The Great Bible* is published. It would become the first Bible to be specifically prescribed for use in English churches.

III. Edward VI 1547-1553; he was the young son of Henry VIII, and a
Protestant. During these years, Calvin was at Geneva and reformer
John Knox (c. 1505-1572) was in England. Edward VI comes to Eng-
land's throne at the age of nine and receives a Protestant education.
The lad is hailed by many as "a new Josiah to purify the temple."
Reformed theologians are now becoming professors at Cambridge.

1549 *Book of Common Prayer* is published (revised in 1552);
largely the work of Thomas Cranmer, who is being influenced
by the writings of Zwingli, Luther and Calvin.

1553 Forty-two Articles published; Edward dies three weeks after
signing them. During these years, John Hooper, bishop of
Gloucester, is trying to discourage "popish" vestments, ceremonies, etc. and has been called the "Father of Puritanism."

IV. Mary I 1553-1558; she is the daughter of Henry VIII and the wife of
the Roman Catholic Philip II of Spain; she forces the restoration of
Roman Catholicism in England. During her five-year reign, three
hundred Protestants are burned at the stake. It is during this time that
William Hickman's family goes into religious exile in Antwerp.

1554 6 Articles of Religion reestablished.

1554-1555 - Protestant Bishops Hugh Latimer, Nicholas Ridley, and
John Hooper are burned at stake.

1556 Thomas Cranmer is burned; Cardinal Reginald Pole becomes
archbishop the next day. Three hundred others are burned in
"the fires of Smithfield."

1558 Almost simultaneously, Mary and her archbishop die by what
John Foxe described as a "divine stroke of Providence."

V. Elizabeth I 1558-1603; this daughter of Henry VIII restores Protestantism to England. The Church of England under Elizabeth is a
compromise between the Protestant/Reformed churches of the continent and the old Roman Catholic tradition. The Church of England
retains her rule of bishops, liturgy, and ceremony. This prompts the
rise of Puritanism. The name "Puritan" was first used in the 1560s.
This period includes the rise of Separatist movements such as the
Mayflower Pilgrims. Such Separatists would view the Church of

England's similarity to Catholicism as "a huge mass of old and stinking works, a pack of popery and a puddle of corruption."

1558   Elizabeth appoints Matthew Parker as Archbishop of Canterbury. The fact that Parker had been ordained as a Roman Catholic in 1527, before the break with Rome, indicates her concern for the continuity of the so-called "apostolic succession" of the Anglican episcopacy.

1560   *Geneva Bible* is published.

1562   French Huguenots attempt to colonize in South Carolina.

1563   Thirty-nine Articles of Religion are published.

1564   The beginning of organized Puritanism as a movement

1568   *Bishops' Bible* is published.

1570   Thomas Cartwright is ousted from Cambridge for teaching Presbyterianism as the only biblical polity.

1579   Union of Utrecht marks independence for Protestant Holland.

1581   Robert Browne begins a separatist congregation at Norwich, England. He later suffers imprisonment and flees to Holland with his congregation. (Within ten years, he would desert his people and accept Anglican ordination.)

1582   Publication of the Catholics' *Douai-Rheims N. T.*

1584   England attempts to colonize in North Carolina.

1587   Execution of Mary Stuart of Scotland.

1588   Defeat of Spanish Armada.

1592   Francis Johnson becomes pastor of the secret Separatist church, established with the help of John Greenwood, Henry Barrowe, and John Penry in London.

1598   Edict of Nantes grants concessions to French Protestants.

STUART MONARCHS 1603-1714

I. James I 1603-1625; son of Mary, Queen of Scots and Lord Darnley, he had been King James VI of Scotland, where he had learned to hate Presbyterianism.

1603   Puritans present James with Millenary Petition.

1604   At Hampton Court Conference, James "authorizes" translation of Bible, and threatens dissenters that they must conform or else he will "harry them out of the land." Cambridge University, especially its Emmanuel College, becomes nursery of English Puritanism.

1607   Anglican settlement of Jamestown, Virginia, on May 24, upon arrival of the three ships.

1608   The Separatists of the Scrooby, England, area flee to Holland.

1609-1610 - Publication of *Douai-Rheims O. T.* for English Catholics.

1610   English laws outlaw the preaching of Puritan doctrine; Puritans begin "lecturing."

1611   *King James Version* is published.

1611-1612 - Earliest English Baptist church established.

1618   Thirty Years War begins in Bohemia.

1620   *Mayflower* sails from Plymouth, England, Sept.16; *Mayflower Compact* is signed, Nov. 21 in Cape Cod Bay. William Bradford later coins term "Pilgrim" in describing this group of Separatists as "Pilgrims and strangers upon the earth."

1624-1625 - Virginia becomes a royal colony.

II. Charles I 1625-1649; marries a French Roman Catholic and makes William Laud of London one of his advisors. Charles would soon make English ships available to Cardinal Richelieu to fight against the French Protestants.

1628   Nonconformist Puritans arrive at Salem, Massachusetts.

1630   Nonconformist Puritans arrive at Boston, Massachusetts.

1633   William Laud becomes Archbishop of Canterbury. Maryland is settled by Roman Catholics under Lord Baltimore.

1635   Great Puritan migration increases as "Laudian" persecution rages in England.

1636   Harvard College founded in Cambridge, Massachusetts.

1638-1639 - First Baptist churches in America founded in Rhode Island.

1642-1648 - Civil War in England: Oliver Cromwell's Independent army defeats the forces of Charles I.

1642   Puritan migration to New World slows.

1643   Westminster Assembly begins in London.

1645   Archbishop Laud beheaded for treason.

1646   Formation of Presbyterian Westminster Standards by the Assembly

1648   New England Puritans, in their Cambridge Platform, adopt Westminster Standards of doctrine, but continue congregational polity.

1649-1660 - The Interregnum: The Protectorate Government of Oliver Cromwell and his son, Richard;

1649   Charles I is beheaded. Cavaliers flee to Virginia, which remains loyal to Crown.

1658   Death of Oliver Cromwell. English Independents stop striving for Presbyterian polity. In their Savoy Declaration, at Savoy Palace, they affirm Congregational polity. Doctrinally the Savoy Declaration is in full agreement with the Presbyterian Westminster Standards.

1659   Richard Cromwell is forced to abdicate.

III. Charles II 1660-1685; Restoration of the Stuarts and the Church of England

1660   John Bunyan, Baptist preacher, begins his twelve-year imprisonment in a Bedford jail in England, where he writes his *Pilgrim's Progress,* published on Feb. 18, 1678.

1662   Great persecution of nonconformists gets underway in England, prompting increase of migration to New England. - Half-Way Covenant is adopted in New England.

1676   Randolph, special agent of the king, is sent to Massachusetts to enforce submission to England.

1680   The Reforming Synod of Massachusetts adopts the English Savoy Confession of 1658. This represents a continuation of basic congregational polity in New England, but tending towards semi-Presbyterianism.

1682   William Penn comes to America.

1683 Charles II issues his *Quo Warranto* (Declaration) against the Massachusetts Charter, and the government and demands full submission. Boston, under the influence of Increase Mather, votes No!

1684 Massachusetts Charter is declared void by the king, who now begins appointing royal governors in New England (Kirke, Randolph, Dudley, Andros).

1685 Increase Mather becomes president of Harvard.

IV. James II 1685-1689; Catholic sympathizer

1685 Revocation of Edict of Nantes in France sends many Huguenots fleeing to Holland, England, Germany, and the New World—South Carolina, New York, and New Jersey.

1688 Heavy taxes imposed on Massachusetts; some imprisoned; Old South (Third Puritan) Church in Boston is taken over for Anglican services; every citizen is commanded to support English *Book of Common Prayer;* King's Chapel is established as the first official Anglican church in Boston. - English "Glorious Revolution" deposes the king.

V. William III 1689-1702 and Mary II 1689-1694

1689 Bill of Rights to protect English Protestants from any future royal attack;

1690 English Toleration Act.

1691 Massachusetts is made an official royal colony, ending the old Puritan rule. Increase Mather was in England from 1688 to 1691 to obtain a charter renewal. This was refused, and the new charter, vastly different from the old one, was imposed. Royal governors would now be formally installed. The franchise (right to vote) was now based, not on church standing, but on property ownership. Religious toleration was to be enforced. Plymouth Colony merges into Massachusetts Bay Colony.

1693 William and Mary College is founded in Williamsburg, Virginia.

1699 Scottish Woolens Act causes many Scotch-Irish Presbyterians to migrate to America.

- Brattle Street Church, a professing Puritan church in Boston, is founded and issues its famous Manifesto. This church symbolizes the fall of the strict, old-line Puritanism. "Puritanism" clearly disintegrates now into two distinct branches—Congregationalism and Presbyterianism.

1701   Yale College founded in New Haven, Connecticut by Congregationalists.

VI. Anne 1702-1714

1706   Founding of First Presbyterian presbytery in America.

1708   The Saybrook Platform in Connecticut is adopted by Congregationalists, allowing for ministerial "Consociations," which resemble Presbyterian synods (semi-Presbyterian polity).

HANOVERIAN MONARCHS 1714-1820

I. George I 1714-1727. Elector of Hanover in Germany, he is crowned King of England in preference to an English Roman Catholic pretender. This period witnesses an increase in German immigration to New York and Pennsylvania.

II. George II 1727-1760. Georgia is founded and named for the king in 1733. The Great Awakening is the most significant movement in the colonies during this time.

III. George III 1760-1820. During this period, America becomes an independent nation and the Second Great Awakening occurs.

1765   Stamp Act.

1776   Declaration of Independence.

1781   Surrender of British at Yorktown.

1787   American Constitutional Convention.

1789   George Washington inaugurated. First Presbyterian General Assembly.

APPENDIX B

MARTYRDOM OF HUGH LATIMER, NICHOLAS RIDLEY, AND THOMAS CRANMER OXFORD—1555-1556

Hugh Latimer[1] was born about 1480 in County Leicester in England. At Christ College, Cambridge, Latimer early distinguished himself as an outspoken opponent of the Reformation. However, as Latimer began studying the Scriptures, he became convicted of his sin and was converted to Christ. When the government granted him permission to preach anywhere in England, he took the opportunity joyfully. His fervent sermons so stirred the hearts of audiences that one man exclaimed, "I have an ear for other preachers, but I have a heart for Latimer." Henry VIII quickly ordered the preacher silenced, and for several years Latimer remained in prison. With the ascension of Edward VI to England's throne, Latimer again began his preaching tours, which continued until 1553, when "Bloody Mary" became queen. Mary was a fanatical Roman Catholic who desired to return England to the domination of Rome. She had Latimer imprisoned in the tower of London.

Nicholas Ridley,[2] the younger of the two martyrs, was born about 1500. He too studied at Cambridge. Following additional studies in France he returned to England and became senior procurator at Cambridge. In 1547 Ridley became Bishop of Rochester and in 1550 Bishop of London. In both positions he remained above reproach and manifested a life of hard work and fervent prayer. Following the death of Edward VI, Ridley remained at his post until July 1553, when Mary deposed him and imprisoned him in the Tower of London in the same room with Latimer. Both men patiently awaited trial.

Finally in April of 1554, Ridley and Latimer were taken before the Divinity School at Oxford and charged with heresy. Their trials took place in the University Church of St. Mary in 1555. "Christ," Latimer said, "made one perfect sacrifice for all the whole world; neither can any man offer him again, neither can the priest offer up Christ again for the sins of men, which he took away by offering himself once for all, as Saint Paul saith, upon the cross; neither is there propitiation for our sins, saving his cross only." Ridley too answered the charges of heresy clearly and forcefully. Since neither man would recant nor moderate his position, the court ordered their imprisonment to continue. When the court called them forth for a final hearing and sentencing, the judges urged Ridley and Latimer to recant but both remained steadfast. On October 1 the court handed down its sentence—death by burning.

On the morning of October 16, 1555, amidst a great crowd of soldiers and onlookers, Ridley and Latimer walked to the stakes which had been set up outside Balliol College, Oxford. When they reached the place of execution Ridley embraced Latimer and said, "Be of good cheer brother Latimer, for God will either lessen the fury of the flames or else strengthen us to bear them." Both then knelt and prayed. Following prayer, both men were quickly bound to the stake, and the guards piled the fagots about them. As the lighted torch touched the pile heaped about them, Latimer spoke those timeless, stirring words: "Be of good courage, brother Ridley, and play the man: For we shall this day light such a candle by God's grace in England, as I trust shall never be put out."

Below is the account as it appears in *Foxe's Book of Martyrs,* along with the final moments of Thomas Cranmer,[3] who under severe torture had signed a recantation. Cranmer withdrew the recantation, but always despised the hand that signed it. Dying at the stake he holds to the flames "this wicked hand."

The Oxford Martyrs as Told by John Fox(e) (1516-1587), of Boston, England, in His Eight-Volume *Actes and Monuments of these Latter and Perilous Dayes Touching Matters of the Church* (1563), commonly known as "The Book of Martyrs:"

Upon the north-side of the town, in the ditch over against the Balliol-college, the place of execution was appointed: and for fear of any tumult that might arise, to let the burning of them, the Lord Williams was commanded, by the Queen's letters and the house-holders of the city, to be there [their] assistant, sufficiently appointed. And when everything was in a readiness, the prisoners were brought forth by the mayor and the bailiffs.

Master Ridley had a fair black gown furred, and faced with foins, such as he was wont to wear being bishop, and a tippet of velvet, furred likewise[,] about his neck, a velvet night-cap upon his head, and a corner cap upon the same, going in a pair of slippers to the stake, and going between the mayor and an alderman, etc.

After him came master Latimer in a poor Bristol frieze frock all worn, with his buttoned cap, and a kerchief on his head, all ready to the fire, a new long shroud hanging over his hose, down to the feet: which at the first sight stirred men's hearts to rue upon them, beholding on the one side, the honor they sometime had, and on the other, the calamity whereunto they were fallen.

Master Doctor Ridley, as he passed toward Bocardo, looked up where master Cranmer did lie, hoping belike to have seen him at the glass-window, and to have spoken unto him. But then master Cranmer was busy with Friar Soto and his fellows, disputing together, so that he could not see him, through that occasion. Then master Ridley, looking back, espied master Latimer coming after, unto whom he said, "Oh, be ye there?" "Yea," said master Latimer, "have after as fast as I can follow." So he, following a pretty way off, at length they came both to the stake, the one after the other, where first Dr. Ridley entering the place, marvelous earnestly holding up both his hands, looked towards heaven. Then shortly after espying master Latimer, with a wondrous cheerful look he ran to him, embraced, and kissed him; and, as they that stood near reported, comforted him, saying, "Be of good heart, brother, for God will either assuage the fury of the flame, or else strengthen us to abide it."

With that went he to the stake, kneeled down by it, kissed it, and most effectuously prayed, and behind him master Latimer kneeled, as earnestly calling upon God as he. After they arose, the one talked with the other a little while, till they which were appointed to see the execution, removed themselves out of the sun. What they said I can learn of no man.

Then Dr. Smith, of whose recantation in King Edward's time ye heard before, began his sermon to them upon this text of St. Paul [in I Corinthians 13], "If I yield my body to the fire to be burnt, and have not charity, I shall gain nothing thereby." Wherein he alleged that the goodness of the cause, and not the order of death, maketh the holiness of the person; which he confirmed by the examples of Judas, and of a woman in Oxford that of late hanged herself, for that they, and such like as he recited, might then be adjudged righteous, which desperately sundered their lives from their bodies, as he feared that those men that stood before him would do. But he cried still to the people to beware of them, for they were heretics, and died out of the church. And on the other side, he declared their diversity in opinions, as Lutherans, Oecolampadians, Zwinglians, of which sect they were, he said, and that was the worst: but the old church of Christ, and the catholic faith believed far otherwise. At which place they lifted up both their hands and eyes to heaven, as it were calling God to witness of the truth: the which countenance they made in many other places of his sermon, whereas they thought he spake amiss. He ended with a very short exhortation to them to recant, and come home again to the church, and save their lives and souls, which else were condemned. His sermon was scant; in all, a quarter of an hour.

Doctor Ridley said to master Latimer, "Will you begin to answer the sermon, or shall I?" Master Latimer said, "Begin you first, I pray you." "I will," said master Ridley.

Then, the wicked sermon being ended, Dr. Ridley and master Latimer kneeled down upon their knees towards my Lord Williams of Thame, the vice-chancellor of Oxford, and divers other commissioners appointed for that purpose, which sat upon a form thereby; unto whom master Ridley said, "I beseech you, my lord, even for Christ's sake, that I may speak but two or three words." And whilst my lord bent his head to the mayor and vice-chancellor, to know (as it appeared) whether he might give him leave to speak, the bailiffs and Dr. Marshall, vice-chancellor, ran hastily unto him, and with their hands stopped his mouth, and said, "master Ridley, if you will revoke your erroneous opinions, and recant the same, you shall not only have liberty so to do, but also the benefit of a subject; that is, have your life." "Not otherwise?" said master Ridley. "No," quoth Dr. Marshall. "Therefore if you will not so do, then there is no remedy but you must suffer for your deserts." "Well," quoth master Ridley, "so long as the breath is in my body, I will never deny my Lord Christ, and his known truth: God's will be done in me!" And with that he rose up, and said with a loud voice, "Well then, I commit our cause to Almighty God, which shall indifferently judge all." To whose saying, master Latimer added his old poise, "Well! there is nothing hid but it shall be opened." And he said, he could answer Smith well enough, if he might be suffered.

Incontinently they were commanded to make them ready, which they with all meekness obeyed. Master Ridley took his gown and his tippet, and gave it to his brother-in-law, master Shipside, who all his time of imprisonment, although he might not be suffered to come to him, lay there at his own charges to provide him necessaries, which from time to time he sent him by the serjeant that kept him. Some other of his apparel that was little worth, he gave away; other the bailiffs took.

He gave away besides, divers other small things to gentlemen standing by, and divers of them pitifully weeping, as to Sir Henry Lea he gave a new groat: and to divers of my lord Williams gentlemen some napkins, some nutmegs, and races of ginger: his dial, and such other things as he had about him, to every one that stood next him. Some plucked the points off his hose. Happy was he that might get any rag of him.

Master Latimer gave nothing, but very quickly suffered his keeper to pull off his hose, and his other array, which to look unto was very simple: and being stripped into his shroud, he seemed as comely a person to them that were there present, as one should lightly see; and whereas in his clothes he appeared a withered and crooked silly old man, he now stood bolt upright, as comely a father as one might lightly behold.

Then master Ridley, standing as yet in his truss, said to his brother, "It were best for me to go in my truss still." "No," quoth his brother, "it will put you to more pain: and the truss will do a poor man good." Whereunto master Ridley said, "Be it, in the name of God;" and so unlaced himself. Then, being in his shirt, he stood upon the foresaid stone, and held up his hand and said, "O heavenly Father, I give unto thee most hearty thanks, for that thou hast called me to be a professor of thee, even unto death. I beseech thee, Lord God, take mercy upon this realm of England, and deliver the same from all her enemies."

Then the smith took a chain of iron, and brought the same about both Dr. Ridley's and master Latimer's middles: and, as he was knocking in a staple, Dr. Ridley took the chain in his hand, and shaked the same, for it did gird in his belly, and looking aside to the smith, said, "Good fellow, knock it in hard, for the flesh will have his course." Then his brother did bring him gun-powder in a bag, and would have tied the same about his neck. Master Ridley asked, what it was. His brother said, "Gunpowder." "Then," said he, "I take it to be sent of God; therefore I will receive it as sent of him. And have you any," said he, "for my brother?" meaning master Latimer. "Yea sir, that I have," quoth his brother. "Then give it unto him," said he, "betime; lest ye come too late." So his brother went, and carried of the same gunpowder unto master Latimer.

In the mean time Dr. Ridley spake unto my lord Williams, and said, "My lord, I must be a suitor unto your lordship in the behalf of divers poor men, and especially in the cause of my poor sister: I have made a supplication to the queen's majesty in their behalves. I beseech your lordship for Christ's sake, to be a mean to her grace for them. My brother here hath the supplication, and will resort to your lordship to certify you hereof. There is nothing in all the world that troubleth my conscience, I praise God, this only excepted. Whilst I was in the see of London, divers poor men took leases of me, and agreed with me for the same. Now I hear say the bishop that now occupieth the same room, will not allow my grants unto them made, but contrary unto all law and conscience, hath taken from them their livings, and will not suffer them to enjoy the same. I beseech you, my lord, be a mean for them: you shall do a good deed, and God will reward you."

Then they brought a faggot, kindled with fire, and laid the same down at Dr. Ridley's feet. To whom master Latimer spake in this manner: "Be of good comfort, master Ridley, and play the man. We shall this day light such a candle, by God's grace, in England, as I trust shall never be put out."

And so the fire being given unto them, when Dr. Ridley saw the fire flaming up towards him, he cried with a wonderful loud voice, *"In manus tuas, Domine, commendo spiritum meum; Domine recipe spiritum meum."* And after, repeated this latter part often in English, "Lord, Lord, receive my spirit;" master Latimer crying as vehemently on the other side, "O Father of heaven, receive my soul!" who received the flame as it were embracing of it. After that he had stroked his face with his hands, and as it were bathed them a little in the fire, he soon died (as it appeared) with very little pain or none. And thus much concerning the end of this old and blessed servant of God, master Latimer, for whose laborious travails, fruitful life, and constant death, the whole realm hath cause to give great thanks to Almighty God.

But master Ridley, by reason of the evil making of the fire unto him, because the wooden faggots were laid about the gorse, and over-high built, the fire burned first beneath, being kept down by the wood; which when he felt, he desired them for Christ's sake to let the fire come unto him. Which when his brother-in-law heard, but not well understood, intending to rid him out of his pain (for the which cause he gave attendance), as one in such sorrow not well advised what he did, heaped faggots upon him, so that he clean covered him, which made the fire more vehement beneath, that it burned clean all his nether parts, before it once touched the upper; and that made him leap up and down under the faggots, and often desire them to let the fire come unto him, saying, "I cannot burn." Which indeed appeared well; for, after his legs were consumed by reason of his struggling through the pain (whereof he had no release, but only his contentation in God), he showed that side toward us clean, shirt and all untouched with flame. Yet in all this torment he forgot not to call unto God still, having his mouth, "Lord have mercy upon me," intermingling his cry, "Let the fire come unto me, I cannot burn." In which pangs he labored till one of the standers by with his bill pulled off the faggots above, and where he saw the fire flame up, he wrested himself unto that side. And when the flame touched the gunpowder, he was seen to stir no more, but burned on the other side, falling down at master Latimer's feet; which, some said, happened by reason that the chain loosed; others said, that he fell over the chain by reason of the poise of his body, and the weakness of the nether limbs.

Some said, that before he was like to fall from the stake, he desired them to hold him to it with their bills. However it was, surely it moved hundreds to tears, in beholding the horrible sight; for I think there was none that had not clean exiled all humanity and mercy, which would not have lamented to behold the fury of the fire so to rage upon their bodies. Signs there were of sorrow on every side. Some took it grievously to see their deaths, whose lives they held full dear: some pitied their persons, that thought their souls had no need thereof. His brother moved many men, seeing his miserable case, seeing (I say) him compelled to such infelicity, that he thought then to do him best service, when he hastened his end. Some cried out of the fortune, to see his endeavor (who most dearly loved him, and sought his release) turn to his greater vexation and increase of pain. But whoso considered their preferments in time past, the places of honor that they sometime occupied in this commonwealth, the favor they were in with their princes, and the opinion of learning they had in the university where they studied, could not choose but sorrow with tears, to see so great dignity, honor, and estimation, so necessary members sometime accounted, so many godly virtues, the study of so many years, such excellent learning, to be put into the fire, and consumed in one moment. Well! dead they are, and the reward of this world they have already. What reward remaineth for them in heaven, the day of the Lord's glory, when he cometh with his saints, shall shortly, I trust, declare. . . .[4]

But when he [Thomas Cranmer] came to the place where the holy bishops and martyrs of God, Hugh Latimer and Nicholas Ridley, were burnt before him for the confession of the truth, kneeling down, he prayed to God; and not long tarrying in his prayers, putting off his garments to his shirt, he prepared himself to death. His shirt was made long, down to his feet. His feet were bare; likewise his head.

. . . Then was an iron chain tied about Cranmer, whom when they perceived to be more steadfast than that he could be moved from his sentence, they commanded the fire to be set unto him.

And when the wood was kindled, and the fire began to burn near him, stretching out his arm, he put his right hand into the flame, which he held so steadfast and immovable (saving that once with the same hand he wiped his face), that all men might see his hand burned before his body was touched. His body did so abide the burning of the flame with such constancy and steadfastness, that standing always in one place without moving his body, he seemed to move no more than the stake to which he was bound; his eyes were lifted up into heaven, and oftentimes he repeated[,] "[t]his unworthy right hand," so long as his voice would suffer him; and using often the words of Stephen, "Lord Jesus, receive my spirit," in the greatness of the flame he gave up the ghost.[5]

---

1. Recommended sources with good bibliographies for further study of Latimer are Harold S. Darby, *Hugh Latimer* (London: The Epworth Press, 1953); and R. M. Carlyle and A. J. Carlyle, *Hugh Latimer* (London: Methuen and Co., 1899).

2. For further study of Ridley, a good source with an excellent bibliograhpy is Jasper Godwin Ridley, *Nicholas Ridley: A Biography* (London: Longmans, Green and Co., 1957).

3. For further study of Cranmer, see Jasper Ridley, *Thomas Cranmer* (Oxford: Oxford University Press, 1962); Ridley's work also has an excellent bibliography; see also Arthur James Mason, *Thomas Cranmer* (London: Methuen and Co., 1898).

4. John Foxe, *Actes and Monuments of These Latter and Perilous Dayes Touching Matters of the Church* (1563; revised rpt. 8 vols. London: Seeley, Burnside, and Seeley, 1843-49), VII:547-51. Volume one of this edition includes a "Life of the Martyrologist, and Vindication of the Work," by the Rev. George Townsend; for a good evaluation of Foxe's writings, along with a discussion of their impact, see William Haller, *The Elect Nation: The Meaning and Relevance of Foxe's Book of Martyrs* (NY: Harper & Row, 1963).

5. Foxe, VIII:89-90.

APPENDIX C

OVERVIEW OF OXFORD:
THE CITY AND THE UNIVERSITY:
THEIR PLACE IN PILGRIM HISTORY

The River Thames, on the west side, and Cherwell, on the east side, meander through Oxford and provide great natural beauty for this city of some 117,000 people. Oxford's original coat of arms contained an "ox" crossing a "ford." Across the bottom are the words *Fortis est Veritas* (Mighty is Truth). Added to the arms at a later time were a leopard, an elephant, and a beaver. With eight centuries of continuous existence, Oxford is the oldest English-speaking university in the world. The city itself is only a bit older than the university. There is no clear date of the university's beginnings, but teaching existed here in some form in 1096 and developed rapidly from 1167, when Henry II banned English students from attending the University of Paris. By 1201, the university was headed by a *magister scholarum Oxonie,* on whom the title of "chancellor" was conferred in 1214. In 1231 the masters were recognized as a *uniuersitas,* or corporation. It was also in the thirteenth century that rioting between town and gown (students and townspeople) hastened the establishment of primitive halls of residence. These were succeeded by the first of Oxford's "colleges," or endowed houses, whose architectural splendor, together with the university's libraries and museums, give the city its unique character. Balliol, Merton, and University Colleges, established between 1249 and 1264, are the three oldest. In 1355, King Edward III paid tribute to the university for its invaluable contribution to learning; he also commented on the services rendered to the state by distinguished Oxford graduates.

John Wyclif (c. 1320-1384), Morning Star of the Reformation, was Master of Balliol College when he called for a Bible translation in the language of the people. Today, across from Balliol College, on Broad Street, one can experience "The Oxford Story," an audio-visual introduction to the city. On St. Giles Street, the Martyrs' Memorial, designed by George Gilbert Scott and erected in the early 1840s, honors Protestant martyrs, Hugh Latimer, Nicholas Ridley, and Thomas Cramner. The scene of their trials was the University Church of St. Mary the Virgin, on High Street. A cross in the pavement of Broad Street marks the spot where in 1555-1556 the three martyrs were placed on stakes and burned to death in the city ditch (now Broad Street), under the reign of the Roman Catholic Queen Mary. Nearby, a plaque affixed to Balliol College wall reads:

Opposite this point
near the cross in the
middle of Broad Street

HUGH LATIMER
one-time Bishop of Worcester,

NICHOLAS RIDLEY
Bishop of London, and

THOMAS CRANMER
Archbishop of Canterbury,

were burnt for their faith
in 1555 and 1556.

From 1642 to 1646, during the Civil War, Oxford was the capital of Royalist England and headquarters of the king's army. Charles I took over the city and university, exploiting their resources to finance military campaigns. While the queen, Henrietta Maria, lodged at Merton College, the king lodged at Christ Church College, where he held his counter-Parliament. Following the War, Oliver Cromwell became chancellor and remained such until the Restoration of the Stuarts (Charles II) in 1660.

Meanwhile, the university's contribution to intellectual life during Cromwell's Interregnum was notable; for it was then that a group of mathematicians and scientists, including Robert Boyle and Sir Christopher Wren, began to meet at Wadham College, forming the nucleus of what was to become the Royal Society. Another Oxford graduate and professor, Sir Edmund Halley—astronomer, mathematician, and friend of Sir Isaac Newton—later became secretary of the society. John Penry, one the Separatist martyrs of 1593, received a degree in 1586 from St. Alban's Hall, which later merged with Merton College. Notable Puritans educated at Oxford included John Owen, Thomas Manton, John Jewell, John Howe, John Davenport, and Henry Jacob (Separatist founder of London's J-L-J Church, which gave rise to the English Particular Baptist movement). In the late seventeenth century, the Oxford philosopher John Locke, suspected of treason, was forced to flee the country.

John Wesley (1703-1791) was educated in Christ Church College on St. Aldate's Street. Here, the Christ Church chapel serves as "Oxford Cathedral," the only college chapel in the world designated as a cathedral. Above its main gate, "Tom Tower" houses Great Tom, the bell which rings 101 times every night at 9:00 PM to commemorate the original number of Christ Church scholars. In Wesley's day, the same bell tolling signaled the time for closing the gate; latecomers were required to pay a "gate fee." The Christ Church picture gallery offers a huge collection of the Old Masters. Several years after his graduation, John Wesley returned to Oxford and served as a Fellow of Lincoln College, on Turl Street, where he joined the "Holy Club" with his brother Charles and his friend George Whitefield. John Wesley's room in Lincoln College can be visited at designated times. During the second half of the eighteenth century, Sir William Blackstone served as Professor of Law at Oxford, later became a member of Parliament, and wrote his *Commentaries on the Laws of England* (published in four volumes, 1765-1769). During the 1840s, the "Oxford Movement" or "Tractarian Movement," led by Cardinal John Henry Newman and John Keble, broke from the Anglican Church, led many Englishmen into the Church of Rome, and created an even greater "High Church" emphasis within the Church of England. Newman was vicar of the University Church of St. Mary the Virgin from 1828 to 1841.

How does Oxford function? Administratively, a chancellor serves as the ultimate figure head of the university, presiding over all major ceremonies. A vice-chancellor presides over council, an elected board of academics responsible for day-to-day governance of the university. The university's academic affairs are governed by a general board, whose chairman is elected every two years. The registrar is responsible for running the university's central administration. Thirty-nine independent, self-governing colleges are related to the university in a type of federation similar to the United States government. The colleges fiercely guard their own autonomy, and the university respects such autonomy. Each college is governed by a head of house and a number of fellows who are academics, specializing in a wide variety if disciplines. Most fellows also hold university posts. In addition to the colleges, there are six "Permanent Private Halls," which were founded by different Christian denominations, and still retain their religious charters. The halls have similar powers and duties as colleges. Thirty of the colleges and all six halls admit students for both undergraduate and graduate degrees. Seven colleges are for graduates only. All Souls College, having fellows only, admits only undergraduates, and Kellogg College specializes in part-time and continuing education. Since 1974, all but one of Oxford's colleges have admitted both men and women. St. Hilda's remains the only women's college.

Oxford University has no "campus" *per se*. Most of the buildings are located within an approximate one-square-mile area in the heart of the city. There are about 14,000 students, including about 4,000 graduate students and around 5,000 women students. Graduation ceremonies are held in the Sheldonian Theatre, designed like a Roman theatre by Sir Christopher Wren and built in 1669. Especially noticeable are the heads of the thirteen emperors along the fence outside. A nice view of the city's spires can be seen from the cupola on the top of this building. Bodleian Library, the most famous library at Oxford, is one of only six British libraries entitled to a copy of every book published in the United Kingdom. It houses some six million books and 50,000 manuscripts. Here, books cannot be borrowed, only read. The classical, domed building, Radcliffe Camera (built in 1737), is a reading room of the Bodleian. ("Camera" was the medieval term for "room.") Oxford Divinity School's fifteenth-century Gothic building is used as an exhibition room for the Bodleian. The vaulted ceiling of the Divinity School has been described as the most beautiful room in Europe. The room's treasures include a 1478 William Caxton folio, thought to be the first book ever printed in England.

C. S. Lewis taught at Oxford for many years. One week before his sixty-fifth birthday, Lewis died in his Oxford home, the Kilns, on Friday November 22, 1963, at 5:30 P.M., the same day on which John F. Kennedy was assassinated.

In the following chart, PPH signifies the Permanent Private Halls.

THE OXFORD COLLEGES AND HALLS:	
All Souls College	Oriel College
Balliol College	Pembroke College
Blackfriars (PPH)	Regent's Park College (PPH)
Brasenose College	Somerville College
Campion Hall (PPH)	St. Anne's College
Christ Church	St. Antony's College
Corpus Christi College	St. Benet's Hall (PPH)
Exeter College	St. Catherine's College
Green College	St. Cross College
Greyfriars (PPH)	St. Edmund Hall
Harris Manchester College	St. Hilda's College
Hertford College	St. Hugh's College
Jesus College	St. John's College
Keble College	St. Peter's College
Kellogg College	Templeton College
Lady Margaret Hall	The Queen's College
Linacre College	Trinity College
Lincoln College	University College
Magdalen College	Wadham College
Mansfield College	Wolfson College
Merton College	Worcester College
New College	Wycliffe Hall (PPH)
Nuffield College	

APPENDIX D

UNIVERSITY OF CAMBRIDGE:
PURITANS, PILGRIMS, AND NOW

The University of Cambridge is the second oldest university in Great Britain, after the University of Oxford. Cambridge University is a system of thirty-one independent Colleges and collegiate institutions:

College:	Date Founded:	College:	Date Founded:
Christ's	1505	Magdalene	1428
Churchill	1960	New Hall (women)	1954
Clare	1326	Newnham (women)	1871
Clare Hall (grad)	1966	Pembroke	1347
Corpus Christi	1352	Peterhouse	1284
Darwin (grad)	1964	Queens'	1448
Downing	1800	Robinson	1979
Emmanuel	1584	St. Catherine's	1473
Fitzwilliam	1966	St. Edmund's	1896
Girton	1869	St. John's	1511
Gonville and Caius	1348	Selwyn	1882
Homerton	1976	Sidney Sussex	1596
Hughes Hall	1885	Trinity	1546
Jesus	1497	Trinity Hall	1350
King's	1441	Wolfson	1965
Lucy Cavendish (women over 21)			1965

Students from the Universities of Oxford and Paris left to study in Cambridge in the thirteenth century. The origin of Cambridge University is traced to these associations of students, who resided in hostels, or halls. Over the centuries these halls were endowed by private benefactors, beginning with Hugh de Balsham, Bishop of Ely, who in 1284 founded Peterhouse as the first of Cambridge's colleges. In 1318 Pope John XXII issued a bull recognizing Cambridge as a *studium generale* (general place of study), or "university." Five new colleges were established during the fourteenth century, four in the fifteenth, and six in the sixteenth; not until the nineteenth century were other colleges founded.

The University of Cambridge figured prominently in the Protestant Reformation. The Dutch scholar Desiderius Erasmus was a professor of Greek and divinity at Cambridge from 1511 to 1514. The reformers William Tyndale, Hugh Latimer, and Thomas Cranmer were educated at Cambridge, as were Oliver Cromwell and John Milton. During the reign of Queen Elizabeth I Cambridge became a stronghold of Puritanism. The Cambridge University Press was established in 1521. It was during this century that the university became the real nursery of the English Puritan movement. Separatist Henry Barrowe received his education at Clare College, and William Brewster took a copy of Barrowe's *Brief Discoverie of the False Church* to Plymouth Colony. Separatists John Penry and William Brewster trained together at Peterhouse College. Separatists Robert Browne, John Greenwood, and John Robinson were educated at Corpus Christi College. Puritan theologian John Preston trained and taught at Queen's College and Emmanuel College. The Puritan-Presbyterian Thomas Brightman graduated at Queen's College. Brightman's commentaries made a powerful impact upon his age. William Brewster printed Brightman's collected commentaries on the *Apocalypse, Daniel and the Canticles* in one volume and brought it with him on the *Mayflower.*

Puritan theologian William Ames studied at Christ's College and served as a chaplain there. Ames went to the Netherlands in 1611 and remained there for the rest of his life, serving as a chaplain to English troops at the Hague, teaching divinity at Franeker in Friesland, attending the Synod of Dort, and ministering to the English church in Rotterdam. The Pilgrims knew him well and used his *Medulla Theologica* (1623) in Plymouth. One of William Ames' Cambridge teachers in Christ's College was William Perkins, whose preaching and scholarship were held in the highest regard by the Pilgrims. John Robinson later edited Perkins' *Catechism,* recommending it as "fully containing what every Christian is to believe touching God and himself." Robinson saw to it that it became the standard handbook of the Pilgrim church. William Brewster published a volume of Perkins' sermons and brought eleven of his treatises on board the *Mayflower.* The Puritan Thomas Goodwin, known for his outstanding commentaries, received his education at Christ's College. English Separatists who trained at Christ's College included Richard Clyfton of Babworth, John Smyth of Gainsborough, and Francis Johnson of the Ancient Church of Amsterdam. William Brewster took three of Johnson's books to Plymouth Plantation. Emmanuel College provided training for New England Puritans John Winthrop (first governor of Massachusetts), John Cotton (former fellow who founded Boston, Massachusetts), Thomas Hooker (founder of Connecticut), John Harvard (contributor to the college named for him), Nathaniel Ward (pastor in Agawam or Ipswich, Massachusetts), and Thomas Shepard. Roger Williams, founder of the First Baptist Church in America, was an Emmanuel College graduate. Still other notable Cambridge men include Henry Ainsworth, the Separatist; John Lathrop, the Independent Separatist of London's J-L-J Church; William Bradshaw, whose *English Puritanism* (1605) is one of the earliest accounts of English nonconformity; and Thomas Cartwright, fellow of St. John's and Trinity Colleges and Father of English Presbyterianism. William Brewster's library included several volumes by Cartwright.

The Cambridge colleges are independent, self-governing corporate bodies, with their own property and income, distinct from the university. Each college, however, is part of an integrated educational entity. Each college regulates its affairs by its own statutes, which can be altered only after consultation with the university and approval of the queen in Council. The colleges are also bound by some university statutes. The governing body of each college consists of a master (provost, president, principal, warden or mistress) and a number of fellows. Every Cambridge student must belong to a college. The academic year is divided into three terms of approximately eight weeks each: autumn, late winter, and spring. Charles, Prince of Wales, studied at Trinity College (as did his forebears Edward VII and George VI), receiving his degree in June 1970. The individual colleges confer all Bachelor of Arts degrees upon satisfactory completion of nine terms (three years), of residency. Candidates for degrees with honors (the majority of students), must take a special examination called the "tripos," named for the three-legged stools on which examiners once sat. Successful candidates for triposes are classified according to their examination results—first, second, or third class. The university itself confers all Master of Arts and Doctor of Philosophy degrees, most of which are in law, theology, medicine, science, and music. The most notable twentieth-century change in the colleges was the introduction of co-residence for men and women; there are now twenty-eight mixed colleges, and three for women only. State aid has been granted to all British universities since 1926.

APPENDIX E

RECONCILING THOSE CONFLICTING CALENDAR DATES

Until 1752, England and her colonies used the Julian Calendar (begun under Julius Caesar in 46 BC), which started the New Year on March 25 and was based on a miscalculation of the length of a year by eleven minutes and fourteen seconds (making a difference of one day every 128 years). In 1582, the time of Pope Gregory XIII, when the Julian Calendar had gotten ten days behind the solar year, a group of brilliant astronomers and mathematicians created the New Style (N.S.) "Gregorian Calendar," adjusting the astronomical errors of the old Julian calendar. They simply advanced the 1582 calendar ten days (omitting October 5 through 14), in conformity with the solar year, and started the New Year at January 1. England refused to use "the Pope's calendar" for the period from 1582 to 1752. This explains why historical markers and books often use double dates for any dates of that period falling between January 1 and March 24. For example, the date March 5, 1621/2 (O.S.) means it was March 5, 1621 to the Pilgrims, since the New Year would not occur until March 25. The same date expressed in New Style would be March 15, 1622 (N.S.). Just remember, when a reference has an O.S. date you must add ten days to get the modern (N.S.) equivalent. I always translate the O.S. dates into N.S. dates, so that they can relate more readily to our own calendars.

By the way, in order finally to make that transition to the N.S. Gregorian calendar, the British and Americans simply advanced the 1752 calendar eleven days (omitting September 3 through 13), in conformity with the solar year, and started their New Year at January 1. Many then complained that the new calendar had robbed their lives of eleven days!

APPENDIX F

PILGRIM WALKING TOUR OF LEIDEN:
LEIDEN AMERICAN PILGRIM MUSEUM
(copyrighted, 1999 edition)

The Museum occupies the ground floor of a beautiful, restored
fifteenth-century house at Beschuitsteeg 9, in front of the tower
of the medieval Hooglandse kerk.

Used by permission of Dr. Jeremy D. Bangs, Director.

Mailing address: Mandenmakerssteeg 11, 2311 ED Leiden, The Netherlands

Beginning in front of the—
LEIDEN AMERICAN PILGRIM MUSEUM: House built ca. 1375, probably as a residence for priests of the Hooglandsekerk.

HOOGLANDSEKERK: Built in the 15th century; the clock tower remains from an earlier smaller church of the first half of the 14th century.

Turning left in front of the tower, walk one block and enter the arch with the lion on top, to see the—
BURCHT: Castle of the medieval viscounts of Leiden, built ca. 1200 to replace an earlier wooden castle on the man-made hill, which is probably from the 10th or 11th century.

Leaving under the lion arch, turn right and walk one block to the covered bridge—
COORNBRUG (Corn Bridge): First bridge over the Rijn River at Leiden. The markets held here on Wednesdays and Saturdays have been here continuously since the 13th century and are the oldest in Holland.

From the Coornbrug there is a view to the Visbrug and beyond it, to the Weigh House. This is where the city crane unloaded all the boats that brought produce for Leiden's markets. Here, also, the passenger boats that provided regular service two or three times a week to the other Dutch cities loaded and unloaded. The Pilgrims landed by the city crane when they arrived from Amsterdam on May Day, 1609.

Continue one block beyond the bridge to the Breestraat and turn right for a view of the—
STADHUIS (Town Hall): Facade 1595; represents the attempt to revive Leiden's importance as a commercial center after the fall of Antwerp to Catholic armies in 1585 and the closing of Antwerp's port. The money for the new town hall was arranged by the leading banker of the Walloon refugees, Daniel van der Meulen. He nominated the architect, Lieven de Key, also a refugee, and the sculptor, Luder van Benthem, who altered the designs while carving the facade stones at his quarry near Bremen in Germany. Various Pilgrim couples were married in civil ceremonies before magistrates in Leiden's city hall—for example, William Bradford and Dorothy May's marriage was registered here.

Walking along the front of the city hall to the far end, across the street is the carved doorway of the—
PENSHAL (Tripe Market): Entry, dated 1607, to the market for cheap meat where liver, tripe, kidneys, etc. were sold, as well as chickens and rabbits. More expensive meat was sold in the main meat market across the street. Poorer people, such as many of the Pilgrims, could only afford the cheaper fare available in the Tripe Market.

Beyond the Penshal at the next corner, in the middle of the Breestraat is the—
BLAUWESTEEN (Blue Stone): In the center of the Breestraat, an old Roman road that marked the northern boundary of the Roman Empire; the Blue Stone was the place of justice in early medieval Leiden. Thieves had fingers cut off; faulty products were burned here. There was also a stone pedestal on the front on the town hall where gossips and scolds had to stand for a set length of time to be jeered at.

Looking farther down the Breestraat, the 17th-cent. house with pillars and carving is the "Vergulden Turk"—
JAN VAN HOUT'S HOUSE (to the right of the Vergulden Turk): Where William Brewster must have gone to discuss obtaining permission for the Pilgrims to stay in Leiden. The English poet Sir Philip Sidney stayed here as a guest of Jan van Hout in 1586, and Brewster probably met both Sidney and van Hout then. Brewster was an assistant Sir William Davison, England's Secretary of State, who was visiting Leiden at the same time as Sidney.

DE VERGULDEN TURK (The Gilded Turk): The mansion of a wealthy merchant. The figures in the gable, Neptune and Mercury, gods of the sea and of communication, and the turbanned Turk, suggest that the merchant traded with Constantinople. The first Dutch trader with Constantinople on a large scale was Bartholomeus van Panhuysen of Leiden. Van Panhuysen was a family connection of van der Meulen, the merchant banker who organized the construction of the new front of the town hall.

Farther down the Breestraat one can see the bell tower of—
DE WAALSE KERK (Walloon Church): Now used by the Walloon church (French-speaking Protestants), in Pilgrim times it was the chapel of the St. Catharine's Hospital. Myles Standish is mentioned in a list of soldiers who were taken care of in this hospital in 1601, although his name was mis-spelled as "Myls Stansen." The Pilgrims found much in common with these French Reformed churches in the Netherlands.

Turning off the Breestraat at the intersection where the Blue Stone is, we—
Enter the PIETERSKERKKOORSTEEG: The Hunkemoller building is Leiden's oldest complete house, dating from ca. 1300.

The first cross street is called the—
LANGE BRUG: Originally an open canal, it was vaulted over in the early seventeenth century and then became known as the Lange Brug, or Long Bridge. Pilgrim James Chilton and his family lived here, although exactly where is unknown. In 1619, coming home from church, he was surrounded by stone-throwing youths. Hit by a paving stone or brick, he was knocked unconscious. The crowd had attacked him and his daughter because it was suspected that illegal religious gatherings of the Arminians (called Remon-strants) were being held in the Chilton's house.

Continuing in the PIETERSKERKKOORSTEEG: The Leiden burgomaster and historian, and also book publisher, Jan Orlers, lived here, just around the corner from William Brewster, whose house opened onto the alley now called the William Brewstersteeg.

Turning into the little alley through the archway on the right, we walk along the—
WILLIAM BREWSTERSTEEG. It was here that Brewster and his assistant Edward Winslow printed books that were forbidden in England. Many were smuggled into England for distribution there. Others were sold at the Frankfurt Book Fair, taken along by Orlers. Through pressure exerted by the English ambassador, the Pilgrims' printing activities were suppressed. Brewster was arrested along with Thomas Brewer, who had helped finance the printing projects. Brewster was released by Leiden's sheriff, which angered the English. Brewster went into hiding in the next village, Leiderdorp, and escaped further pursuit by emigrating to New England in 1620 on the *Mayflower.*

At the end of the alley, turn left in another alley leading to the Pieterskerkstraat and a view of the—
LOKHORSTKERK: an example of a "hidden church," the actual church was built behind houses in the 17th century, so that it was not visible from the street. Those houses were replaced in 1860 by the present entrance. This church was built by Mennonites, who were already here when the Pilgrims arrived. Now the church is also used by the Remonstrants, a denomination that was organized in 1619 by the followers of Jacobus Arminius, after they were forced out of the Dutch Reformed Church. Other groups that had hidden churches in Leiden included Lutherans and Catholics.

Passing in front of the Lokhorskerk, at the corner turn left and walk one block. On the right is the—
LATIJNSE SCHOOL (Latin School): While the Pilgrims lived in Leiden, the Latin School prepared students for university study. Rembrandt was a pupil here. The school was founded in the middle ages to provide training for the boys' choir of the Pieterskerk. The music sung before the Reformation was famous throughout Europe, and the church was visited by other choirs in the 16th century, including the cathedral of San Marco in Venice. The Latin School received a new facade in 1599. In the Schoolsteeg (School Alley) there was a Jesuit "hidden church" in Pilgrim times.

Farther along the open square, on the left is the—
GRAVENSTEEN. This was the residence of the Counts of Holland around 1200, before they moved their residence to The Hague. It later became a prison and presently is part of the Law School of the University of Leiden. Many Protestants were martyred here under the Inquisition.

To the left of the Gravensteen is a short alley called the—
MUSCADELSTEEG: Rembrandt may have shared a studio here with the painter Jan Lievens.

Going through the Muscadelsteeg, we reach the Pieterskerk and walk into the churchyard in front of it.—
PIETERSKERK: The present church was built between 1390 and 1565; different parts were designed by several of the most famous architects in the Low Countries. It contains an important organ from 1637, parts of which date from the 15th and 16th centuries. Many famous university professors are buried here, as well as the printer Jan Steen and the Pilgrims' minister John Robinson.

PIETERSKERKHOF (churchyard): The theologian Jacobus Arminius lived in a house facing the church. The white house on the corner of the Kloksteeg was where the family of Pilgrim Thomas Rogers lived briefly while he and his son Joseph went to Plymouth on the *Mayflower* in 1620. Thomas died during the first winter but other family members later joined Joseph. Thomas Brewer lived in the house with the stepped gable on the opposite side of the Kloksteeg. The tall Pieterskerk tower at the west front of the church collapsed in 1512, but the bell was unbroken and was hung in a stubby free-standing tower at the corner of the church yard, giving the name Bell Alley or Kloksteeg to the street. Brewer was a friend of the Pilgrims and provided financial support for William Brewster's printing activities. The minister of the English Reformed Church, a friend of the Pilgrims, lived in Brewer's house.

On the far side of the churchyard is the formal entrance to the almshouse called the—
JEAN PESYNHOF: Built in 1683 on the spot where the Pilgrims' minister John Robinson's house was. The Pilgrims built 21 small houses in the garden behind Robinson's house. These were smaller than the dwellings that

are now part of the almshouse. It is possible to see the chapel of the Begijnhof from the almshouse garden. The almshouse was built for members of the Walloon church, through a legacy from Jean Pesyn and his wife Marie de la Noy, who was probably a distant relative of Philip Delanoy, the Pilgrim ancestor of Franklin Delano Roosevelt. You may view the garden, but please respect the quiet of the residents.

From the almshouse, enter the alley leading away from the church, and walk one block to the canal.—
CORNER OF KLOKSTEEG AND RAPENBURG: In Pilgrim times this pub (Barerra) was an English book shop operated by the publishers Thomas and Govert Basson. Although the Bassons were friends of John Robinson, Govert Basson supported the followers of Arminius (whom Robinson opposed) and Govert Basson published the complete writings Arminius in 1617.

ACADEMIEGEBOUW: Theological debates were held in the lower room on the right end of this medieval convent chapel, which is the oldest part of the University of Leiden. This is probably where Robinson debated with Arminius's successor Simon Episcopius. Now the room is part of the Museum of University History. Gomarus, the strict Calvinist opponent of Arminius, lived across the bridge in the Nonnensteeg.

Turning left without crossing the bridge, follow the Rapenburg canal and notice the—
STEPS DOWN TO THE WATER: These steps may have been used by the Pilgrims to embark on the boats that took them to Delfshaven, although the boats ordinarily started at the Weigh House center of town.

A little farther along the curve of the canal, just past a fenced garden is an alley leading to the—
BEGIJNHOFKAPEL (Beguinage Chapel): This chapel was used by the university for its library and anatomy theater. The Pilgrims were allowed to use a large groundfloor room on Sundays in the last years of their stay in Leiden, when religious meetings in private homes were made illegal.

Farther along the curving Rapenburg canal, on the opposite side is an arched bridge over the—

VLIET RIVER: The Pilgrims began their migration to America in 1620, departing Leiden in boats that went along the Vliet River to Delfshaven, where they got on their ship the *Speedwell*. The *Speedwell* took them to England, where they met the *Mayflower,* which their agents had hired. Both ships were intended to go to America, but the *Speedwell* was leaky, and so the ships turned back and many *Speedwell* passengers got on the *Mayflower* which continued on alone to America. Some passengers came back to Leiden, and joined other Leiden Pilgrims in the later ships, *Fortune, Anne, Little James,* and another ship also called the *Mayflower.*

A small house on the left as we continue along the Rapenburg has a carved coat-of-arms. This is the—
HOUSE OF THE VAN DUIVENBODE BROTHERS: Two brothers who kept carrier pigeons lived here. Their pigeons were used during the Siege of Leiden in 1573-1574 to send and bring messages between the people in Leiden and the navy of William of Orange, which eventually was able to sail up to the city walls to relieve the siege, once they had flooded the farmland south of town. The city granted the coat of arms seen on the house to the brothers to commemorate their contribution to the city; and the brothers took the surname "van Duivenbode" which means "of the carrier pigeons."

A larger house farther along the Rapenburg, identified by a stone inscription, was—
JEAN LUZAC'S HOUSE: America's first ambassador, the future president John Adams, visited Leiden's publisher Jean Luzac in the 1780s here, where the French-language "Gazette de Leyde" was produced. That newspaper carried favorable news and editorials about the American Revolution, distributed throughout Europe. Luzac was killed in 1807, when a boat full of gunpowder exploded further along the canal, destroying about eight square blocks of houses and killing 155 people.

Crossing the bridge, we enter the—
VAN DER WERFF PARK: The gunpowder explosion cleared the space for this park. The Kamerlingh-Onnes laboratory, across the canal, was the center of Leiden University's pioneering physics research into temperatures near absolute zero.

The elaborate tower across the canal belongs to the—
LODEWIJKSKERK (Church of St. Louis): Built as a hospice chapel for a stopping place on the medieval pilgrimage route to Santiago da Compostella in Spain, the building became a guildhall after the Reformation. William Bradford belonged to the cloth guild that met here, and this was where cloth approved by the guild was sold. When the chapel was spared on the edge of the destruction caused by the gunpowder explosion, it once again became a Roman Catholic church. It was renamed after St. Louis, the patron saint of France, to honor Louis Napoleon, who had been appointed king of the Netherlands by his brother, the French Emperor Napoleon. Louis Napoleon had personally come from The Hague to help in the rescue efforts the day after the explosion, which could be heard as far away as The Hague, Delft, and Amsterdam.

At the end of the park, a small street next to a parking lot is the beginning of the—
LEVENDAAL: Somewhere on this canal, now filled in, Pilgrim Francis Cook and Hester Mahieu lived. They were among the French-speaking Protestants who joined the English Pilgrims in Leiden. Here also is Leiden's Synagogue, whose congregation was founded in the 18th century, although there are references to Jews in Leiden as early as the 15th century.

*To return to the **Leiden American Pilgrim Museum,** turn left at the Synagogue, then right at the first intersection. Walk about half a block to the Nieuwe Rijn River. Follow the River to the footbridge you can see. This footbridge takes you to the Beschuitsteg, where the museum is # 9. The museum is open Wednesday through Saturday, 1:00 - 5:00 PM.*

Another important Pilgrim site is the Vrouwekerk, whose picturesque ruins still stand in the public square in front of the Boerhaave Museum, just north of the Haarlemmerstraat. In Pilgrim times, this was the Walloon Church (now the congregation uses a small chapel on the Breestraat instead). Francis Cook and Hester Mahieu were married here in 1603, and their nephew Philipe de la Noye (Philip Delano) was baptized here the same year. These Pilgrims became ancestors of United States presidents Ulysses S. Grant, Franklin Delano Roosevelt, and George H. W. Bush. The church is presently threatened with imminent demolition. One of Leiden's aldermen, responsible for urban development, considers the ruin an eyesore in the way of the view from a modern commercial property which he wants as a replacement for the medieval houses across the street from the ruin. See this historic site before it is flattened for short-term profit.

APPENDIX G

EIGHTEEN TITLES PRINTED BY WILLIAM BREWSTER'S PILGRIM PRESS IN LEIDEN

One of the books is in Dutch; four are in Latin; and thirteen are in English.

1. *Thien Gheboden etc.* (A Dutch Version of Dod and Cleaver's *Tenne Commandments*) Anno 1617.

2. *Guil. Amesii ad Responsum Nic. Grevinchovii Rescriptio Contracta etc.* In Vico Chorale 1617.

3. *Commentarii Succincti & Dilucide in Proverbia Salomonis.* Authore Thoma Cartwrighto SS. etc. In Vico Chorali. 1617.

4. *An Abridgement of that Booke Which the Ministers of Lincolne Diocesse Delivered to His Maiesti Upon the first of December 1605 etc.* Reprinted Anno Domini. 1617.

5. *A Plaine and Familiar Exposition of the Tenne Commandments With a Methodicall Short Catechisme* . . . by the Author, Mr. John Dod etc. Printed Anno Dom. 1617.

6. *An Admonition to the Parliament Holden in the 13 Yeare of the Reigne of Queene Elizabeth of Blessed Memorie etc.* Imprinted Anno 1617.

7. *A Full and Plaine Declaration of Ecclesiastical Discipline out of the Word of God, and of the Declining of the Church of England from the Same.* (Travers). Reprinted, Anno 1617.

8. *De Vera et Genuina Jesu Christi Domini et Salvatoris Nostri Religione* Authore Minist. Angl. Impressus Anno Dom. 1618.

9. *De Regimine Ecclesiae Scoticanae Brevis Relatio.* (Calderwood) Impressus Anno Dom. 1618.

10. *A True, Modest and Just Defence of the Petition for Reformation, Exhibited to the King's Most Excellent Maiestie. Containing an Answere to the Confutation Published under the Names of Some of the Universitie of Oxford etc.* Imprinted 1618.

11. *Certain Reasons of A Private Christian Against Conformitie to Kneeling in the Very Act of Receivng the Lord's Supper.* By Tho. Dighton Gent. Anno 1618.

12. *The Peoples' Plea For the Exercise of Prophesie. Against Mr. John Yates his Monopolie.* By John Robinson. Printed in the yeare 1618.

13. *A Little Treatise Upon The First Verse of the 122 Psalme etc.* By R. Harrison. Reprinted An. Dom. 1618.

14. *A Fruitful Sermon upon the 3, 4, 5, 6, 7 and 8 Verses of the 12 Chapter of the Epistle of S. Paul to the Romaines.* (Chaderton. Title page missing).

15. *A Confutation of The Rhemists Translation, Glosses And Annotations on The New Testament etc. . . .* By that Reverend, Learned and Judicious Divine, Thomas Cartwright . . . Printed in the yeare 1618.

16. *The Second Part of a Plaine Discourse of An Unlettered Christian . . . in Refusing Conformity to Kneeling in the Act of Receivng the Lords Supper.* Printed in the yeare 1619.

17. *An Answer to the Ten Counter Demands Propounded by T. Drakes, Preacher of the Word at H. & D. in the County of Essex.* By Wil. Euring. Printed in the yeare 1619.

18. *Perth Assembly. Containing 1. The Proceedings thereof etc.* MDCXIX (Calderwood, D.).

An excellent source is Rendel Harris and Stephen K. Jones, *The Pilgrim Press: A Bibliographical & Historical Memorial of the Books Printed at Leyden by the Pilgrim Fathers* (Cambridge: W. Heffer and Sons, 1922), 72ff. Although not included by Harris and Jones, two others could have possibly been printed by Brewster's Press: *A Christian Plea* (1617) by Francis Johnson and *Apologia Justa et Necessaria* (1619) by John Robinson.

APPENDIX H

The Farewell Letter
from John Robinson to the Pilgrims

Dated July 27, 1620

Read at Southampton, England,
Just Prior to Their August 15 (N.S.) Departure:

Loving and Christian friends, I do heartily and in the Lord salute you all as being they with whom I am present in my best affection, and most earnest longings after you. Though I be constrained, God knowing how willingly and much rather than otherwise, I would have borne my part with you in this first brunt, were I not by strong necessity held back for the present. Make account of me in the meanwhile as of a man divided in myself with great pain, and as (natural bonds set aside) having my better part with you. And though I doubt not but in your godly wisdom you both foresee and resolve upon that which concerneth your present state and condition, both severally and jointly, yet have I thought it but my duty to add some further spur of provocation unto them who run already; if not because you need it, yet because I owe it in love and duty. And first, as we are daily to renew our repentance with our God, especially of our sins known, and generally for our unknown trespasses; so doth the Lord call us in a singular manner upon occasions of such difficulty and danger as lieth upon you, to a both more narrow search and careful reformation of your ways in His sight; lest He, calling to remembrance our sins forgotten by us or unrepented of, take advantage against us, and in judgment leave us for the same to be swallowed up on one danger or other. Whereas, on the contrary, sin being taken away by earnest repentance and the pardon thereof from the

Lord, sealed up unto a man's conscience by His Spirit, great shall be his security and peace in all dangers, sweet his comforts in all distresses, with happy deliverance from all evil, whether in life or in death.

Now, next after this heavenly peace with God and our own consciences, we are carefully to provide for peace with all men what in us lieth, especially with our associates. And for that, watchfulness must be had that we neither at all in ourselves do give, no, nor easily take offense being given by others. Woe be unto the world for offenses, for though it be necessary (considering the malice of Satan and man's corruption) that offenses come, yet woe unto the man, or woman either, by whom the offense cometh, saith Christ, Matthew xviii.7. And if offenses in the unseasonable use of things in themselves indifferent, be more to be feared than death itself (as the Apostle teacheth, I Corinthians ix.15) how much more in things simply evil, in which neither honour of God nor love of man is thought worthy to be regarded. Neither yet is it sufficient that we keep ourselves by the grace of God from giving offense, except withal we be armed against the taking of them when they be given by others. For how unperfect and lame is the work of grace in that person who wants charity to cover a multitude of offenses, as the Scriptures speak [I Peter 4:8]!

Neither are you to be exhorted to this grace only upon the common grounds of Christianity, which are, that persons ready to take offense either want charity to cover offenses, or wisdom duly to weigh human frailty; or lastly, are gross, though close hypocrites as Christ our Lord teacheth (Matthew vii.1, 2, 3), as indeed in my own experience few or none have been found which sooner give offense than such as easily take it. Neither have they ever proved sound and profitable members in societies, which have nourished this touchy humor.

But besides these, there are divers motives provoking you above others to great care and conscience this way: As first, you are many of you strangers, as to the persons so to the infirmities one of another, and so stand in end of more watchfulness this way, lest when such things fall out in men and women as you suspected not, you be inordinately affected with them; which doth require at your hands much wisdom and charity for the covering and preventing of incident offenses that way. And, lastly, your intended course of civil community will minister continual occasion of offense, and will be as fuel for that fire, except you diligently quench it with brotherly forbearance. And if taking of offense causelessly or easily at men's doings be so carefully to be avoided, how much more heed is to be taken that we take not offense at God Himself, which yet we certainly do so oft as we do murmur at His providence in our crosses, or bear impatiently such afflictions as wherewith He pleaseth to visit us. Store up, therefore, patience against that evil day, without which we take offense at the Lord Himself in His holy and just works.

A fourth thing there is carefully to be provided for, to wit, that with your common employments you join common affections truly bent upon the general good, avoiding as a deadly plague of your both common and special comfort all retiredness of mind for proper advantage, and all singularly affected any manner of way. Let every man repress in himself and the whole body in each person, as so many rebels against the common good, all private respects of men's selves, not sorting with the general convenience. And as men are careful not to have a new house shaken with any violence before it be well settled and the parts firmly knit, so be you, I beseech you, brethren, much more careful that the house of God, which you are and are to be, be not shaken with unnecessary novelties or other oppositions at the first settling thereof.

Lastly, whereas you are become a body politic, using amongst yourselves civil government, and are not furnished with any persons of special eminence above the rest, to be chosen by you into office of government; let your wisdom and godliness appear, not only in choosing such persons as do entirely love and will promote the common good, but also in yielding unto them all due honour and obedience in their lawful administrations, not beholding in them the ordinariness of their persons, but God's ordinance for your good; not being like the foolish multitude who more honour the gay coat than either the virtuous mind of the man, or glorious ordinance of the Lord. But you know better things, and that the image of the Lord's power and authority which the magistrate beareth [Romans 13:4], is honourable, in how mean persons soever. And this duty you both may the more willingly and ought the more conscionable to perform, because you are at least for the present to have only them for your ordinary governors, which yourselves shall make choice of for that work.

Sundry other things of importance I could put you in mind of and of those before mentioned in more words, but I will not so far wrong your godly minds as to think you heedless of these things, there being also divers among you so well able to admonish both themselves and others of what concerneth them. These few things, therefore, and the same in few words I do earnestly commend unto your care and conscience, joining therewith my daily incessant prayers unto the Lord, that He who hath made the heavens and the earth, the sea and all rivers of waters, and whose providence is over all His works, especially over all His dear children for good, would so guide and guard you in your ways, as inwardly by His Spirit, so outwardly by the hand of His power, as that both you and we also, for and with you, may have after matter of praising his name all the days of your and our lives. Fare you well in Him whom you trust, and in whom I rest.

An unfeigned wellwiller of your happy success in this hopeful voyage,

John Robinson

Source:
William Bradford, *Of Plymouth Plantation 1620-1647,* ed. Samuel Eliot Morison (1952; rpt. NY: Alfred A. Knopf, 1998), 368-71.

APPENDIX I

The Peirce Patent (1621):

The second *Peirce Patent,* issued June 1, 1621, confirmed and super-seded the *Mayflower Compact.* The original document is in Pilgrim Hall Museum in Plymouth, Massachusetts. With rare and slight editing, the text below is from William Bradford, *Of Plimmoth Plantation,* ed. Worthington C. Ford (Boston: Massachusetts Historical Society, 1912), I:246-51. The text contains almost no punctuation, and this has been left unchanged below. The few changes include "Yf" being changed to "If," and "vnto" being changed to "unto." Most other editing appears in brackets. The text is as follows:

> This Indenture made the First Day of June 1621 And in the yeeres of the raigne of our soveraigne Lord James by the grace of god King of England Scotland Fraunce and Ireland defendor of the faith etc. That is to say of England Fraunce and Ireland the Nyne-tenth and of Scotland the fowre and fiftith. Betwene the President and Counsell of New England of the one partie And John Peirce Citizen and Clothworker of London and his Associates of the other partie Witnesseth that whereas the said John Peirce and his Associates have already transported and undertaken to transporte at their cost and chardges themselves and dyvers persons into New England and there to erect and build a Towne and settle dyvers Inhabitantes for the advancemt of the generall plantacon of that Country of New England Now the sayde President and Coun-sell in consideracon thereof and for the furtherance of the said plantacon and incoragemt of the said Undertakers have agreed to

graunt assigne allott and appoynt to the said John Peirce and his associates and every of them his and their heires and assignes one hundred acres of grownd for every person so to be transported besides dyvers other pryviledges Liberties and commodyties hereafter menconed. And to that intent they have graunted allotted assigned and confirmed, And by theis pre[sen]ntes doe graunt allott assigne and confirme unto the said John Peirce and his Associates his and their heirs and assignes and the heires and assignes of every of them severally and respectivelie one hundred severall acres of grownd in New England for every person so transported or to be transported, If the said John Peirce or his Associates contynue there three whole yeeres either at one or severall tymes or dye in the meane season after he or they are shipped with intent there to inhabit. The same Land to be taken and chosen by them their deputies or assignes in any place or plaes wheresoever not already inhabited by any English and where no English person or persons are already placed or settled or have by order of the said President and Councell made choyce of, nor within Tenne myles of the same, unles it be the opposite syde of some great or Navigable Ryver to the former particuler plantacon, together with the one half of the Ryver or Ryvers, that is to say to the middest thereof, as shall adjoyne to such landes as they shall make choyce of together with all such Liberties pryviledges proffittes and commodyties as the said Land and Ryvers which they shall make choyce of shall yeild together with free libertie to fishe in and upon the Coast of New England and in all havens portes and creekes Thereunto belonging and that no person or persons whatsoever shall take any benefitt or libertie of or to any of the grownds or the one half of the Ryvers aforesaid, excepting the free use of highwayes by land and Navigable Ryvers, but that the said undertakers and planters their heirs and assignes shall have the sole right and use of the said grownds and the one half of the said Ryvers with all their proffittes and appurtennces. And forasmuch as the said John Peirce and his associates intend to have undertaken to build Churches, Schooles, Hospitalls Towne howses, Bridges and such like workes of Charytie As also for the maynteyning of Magistrates and other inferior Officers, In regard whereof and to the end that the said John Peirce and his Associates his and their heires and assignes may have wherewithall to beare and support such like charges. Therefore the said President and Councell aforesaid to graunt unto the said Undertakers their heires and assignes Fifteene hundred acres of Land more over and above the aforesaid proporcon of one hundred the person for every undertaker and Planter to be imployed upon such publique uses and the said Undertakers and Planters shall thinck fitt. And they do further graunt unto the said John Peirce and his Associates their heires and assignes, that for every person that they or any of them shall transport at their owne proper costes and charges into New England either unto the Lands hereby graunted or adjoyninge to them within Seaven Yeeres after the feast of St. John Baptist next comming If the said person transported contynue there three whole yeeres either at one or severall tymes or dye in the mean season after he is shipped with intent there to inhabit that the said person or persons that shall so at his or their owne charges transport any other shall have graunted and allowed to him and them and his and their heires respectyvelie for every person so transported or dyeing after he is shipped one hundred acres of Land, and also that every person or persons who by contract and agream[en]t to be had and made with the said Undertakers shall at his and their owne charge transport him and themselves or any other and setle and plant themselves in New England within the said Seaven Yeeres for three yeeres space as aforesaid or dye in the mean tyme shall have graunted and allowed unto every person so transporting or transported and their heires and assignes respectyvely the like nomber of one hundred acres of Land as aforesaid the same to be by him and them or their heires and assignes chosen in any entyre place together and adjoyning to the aforesaid Landes and not straglingly not before the type of such choyce made possessed or inhabited by any English Company or within tenne myles of the same, except it be on the opposite side of some great Navigable Ryver as aforesaid Yeilding and paying unto the said President and Counsell for every hundred acres so obteyned and possessed by the said John Peirce and his said Associates and by those said other persons and their heires and assignes who by Contract as aforesaid shall at their owne charges transport themselves or others the Yerely rent of Two shillings at the feast of St. Michaell Tharchaungell to the hand of the Rentgatherer of the said President and Counsell and their successors forever, the first payment to begyn after the expiracon of the first seaven Yeeres next after the date hereof And further it shal be lawfull to and for the said John Peirce and his Associates and such as contract with them as aforesaid their Tennantes and servantes upon dislike of or in the Country to returne for England or elsewhere with all their goodes and chattells at their will and pleasure without lett or disturbaunce of any paying all debtes that justly shalbe demaunded And likewise it shalbe lawfull and is graunted to and for the said John Peirce and his Associates and Planters their heires and assignes their Tennantes and servantes and such as they or any of them shall contract with as aforesaid and send and imploy for the said plantacon to goe and returne trade traffique inport or transport their goodes and merchaundize at their will and pleasure into England or elswhere paying onely such dueties to the Kinges ma[jes]tie his heires and succesors as the President and Counsell of New England doe pay without any other taxes Imposicons burthens or restraintes whatsoever upon them to be imposed (the rent hereby reserved being onely excepted) And it shalbe lawfull for the said Undertakers and Planters, their heires and successors freely to truck trade and traffique with the Salvages in New England or neighboring thereabouts at their wills and pleasures without lett or disturbaunce. As also to have libertie to hunt hauke fish or fowle in any place or places not now or hereafter by the English inhabited. And the said President and Counsell do covenant and promyse to and with the said John Peirce and his Associates and others contracted with as aforesaid his and their heires and assignes, That upon lawfull survey to be had and made at the charge of the said Undertakers and Planters and lawfull informacon geven of the bowndes, meetes, and quantytie of Land so as aforesaid to be by them chosen and possessed they the said President and Counsell upon surrender of this p[rese]nte graunt and Indenture and upon reasonable request to be made by the said Undertakers and Planters their heires and assignes within seaven Yeeres now next coming, shall and will by their Deede Indented and under their Common seale graunt infeorre and confirme all and every the said landes so sett out and bownded as aforesaid to the firme all and every the said landes so sett out and bownded as afiresaid to the said John Peirce and his Associates and such as contract with them their heires and assignes in as large and beneficiall manner as the same are in theis p]rese]ntes graunted or intended to be graunted to all intentes and purposes with all and every particular pryviledge and freedome reservacon and condicon with all dependances herein specyfied and graunted. And shall also at any tyme within the said terme of Seaven Yeeres upon request unto the said President and Counsell made, graunt unto them the said John Peirce and his Associates Undertakers and Planters their heires and assignes, Letters and Grauntes of Incorporacon by some usuall and fitt name and tytle with Liberty to them and their successors from tyme to tyme to make orders Lawes Ordynaunces and Constitucons for the rule governement ordering and dyrecting of all persons to be transported and settled upon the landes hereby graunted, intended to be graunted or hereafter to be granted and of the said Landes and proffittes thereby arrysing. And in the meane tyme untill such graunt made, It shalbe lawfull for the said John Peirce his Associates Undertakers and Planters their heires and assignes by consent of the greater part of them to establish such lawes and ordynaunces as are for their better governemt, and the same by such Officer or Officers as they shall by most voyces elect and choose to put in execucon And lastly the said President and Counsell do graunt and agree to and with the said John Peirce and his Associates and others contracted with and imployed as aforesaid their heires and assignes, That when they have planted the Landes hereby to them assigned and appoynted, That then it shalbe lawfull for them with the pryvitie and allowaunce of the President and Counsell as aforesaid to make choyce of and to enter into and have an addition of fiftie acres more for every person transported into New England wiht like reservacons condicons and pryviledges as are above granted to be had and chosen in such place or places where no English shalbe then setled or inhabiting or have made choyce of and the same entered into a booke of Actes at the tyme of such choyce so to be made or within thenne Myles of the same, excepting on the opposite side of some great Navigable Ryver as aforesaid. And that it shall and may be lawfull for the said John Peirce and his Associates their heires and assignes from tyme to tyme and at all tymes hereafter for their severall defence and savetie to encounter expulse repell and resist by force of Armes as well by Sea as by Land and by all wayes and meanes whatsoever all such person or persons as without the especiall lycense of the said President or Counsell and their successors or the greater part of them shall attempt to inhabit within the severall presinctes and lymmyttes of their said Plantacon, Or shall enterpryse or attempt at any tyme hereafter distruccon, Invation, detryment or annoyaunce to the said Plantacon. And the said John Peirce and his associates and their heires and assignes do covennant and promyse to and with the said President and Counsell and their successors, That they the said John Peirce and his Associates from tyme to tyme during the said Seaven Yeeres shall make a true Certificat to the said President and Counsell and their successors from the chief Officers and the places respectyvely of every person transported and landed in New England or shipped as aforesaid to be entered by the Secretary of the said President and Counsell into a Register book for that purpose to be kept And the said John Peirce and his Associates Jointly and severally for them their heires and assignes do covennant promyse and graunt to and with the said President and Counsell and their successors That the persons transported to this their particuler Plantacon shall apply themselves and their Labors in a large and competent manner to the planting setting making and procuring of good and staple commodyties in and upon the said Land hereby graunted unto them as Corne and silkgrasse hemp flaxe pitch and tarre sopeashes and potashes Iron Clapbord and other the like materialls. In witnes whereof the said President and Counsell have to the one part of this p]rese]nte Indenture sett their seales And to th'other part hereof the said John Peirce in the name of himself and his said Associates have sett to his seale geven the day and yeeres first above written.

Lenox   Hamilton   Warwick   Sheffield   Ferd: Gorges

APPENDIX J

TRACING YOUR ROOTS:
HELPFUL RESOURCES FOR GETTING STARTED ON
RESEARCHING FAMILY NAMES

The following list is selected, rather than exhaustive. Most of these sources will lead to others.

http://www.genealogy.com/index.html

http://www.mayflowerfamilies.com

Caleb Johnson's *Mayflower* Web Pages:
http://members.aol.com/calebj/mayflower.html

Connecticut State Library
Genealogy Unit, 231
Capitol Avenue
Hartford, CT 06106
http://www.cslib.org/handg.htm

Genealogical Publishing Company
1001 N Calvert St.
Baltimore, MD 21202
http://www.genealogybookshop.com

General Society of Mayflower Descendants
P. O. Box 3297
Plymouth, MA 02361
http://www.mayflower.org

Heritage Books Inc.
1540-E Pointer Ridge Pl.
Bowie, MD 20716
http://www.heritagebooks.com

Massachusetts Society of Mayflower Descendants
376 Boylston Street—Suite B
Boston, MA 02116
http://www.tiac.net/users/msmd

Mayflower Pilgrim Family Genealogies Through Five Generations is a series of books published by the General Society of Mayflower Descendants. See http://www.mayflowersociety.com/book.htm

National Archives and Records Administration
7th and Pennsylvania Ave. NW
Washington DC 20408
http://www.nara.gov/nhprc/redirect.html

Picton Press
P. O. Box 250
Rockport, ME 04856-0250
http://www.pictonpress.com

Public Records Office
Chancery Lane, London WC2A 1LR
England
http://www.pro.gov.uk/leaflets/riindex.htm

Also helpful, in the bibliography of this book, are the works of Roser, Savage, Sawyer, Shurtleff, Stratton, and Torrey.

SELECT BIBLIOGRAPHY AND ANNOTATIONS

Note on William Bradford's Manuscript History *Of Plimoth Plantation*

In 1630 William Bradford began his *History of the Plimoth Plantation, Containing an Account of the Voyage of the Mayflower.* For the period 1606-1630, he used notes written largely from memory. He wrote and gathered his own annals for the period covering the years 1630-1647. By the time he laid down his pen, his vellum-bound manuscript, measuring eleven and a half by seven and three quarter inches, extended to about 270 folio pages. His last contribution is a list of the *Mayflower* passengers (to which he added notes up to about 1650). The finished work was never intended for publication, but was handed down from father to son for several generations. Nathaniel Morton, Bradford's nephew, however, consulted it and used some extracts from it in compiling his annals of the forefathers, titled *New England's Memorial,* published in 1669. Other historians had used it as well; but a memorandum dated June 4, 1728, shows when Bradford's grandson, Major John Bradford, allowed Rev. Thomas Prince of Boston's Old South Church to borrow it. Prince was researching for his *Chronological History of New England in the Form of Annals* (Boston: Kneeland, 1736). He placed the manuscript into his "New England Library," located in the tower of the Old South Church. Although others may have used it while it was there, it is believed that the manuscript was still in the Old South Church at the time of the American War for Independence.

During the War, the British used Old South Church as a stable and riding academy. When they left, the Bradford manuscript was missing. All hope of ever finding it was lost until 1855, when a couple of readers stumbled upon a clue in a book titled *A History of the Protestant Episcopal Church in America,* written in 1844 by Bishop Samuel Wilberforce of

Oxford. The book contained several quoted passages attributed to an anonymous manuscript which the readers immediately recognized as coming from the long-lost Bradford history. A search for the manuscript soon led to the Fulham Palace Library of the Bishop of London, where the missing manuscript was indeed found. How it had reached there no one knew. A copyist was contracted to make a transcript of the manuscript; and in 1856 it was published in the *Collections* of the Massachusetts Historical Society. The original manuscript remained in London's Fulham Palace Library until 1897, when it was presented to the State of Massachusetts. Typical of Bradford's style is the expression, "Behold, now, another providence of God" (Morison edition, p. 112).

All Saints' Church [of] *Babworth*[,] *1290-1990*. Babworth, England: All Saints' Church, 1990. "A commemorative booklet to celebrate seven hundred years of the church of Babworth."

Anderson, Christopher. *The Annals of the English Bible*. London: Jackson, Walford, and Hodder, 1862.

Anwyl, E. Catherine. *John Smyth: The Se-Baptist at Gainsborough*. Gainsborough, England: G. W. Belton Ltd., 1991. paperback booklet.

Arber, Edward, ed. *The Story of The Pilgrim Fathers, 1606-1623 A.D; as Told by Themselves, Their Friends, and Their Enemies*. London: Ward and Downey, Limited, 1897.

Bacon, Leonard. *The Genesis of the New England Churches*. 1874; rpt. NY: Arno Press, 1972. This is an excellent work, especially for the overall picture of the New England churches.

Bangs, Jeremy Dupertuis. *Church Art and Architecture in the Low Countries Before 1556*. Kirksville, MO: Sixteenth Century Journal Publishers, 1997. This book reconstructs the appearance of Dutch churches prior to the Protestant iconoclasm of 1556.

_____. *Pilgrim Life in Leiden*. Leiden: Leiden American Pilgrim Museum, 1997. The author has served as Chief Curator of the Plimoth Plantation in Plymouth, Massachusetts. He has specialized in researching original documents, including those in the Archives of the City of Leiden. Bangs is director of the Leiden American Pilgrim Museum.

_____, ed. *The Pilgrims in the Netherlands: Recent Research.* 1985; rpt. Leiden: Leiden American Pilgrim Museum, 1998. Papers presented at a symposium held by The Leiden Pilgrim Documents Center and The Sir Thomas Browne Institute, September 7, 1984.

_____. "A Real Leiden Pilgrim House." In *The Pilgrims in the Netherlands: Recent Research,* ed. Jeremy D. Bangs, 44-50. 1985; rpt. Leiden: Leiden American Pilgrim Museum, 1998.

_____, ed. *The Seventeenth-Century Town Records of Scituate, Massachusetts.* 3 vols. Boston, MA: New England Historic Genealogical Society, 1997-2000. Scituate was one of the most important towns in Plymouth Colony. For his first five years in Plymouth Colony, John Lathrop (Lothrop) lived in Scituate. Lathrop had ministered at the "J-L-J Church," established in a London home by Henry Jacob in 1616 as the first designated "Congregationalist" church in England. This set also contains information on John Robinson's son Isaac, who settled in Barnstable when Lathrop moved there. Bangs' introductions include the most recent reviews of current literature on New England Colonial history. The set is a major contribution to the most up-to-date research.

_____. *Strangers on the Mayflower.* Leiden: unpublished paper, 1999.

_____. "Towards a Revision of the Pilgrims: Three New Pictures." *The New England Historical and Genealogical Register* 153, no. 609 (January 1999): 3-28.

Banks, Charles E. *The English Ancestry and Homes of the Pilgrim Fathers, who came to Plymouth on the Mayflower in 1620, the Fortune in 1621, and the Anne and the Little James in 1623.* NY: The Grafton Press, 1929. This is an important and reliable work, cited often by serious authors.

_____. *The Planters of the Commonwealth: a Study of the Emigrants and Emigration in Colonial Times: To Which are Added Lists of Passengers to Boston and to the Bay Colony, the Ships which brought them, their English homes, and the Places of their Settlement in Massachusetts, 1620-1640.* Baltimore: Genealogical Pub. Co., 1967. Another major contribution to further research.

Bartlett, Robert Merrill. *The Faith of the Pilgrims*. New York: United Church Press, 1978. This is an excellent study of such topics as the Pilgrim family, Pilgrim ethics, the sermons, and the sacraments.

_____. *The Pilgrim Way*. Philadelphia: United Church Press, 1971. This in one of best surveys of the topic. It is carefully researched.

Bartlett, William Harry, ed. *The Pilgrim Fathers*. CA: Published by the editor, 1981. This is an update of William Henry Bartlett's *Pilgrim Fathers* (1853), the genealogical index being updated to 1945 by Wilma Hunt Bartlett Grahl, and extended to 1970 by the editor, William Harry Bartlett, whose address is given as 533 Vista del Mar Drive, Aptos, CA 95003.

Bartlett, William Henry. *The Pilgrim Fathers*. NY: T. Nelson, 1853. The 1853 London edition is titled *The Pilgrim Fathers, or The Founders of New England in the Reign of James the First*.

Board, Joan. *The Old North Road Through Babworth Parish*. Derby, England: J. H. Hall & Sons Limited, 1992. Good for background material on the area.

Bögels, Theo. "Govert Basson, English Printer at Leiden." In *The Pilgrims in the Netherlands: Recent Research,* ed. Jeremy D. Bangs, 18-23. 1985; rpt. Leiden: Leiden American Pilgrim Museum, 1998.

Bradford, William. *History of the Plimoth Plantation, Containing an Account of the Voyage of the 'Mayflower' Written by William Bradford, One of the Founders and Second Governor of the Colony*. Facsimile of the handwritten folio manuscript, with an introduction by John A. Doyle. Boston: Houghton Mifflin & Co., 1896. Doyle was Fellow of All Souls College, Oxford. The work was simultaneously published in London by Ward and Downey Ltd.

_____. *Of Plimmoth Plantation,* ed. Worthington C. Ford, 2 vols. Boston: Massachusetts Historical Society, 1912. This edition and Morison's are the best. Ford retains the original spelling and punctuation and provides the most valuable and lengthy footnotes.

_____. *Of Plymouth Plantation 1620-1647,* ed. Samuel Eliot Morison, 1952; rpt. NY: Alfred A. Knopf, 1998. This is the edition used in the present study. Morison slightly edited the work just enough to help the modern reader, without sacrificing any of the original sense. His notes have the advantage of more recent research than Ford's.

Breugelmans, R. "The Pilgrim Press and How its Books were Sold." In *The Pilgrims in the Netherlands: Recent Research,* ed. Jeremy D. Bangs, 24-28. 1985; rpt. Leiden: Leiden American Pilgrim Museum, 1998.

Brewster, Dorothy. *William Brewster of the Mayflower: Portrait of a Pilgrim.* NY: New York University Press, 1970. A brief work, with interesting observations.

Briggs, Rose T., ed. *Picture Guide to Historic Plymouth.* Plymouth, MA: The Pilgrim Society, 1963 (forty-page booklet).

Brook, Benjamin. *The Lives of the Puritans.* 3 vols. Pittsburgh, PA: Soli Deo Gloria, 1994.

Brown, John. *John Bunyan (1628-1688): His Life, Times, and Work.* London: Wm. Isbister Limited, 1885.

_____. *The Pilgrim Fathers of New England and Their Puritan Successors.* London: The Religious Tract Society, 1897.

Burgess, Walter H. *The Pastor of the Pilgrims: A Biography of John Robinson.* NY: Harcourt, Brace & Howe, 1920. A valuable work and enjoyable, even though Timothy George's research has corrected parts of it.

_____. *John Smyth the Se-Baptist, Thomas Helwys, and the First Baptist Church in England with Fresh Light upon the Pilgrim Fathers' Church.* London: James Clarke & Co., 1911.

Burrage, Champlin. *The Early English Dissenters in the Light of Recent Research (1550-1641).* 2 vols. Cambridge: Cambridge University Press, 1912. A major source for any serious research.

Caffrey, Kate. *The Mayflower.* NY: Stein and Day Publishers, 1974.

Carlson, Leland H., ed. *The Writings of Henry Barrow: 1587-1590.* London: George Allen & Unwin Ltd., 1962.

Carter, Alice C. *The English Reformed Church in Amsterdam in the Seventeenth Century.* Amsterdam: Scheltema & Holkema, 1964. This is still perhaps the best source of information on this church.

Clamp, Arthur L. *The Pilgrim Fathers and the Mayflower Ship, 1620.* Plymouth, England: P. D. S. Printers Ltd., n.d.

Clark, Henry W. *History of English Nonconformity: From Wiclif to the Close of the Nineteenth Century.* NY: Russell & Russell, 1965.

Coggins, James R. *John Smyth's Congregation: English Separatism, Mennonite Influence, and the Elect Nation.* Scottdale, PA: Herald Press, 1991.

Creighton, Mandell. *Cardinal Wolsey.* London: Macmillan and Co., Limited, 1921. A basic work on Wolsey.

Cuckson. John. *A Brief History of the First Church in Plymouth.* Boston: Geo. H. Ellis Co., 1902. An overview, but contains much helpful information.

Dale, R. W. *History of English Congregationalism.* London: Hodder and Stoughton, 1907. A valuable old source. Dale pulls together a number of sources.

Davies, Horton. *The Worship of the American Puritans, 1629-1730.* Morgan, PA: Soli Deo Gloria Publishers, 1999. Davies' works are of great value.

_____. *The Worship of the English Puritans.* 1948; rpt. Morgan, PA: Soli Deo Gloria Publishers, 1997.

_____. *Worship and Theology in England,* vol. I., *From Cranmer to Hooker, 1534-1603*, vol. II, *From Andrewes to Baxter and Fox, 1603-1690.* 2 vols., 1970, 1975; rpt. Grand Rapids, MI: William B. Eerdmans Publishing Co., 1996 combined edition.

Davis, Ozora S. *John Robinson: The Pilgrim Pastor.* Boston: The Pilgrim Press, 1903. Largely replaced by Timothy George's work, but still helpful, especially for a basic biography.

Demos, John. *A Little Commonwealth: Family Life in Plymouth Colony.* Oxford: Oxford University Press, 1970. This is one of the best sources on such topics as Pilgrim houses, furnishings, clothing, family relationships, and many others.

Dexter, Henry Martyn. *The Congregationalism of the Last Three Hundred Years, as Seen in Its Literature.* NY: Harper and Brothers, Publishers, 1880. This is still a valuable and classic work.

_____, and Morton Dexter. *The England and Holland of the Pilgrims.* 1906; rpt. Baltimore: Genealogical Publishing Co., Inc., 1978. By far, this is one of the most valuable sources of well-researched material.

Dillon, Francis. *The Pilgrims.* 1973; rpt. NY: Doubleday & Company, Inc., 1975. The original 1973 title is *A Place for Habitation.*

Dolby, Malcolm. *William Bradford of Austerfield: His Life and Work.* England: Doncaster Library and Information Services, 1991.

Dorsten, Jan van. "Why the Pilgrims Left Leiden." *In The Pilgrims in the Netherlands: Recent Research,* ed. Jeremy D. Bangs, 34. 1985; rpt. Leiden: Leiden American Pilgrim Museum, 1998.

Dowsing, James. *Places of the Pilgrim Fathers.* London: Sunrise Press, n.d.

Drysdale, A. H. *History of the Presbyterians in England: Their Rise, Decline, and Revival.* London: Publication Committee of the Presbyterian Church of England, 1889. One of the best works on Presbyterian history.

Earle, Alice Morse. *Child Life in Colonial Days.* NY: Macmillan, 1961.

_____. *Home Life in Colonial Days.* NY: Macmillan, 1961.

Ekkart, R. E. O., et al., ed. *The Pilgrim Fathers in Holland.* Leiden: Stichting Oude Hollandse Kerken, 1993 (twenty-three page booklet). Produced by the Foundation for Old Dutch Churches, this is sold to visitors in Holland. It is a basic, helpful, and detailed overview, correcting some of the popular "American myths." The booklet is written with care and restraint, to aid tourists with an accurate perception of background material related to the Pilgrims.

Fleming, Thomas J. *One Small Candle: The Pilgrims' First Year in America.* New York: W. W. Norton & Co. Inc., 1964. This is for the lazy reader, but a nightmare for the historian. It should not be relied upon for any careful study. Without notice, it constantly enhances and embellishes the narrative far beyond the known facts.

Foxe, John. *Acts and Monuments.* 8 vols. London: Seeley, Burnside, and Seeley, 1843-49. Volume one of this edition includes a "Life of the Martyrologist, and Vindication of the Work," by the Rev. George Townsend. For an excellent evaluation of Foxe as a historian, see Haller's Elect Nation, listed below.

Geller, L. D., ed. *They Knew They Were Pilgrims: Essays in Plymouth History.* NY: Poseidon Books, Inc., 1971. This book offers some helpful discussions, such as the chapter on "Doctrinal Divisions in the Church of Christ at Plymouth 1744-1801."

George, Timothy. *John Robinson and the English Separatist Tradition.* Macon, GA: Mercer University Press, 1982. This is the best study of Robinson.

Gill, Crispin. *Mayflower Remembered: A History of the Plymouth Pilgrims.* NY: Taplinger Publishing Co., 1970. A delightful and helpful study.

Goehring, Walter R. "Henry Jacob (1563-1624) and the Separatists," Ph.D. dissertation, New York University, 1975. The most complete source of information on Jacob.

_____. *The West Parish Church of Barnstable: An Historical Sketch— Being an Account of the Gathering of the Church Body in London in 1616 with Henry Jacob and its Early History in the New World And Particularly of the West Parish Meetinghouse Built in 1717 in West Barnstable, Massachusetts.* West Barnstable, MA: The West Parish Memorial Foundation, 1959.

Goodwin, John A. *The Pilgrim Republic: An Historical Review of the Colony of New Plymouth With Sketches of the Rise of Other New England Settlements, the History of Congregationalism and the Creeds of the Period.* Boston: Houghton Mifflin Company, 1920. Contains some good insight and a broad picture.

Gordon, Rev. J. C. *An Adventure Almost Desperate: The Pilgrim Fathers and Their Associations with the Netherlands.* Amsterdam: The Consistory of the English Reformed Church (Church of Scotland), n.d. (sixteen-page booklet).

Haller, William. *The Elect Nation: The Meaning and Relevance of Foxe's Book of Martyrs.* NY: Harper & Row, 1963.

————. *The Rise of Puritanism.* NY: Harper & Brothers, 1957.

Hardwick, Charles. *A History of the Articles of Religion.* Cambridge: Cambridge University Press, 1859. A good source for some of those documents not found in Schaff's *Creeds of Christendom.*

Harris, Rendel, and Stephen K. Jones. *The Pilgrim Press: A Bibliographical & Historical Memorial of the Books Printed at Leyden by the Pilgrim Fathers.* Cambridge: W. Heffer and Sons, 1922. The best book on the subject.

Haykin, Michael A. G., ed. *The British Particular Baptists: 1638-1910.* Springfield, MO: Particular Baptist Press, 1998.

————. *Kiffin, Knollys and Keach: Rediscovering Our English Baptist Heritage.* Leeds, England: Reformation Today Trust, 1996. The book is distributed by Evangelical Press, Darlington, Co. Durham, England. It is a valuable study.

Heaton, Vernon. *The Mayflower.* Exeter, England: Webb & Bower, 1980.

Helwys, Thomas. *A Short Declaration of the Mystery of Iniquity,* ed. Richard Groves, 1611-12; rpt., Macon, GA: Mercer University Press, 1998.

Hetherington, William Maxwell, *History of the Westminster Assembly of Divines.* 1856; rpt. Edmonton, Canada: Still Waters Revival Books, 1993.

Hills, Leon Clark. *History and Genealogy of the Mayflower Planters and First Comers to Ye Olde Colonie.* 2 vols., 1936, 1941; rpt. (2 vols. in 1) Baltimore: Genealogical Publishing Co., Inc., 1977.

Hoftijzer, Paul. "A Continuing Tradition: English Puritan Booksellers in the Second Half of the Seventeenth Century in Amsterdam." In *The Pilgrims in the Netherlands: Recent Research,* ed. Jeremy D. Bangs, 29-33. 1985; rpt. Leiden: Leiden American Pilgrim Museum, 1998.

Hubbard, William. *General History of New England.* Cambridge: Massachusetts Historical Society, 1815. Although not published until the nineteenth century, this was written in the second half of the seventeenth century and is a good source of study.

James, Sydney V. Jr., ed. *Three Visitors to Early Plymouth.* Plymouth, MA: Plimoth Plantation, 1963. This book offers letters written by John Pory, Emmanuel Altham, and Isaac Rasieres between 1622-1628, relating to their visits to Plymouth. Valuable eye-witness sources.

Jessup, Edmund F. *The Mayflower Story.* 4th ed. Retford, England: Whartons Ltd., 1977, 1984. The author was Rector of Babworth. This twenty-eight-page booklet is carefully written and provides an accurate brief overview of some of the basic facts.

Johnson, Caleb. *Mayflower* Web Pages.
http://members.aol.com/calebj/mayflower.html. This is the single best source of information on the Internet, on the topics of the *Mayflower* and the Pilgrims. Caleb Johnson carefully maintains high standards and updates his material regularly. This is an example of what can be done on the Internet to make the highest quality information accessible.

Jones, R. Tudur, and Alan Tovey. *Some Separatists: The Martyrs of 1593.* North Humberside, England: Evangelical Fellowship of Congregational Churches, 1993. Mailing address is 10 Willow Grove, Beverley, North Humberside, England HU17 8DS. Congregational Studies Conference Papers, commemorating four hundred years since the deaths of Henry Barrow, John Greenwood, and John Penry.

Kardux, Joke, and Eduard van de Bilt. *Newcomers in an Old City: The American Pilgrims in Leiden 1609-1620.* Leiden: Uitgeverij Burgersdijk & Niermans, 1998. This is an excellent and insightful overview.

Kirk-Smith, Harold. *William Brewster 'The Father of New England'—His Life and Times—1567-1644.* Boston, England: Richard Kay, 1992.

This is the most recent study of Brewster. It demonstrates the use of some of the best sources and is a fine contribution. Surprisingly, he entirely omits the events in Dartmouth.

Langdon, George D. Jr. *Pilgrim Colony: A History of New Plymouth 1620 - 1691*. New Haven: Yale University Press, 1966. This is a major and valuable source for serious study.

Leverland, B. N. "Geographic Origins of the Pilgrims." *In The Pilgrims in the Netherlands: Recent Research,* ed. Jeremy D. Bangs, 8-17. 1985; rpt. Leiden: Leiden American Pilgrim Museum, 1998.

Light, Alfred. *Bunhill Fields*. London: C. J. Farncombe & Sons, Ltd., 1913. Contains helpful biographical sketches of dissenters buried in this famous London cemetery. It is a rare and valuable book.

Lumpkin, William L. *Baptist Confessions of Faith.* Valley Forge: The Judson Press, 1969.

McBeth, H. Leon. *The Baptist Heritage.* Nashville: Broadman Press, 1987.

_____. *A Sourcebook for Baptist Heritage.* Nashville: Broadman Press, 1990.

McGinn, Donald J. *John Penry and the Marprelate Controversy.* New Brunswick, NJ: Rutgers University Press, 1966. A valuable study.

McIntyre, Ruth A. *Debts Hopeful and Desperate: Financing the Plymouth Colony.* Plymouth, MA: Plimoth Plantation, 1963. This is probably the best single source of information on the topic.

Mackennal, Alexander. *Homes and Haunts of the Pilgrim Fathers.* London: The Religious Tract Society, 1899. A delightful old book, containing many forgotten treasures of Pilgrim history.

Martyn, W. Carlos. *The Pilgrim Fathers of New England.* NY: American Tract Society, 1867. Helpful, but much of its material is outdated by more recent research.

Mason, Thomas W., and B. Nightingale. *New Light on the Pilgrim Story.* London: Congregational Union of England and Wales, 1920. Some help, but no major breakthroughs.

Mather, Cotton. *Magnalia Christi Americana: or, The Ecclesiastical History of New-England from its first Planting in the year 1620 unto the year of our Lord 1698.* London: T. Parkhurst, 1702 folio.

Mayflower Descendant. 34 vols., compiled and published by George Ernest Bowman, from 1899 to 1937, Massachusetts Society of Mayflower Descendants. "Mayflower Legacy," 43-vol. searchable CD edition, Wheat Ridge, CO: Search & Research Publishing Corporation, 1998, containing *The Mayflower Descendant With Other New England Town Records.* The set contains literal transcripts of vital town records, church records, Pilgrim diaries, inventories, probate records, biographies, cemetery records, wills, letters, etc. The CD is presently available from:
Ancestor Publishers
6166 Janice Way CD1
Arvada, CO 80004-5160
Phone: 1-800-373-0816
e-mail: ancestor@net1comm.com
web address: http://www.firstct.com/fv/mayflow.html

Merle d'Aubigné, J. H. *History of the Reformation of the Sixteenth Century.* 5 vols. Translated by Henry White. NY: Hurst and Co., n.d.

_____. *The Protector: A Vindication.* 1847; rpt. Harrisonburg, VA: Sprinkle Pub., 1983. A biography of Oliver Cromwell.

Miller, Perry, and Thomas H. Johnson, ed. *The Puritans.* NY: American Book Company, 1938.

Mitchell, Alexander F. *The Westminster Assembly: Its History and Standards.* 1883; rpt. Edmonton, Canada: Still Waters Revival Books, 1992.

Morton, Nathaniel. *New England's Memorial.* 1669; rpt. Boston: Congregational Board of Publications, 1855. Morton was about ten years old when he arrived in Plymouth Colony in 1623. He lived with his uncle, William Bradford, and later served as Secretary to the Court for New Plymouth. He was known to be well-read and a careful recorder of the colony's vital information. He would have had constant access to the records of the Colony, as well as to Bradford's

Plymouth Plantation. He would have known as many as fifty of the *Mayflower*'s passengers. Although his *Memorial* repeats much of Bradford's history, it is valuable for its additional "sidelights" not recorded elsewhere; for example, the names of the ships, the size of the *Speedwell,* the names of those who signed the *Mayflower Compact,* and the Pilgrims' belief that the Dutch bribed Captain Jones of the *Mayflower* to take them to New England rather than the Hudson River, since they were making their own plans for a settlement there. The *Memorial* includes Bradford's *Dialogue,* numerous miscellaneous articles of value, and portions of Thomas Prince's *Annals.*

Motley, John Lothrop. *The Rise of the Dutch Republic.* 3 vols. London: Frederick Warne and Co., 1886. A valuable source.

Mourt, G. (Edward Winslow and William Bradford). *Mourt's Relation: A Journal of the Pilgrims at Plymouth,* ed. Dwight B. Heath, 1622; rpt. Bedford, MA: Applewood Books, 1986. The original title is *A Relation or Journal of the Beginnings and Proceedings of the English Plantation Settled at Plymouth in New England, by Certain English Adventurers Both Merchants and Others. . . .* (It continues for some twenty more lines.) Historian Thomas Prince, pastor of Boston's Old South Church, who quotes extensively from the work, mercifully shortened the title to *Mourt's Relation.* The work was prepared as an encouraging report to Plymouth's financial investors in England. Robert Cushman, who had started out on the *Speedwell,* but remained behind, arrived in Plymouth with his son, Thomas, on the *Fortune* in 1621. Leaving Thomas in the care of the Bradfords, Robert returned with the *Fortune* in December 1621. In Cushman's possession was *Mourt's Relation,* which he was taking to London for publication. However, a French ship captured the *Fortune* and confiscated its cargo, the fruits of a year's labor by the Pilgrims. After several months of imprisonment, Cushman finally reached London—with his manuscript! Cushman intended to return to Plymouth, but died in 1625; he accomplished his mission, however, of finding Bradford's Separatist friend, George Morton, who arranged for the 1622 publication of the manuscript in London. The name of the publisher is omitted. The introduction, "To the Reader", is signed by "G. Mourt," who is no doubt George Morton.

It was not an uncommon thing in those days to drop the ending of a name; however, since Morton did not arrive in Plymouth until 1623, the work was most likely written by Edward Winslow and William Bradford. It provides a day-by-day narrative of the time from the *Mayflower's* arrival, up to and including the first Thanksgiving. William Bradford's second wife was George Morton's sister-in-law. Since George Morton died the year after he arrived in Plymouth, the Bradfords raised his eldest son, the well-known chronicler, Nathaniel Morton. (His friend Thomas Cushman succeeded William Brewster as ruling elder of the Plymouth Church.) Other helpful editions of *Mourt's Relation,* especially for their footnotes, are the 1865 edition by Henry Martyn Dexter; and the edition by Jordan D. Fiore, (Plymouth, MA: Plymouth Rock Foundation, 1985).

Neal, Daniel. *The History of the Puritans, or Protestant Nonconformists; from the Reformation in 1517, to the Revolution in 1688.* 2 vols. NY: Harper & Brothers, 1843-44.

Nicholson, H. W. *Boston: the Town, the Church, the People.* Boston, England: Guardian Press Ltd., 1986.

Nickerson, Warren Sears. *Land Ho! — 1620: A Seaman's Story of the Mayflower, Her Construction, Her Navigation, and Her First Landfall.* Boston: Houghton Mifflin Company, 1931.

Noble, Frederick A. *The Pilgrims.* Boston: The Pilgrim Press, 1907. Still helpful, but the research is too outdated in some areas.

Oliver, Robert W. *From John Spilsbury to Ernest Kevan: The Literary Contribution of London's Oldest Baptist Church.* London: Grace Publications Trust, 1985. The address of the publisher is 139 Grosvenor Avenue, London N5 2NH. The book was published in behalf of the Evangelical Library, 78A Chiltern Street, London W1M 2HB. A valuable work.

Payne, Ernest A. *The Free Church Tradition in the Life of England.* London: S.C.M. Press Ltd., 1944. A valuable overview.

_____. *Thomas Helwys and the First Baptist Church in England.* London: The Baptist Union of Great Britain and Ireland, 1966.

Pearson, A. F. Scott. *Thomas Cartwright and Elizabethan Puritanism 1535-1603.* 1925; rpt. Gloucester, MA: Peter Smith, 1966. Excellent material.

Peterson, Harold L. *Arms and Armor in Colonial America,* 1526-1783. Harrisburg, PA: The Stackpole Co., 1956.

————. *Arms and Armor of the Pilgrims 1620—1692.* Plymouth, MA: Plimoth Plantation, Inc. and the Pilgrim Society, 1957. The author is the leading authority on the subject. Informative, well-researched, and illustrated appropriately.

Pierce, William. *John Penry: His Life, Times and Writings.* London: Hodder and Stoughton, 1923. This work is well researched and remains the major source for an in-depth look at John Penry. Penry was a major figure in the Welsh and English Reformation and in Separatist and *Mayflower* history.

Pilgrim Hall Museum. http://www.pilgrimhall.org

Plimoth Plantation. http://www.plimoth.org

Plooij, D., and J. Rendel Harris, ed. *Leyden Documents Relating to the Pilgrim Fathers.* Leyden: E. J. Brill, 1920. A major source.

Plooij, D. *The Pilgrim Fathers from a Dutch Point of View.* 1932; rpt. NY: AMS Press, Inc., 1969. This is one of most valuable sources; its research is among the best.

Plymouth Church Records 1620-1859. 2 vols., 1920-23; rpt. Baltimore, MD: Genealogical Publishing Co., Inc., 1975. Originally published by the New England Society, in the city of New York. In I:115-41 there is provided William Bradford's *Dialogue, or the Sum of a Conference between some Young Men born in New England, and sundry Ancient Men that came out of Holland and Old England.* Volume one begins with Nathaniel Morton's synopsis of the history of Plymouth Church.

Porter, H. C., ed. *Puritanism in Tudor England.* Columbia, SC: University of South Carolina, 1971. A helpful resource.

Powicke, Frederick J. *Henry Barrow, Separatist, and the Exiled Church of Amsterdam.* London: J. Clark & Co., 1900. A fine and valuable study.

_____. *John Robinson.* London: Hodder & Stoughton, Ltd., 1920.

_____. *Robert Browne, Pioneer of Modern Congregationalism.* London: Memorial Hall, 1910. Helpful.

Prince, Thomas. *Chronological History of New England in the Form of Annals.* Boston: Kneeland, 1736. A prime source.

Robinson, John. *Works of John Robinson with a Memoir and Annotations,* ed. Robert Ashton, 3 vols. London: John Snow, 1851.

Roser, Susan E. *Mayflower Births and Deaths: From the Files of George Ernest Bowman at the Massachusetts Society of Mayflower Descendants.* Baltimore, MD: Genealogical Publishing Company, 1992.

_____. *Mayflower Deeds and Probates: From the Files of George Ernest Bowman at the Massachusetts Society of Mayflower Descendants.* Baltimore, MD: Genealogical Publishing Company, 1994.

_____. *Mayflower Increasings.* Baltimore, MD: Genealogical Publishing Company, 1995.

_____. *Mayflower Marriages: From the Files of George Ernest Bowman at the Massachusetts Society of Mayflower Descendants.* Baltimore, MD: Genealogical Publishing Company, 1990.

Rosier, James. *A True Relation of the Most Prosperous Voyage Made this Present Year 1605 by Captain George Weymouth.* Ann Arbor, MI: University Microfilms, 1966.

Savage, James. *Genealogical Dictionary of the First Settlers of New England.* 4 vols. 3rd ed. Baltimore, MD: Genealogical Publishing Company, 1998. This is the basic genealogical dictionary of early New England settlers, giving the name of every settler who arrived in New England before 1692.

Sawyer, Joseph Dillaway. *History of the Pilgrims and Puritans: Their Ancestry and Descendants,* ed. William Elliot Griffis, 3 vols. NY: The Century History Company, Inc., 1922.

Schaff, Philip. *The Creeds of Christendom, with a History and Critical Notes.* 3 vols. NY: Harper & Brothers 1877. Best source for those hard-to-find creeds and confessions.

Sewall, Samuel. *The Diary of Samuel Sewall: 1674—1729,* ed. M. Halsey Thomas, 2 vols. NY: Farrar, Straus and Giroux, 1973.

Sherwood, Mary B. *Pilgrim: Biography of William Brewster.* Falls Church, VA: Great Oak Press of Virginia, 1982.

Shurtleff, Nathaniel B., and David Pulsifer, ed. *Records of the Colony of New Plymouth in New England (1620-1691).* 12 vols., Boston, 1855-61; rpt. (12 vols. in 6) NY: AMS Press 1968. This is a most valuable source of information. Volumes 1-4 are edited by Nathaniel B. Shurtleff and volumes 5-6 are edited by David Pulsifer. Volumes 1-3: Court Orders, 1633-1691; volume 4: Judicial Acts, 1636-1692 and Miscellaneous Records, 1633-1689; volume 5: Acts of the Commissioners, 1643-1679; and volume 6: Laws, 1623-1682 and Deeds, &c., 1620-1651.

Simmons, Charles, ed. *Plymouth Colony Records: Wills & Inventories, 1633-69.* Camden, ME: Picton Press, 1996. This is a vital source of information, with introduction by Jeremy D. Bangs.

Simon, Philip J. *Log of the Mayflower.* Chicago: Priam Press, 1956.

Smith, Bradford. *Bradford of Plymouth.* Philadelphia: J. B. Lippincott Company, 1951.

Smith, H. Shelton, et al., ed. *American Christianity: An Interpretation with Representative Documents.* 2 vols. NY: Charles Scribner's Sons, 1960.

Smyth, John. *The Works of John Smyth Fellow of Christ's College, 1594-8,* ed. W. T. Whitley, 2 vols. Cambridge: Cambridge University Press, 1915. This edition includes a biography and was published for the Baptist Historical Society.

Sprague, William B. *Annals of the American Pulpit; or Commemorative Notices of Distinguished American Clergymen of Various Denominations, From the Early Settlement of the Country to the Close of the Year Eighteen Hundred and Fifty-Five.* 9 vols. NY: Robert Carter & Brothers, 1857-69.

Sprunger, Keith L. *Dutch Puritanism: A History of English and Scottish Churches of the Netherlands in the Sixteenth and Seventeenth Centuries.* Leiden: E. J. Brill, 1982. This is the best and most complete book written on Dutch Puritanism.

Spurrell, Mark. *Boston Parish Church.* Boston, England: Ingelow Press, n.d. Spurrell was lecturer of Boston, England from 1965 to 1976.

Steele, Ashbel. *Chief of the Pilgrims: or the Life and Time of William Brewster.* Philadelphia, PA: J. B. Lippincott and Company, 1857.

Stephen, Sir Leslie, and Sir Sidney Lee, ed. *The Dictionary of National Biography.* 21 vols., 1917; rpt. London: Oxford University Press, 1921-22. This remains a vital source of information.

Stoddard, Francis R. *The Truth About the Pilgrims.* NY: Society of Mayflower Descendants, 1952. Written in popular style; it contains some helpful data.

Stratton, Eugene A. *Plymouth Colony: Its History & People 1620-1691.* Salt Lake City, UT: Ancestry Publishing, 1986. His bibliography on pp. 379-89 is indispensable for tracing family trees. A valuable source.

Tammel, Johanna W., ed. *The Pilgrims and other People from the British Isles in Leiden 1576-1640.* Isle of Man, British Isles: Mansk-Svenska Publishing Company Limited, 1989.

Tanner, J. R., ed. *Constitutional Documents of the Reign of James I A.D. 1603-1625 with an Historical Commentary.* Cambridge: Cambridge University Press, 1930.

Taylor, Dale. *The Writer's Guide to Everyday Life in Colonial America.* Cincinnati, Ohio: Writer's Digest Books, 1997.

Tolmie, Murray. *The Triumph of the Saints: The Separate Churches of London 1616—1649.* Cambridge: Cambridge University Press, 1977.

Torrey, Clarence A. *New England Marriages Prior to 1700.* Baltimore, MD: Genealogical Publishing Company, 1985.

Towns of New England and Old England, Ireland and Scotland. 2 vols. Boston, MA: State Street Trust Company of Boston, 1920-21. Limited Edition. This was written and published to commemorate the tercentenary of the landing of the Pilgrims. It documents connecting links between cities and towns of New England and those of the same names in England, Ireland and Scotland. It contains narratives, descriptions and memorials (on both sides of the Atlantic) of many founders and settlers of New England. Contains many photographs. A valuable resource.

Trap, Bert. *Pilgrim Trail.* Rotterdam: The Pilgrim Fathers Foundation, 1995. Booklet.

Usher, Roland G. *The Pilgrims and Their History.* NY: The Macmillan Company, 1920.

Vernon, Jennifer. *Gainsborough Old Hall and the Mayflower Pilgrim Story.* Gainsborough, England: Friends of the Old Hall Association, 1991.

Villiers, Captain Alan. "How We Sailed the New *Mayflower* to America." *The National Geographic Magazine* 112, no. 5 (November 1957): 627-72.

Walker, Williston. *The Creeds and Platforms of Congregationalism.* Boston: The Pilgrim Press, 1960. A valuable source for hard-to-find documents; it also provides helpful background material.

Walling, R. A. J. *The Story of Plymouth.* NY: William Morrow & Company, 1950. This is a history of Plymouth, England to the mid twentieth century.

Watts, Michael R. *The Dissenters: From the Reformation to the French Revolution.* Oxford: Clarendon Press, 1978. Valuable source.

White, B. R., ed. *Association Records of the Particular Baptists of England, Wales and Ireland to 1660.* London: Baptist Historical Society, 1974.Valuable primary source.

White, B. R., and Roger Hayden, ed. *The English Baptists of the Seventeenth Century.* London: Baptist Historical Society, 1996. Useful source.

White, B. R. *The English Separatist Tradition: From the Marian Martyrs to the Pilgrim Fathers.* London: Oxford University Press, Ely House, 1971. A major source.

Willison, George F. *The Pilgrim Reader: The Story of the Pilgrims as Told by Themselves & Their Contemporaries Friendly & Unfriendly.* NY: Doubleday & Company, 1953. A helpful resource which includes much prime material.

_____. *Saints and Strangers.* NY: Reynal & Hitchcock, 1945. A popular and helpful source; although, much of the material is badly outdated in light of research since 1945.

Winslow, Edward. *Good Newes from New England.* 1623-24; rpt. Bedford, MA: Applewood Books, 1996. First published in London, this work essentially continues the narrative of *Mourt's Relation* and is of much value. It is a journal of events that occurred between 1622 and 1623 at Plymouth Colony. It includes information about Tisquantum's death (November 1622), the sickness of Massasoit, Thomas Weston's Wessagussett Colony, and much more.

_____. *Hypocrisie Unmasked.* London, 1646; reissued in 1649, under the title, *The Danger of Tolerating Levellers in a Civil State;* also appears as volume 27 of the *Mayflower Descendant.*

Wood, Ralph V. *Francis Cooke of the Mayflower: The First Five Generations.* Camden, ME: Picton Press, 1996. Distributed by the General Society of Mayflower Descendants, this work includes a helpful background preface by Jeremy D. Bangs.

Yohn, David Waite. *The Gist of Jacob: Being an Investigation of the Thought of the Rev. Henry Jacob Who Coined the Designation "Congregational" and Gathered the Most Ancient Church Still Called by that Name.* West Barnstable, MA: West Parish Memorial Foundation, Inc., 1982. Yohn wrote as "Pastor/Teacher of the West Parish Congregational Church."

Young, Alexander, ed. *Chronicles of the Pilgrim Fathers of the Colony of Plymouth, from 1602 to 1625.* 1844; rpt. Baltimore: Genealogical Publishing Co., Inc., 1974. This book contains selections from contemporary writings, such as Bradford's and *Mourt's Relation*. The *Mayflower,* which is mentioned by name in only a few passing references in any of the sources, is mentioned by name in *Mourt's Relation,* on page 99. Also of special interest, on pages 409-58 is William Bradford's *Dialogue, or the Sum of a Conference between some Young Men born in New England, and sundry Ancient Men that came out of Holland and Old England.*

Young, G. V. C. "Pilgrim Myles Standish: His European Background." In *The Pilgrims in the Netherlands: Recent Research,* ed. Jeremy D. Bangs, 35-43. 1985; rpt. Leiden: Leiden American Pilgrim Museum, 1998.

INDEX

D

E

F

G

H

Half-Way Covenant: 154, 157, 190
Hampton Court Conference: 20, 21, 34, 41, 174, 189
Hampton Court Palace: 20
Harrison, Robert: 8, 226
Harvard College: 155, 156, 189, 191
Harvard, John: 211
Heale, Giles: 110, 113, 122
Heidelberg Catechism: 73
Henry VII, King: 37, 39, 185
Henry VIII, King: 2, 3, 5, 36, 38, 39, 185, 186, 187, 193
Hickman, Anthony: 35, 36
Hickman, Rose: 35, 36
Hickman, William: 35, 36, 82, 165, 187
Holbeck, William: 119
Hooke, John: 116
Hooker, Thomas: 211, 246
Hooper, John: 5, 187
Hopkins, Oceanus: 113, 120, 123
Hopkins, Stephen: 107, 119, 120, 128, 142
Howard, Catherine: 36
Howland, John: 108, 116, 117, 122, 124, 128

J

J-L-J Church: 175, 176, 177, 178, 205, 211, 243
Jacob, Henry: 97, 174, 175, 177, 205, 243, 248, 260
James I, King of England (James VI of Scotland): 19, 24, 34, 35, 38, 40, 41, 42, 75, 76, 79, 82, 174, 188, 258
James II, King: 27, 153, 191
James IV, King: 38, 39
Jessey, Henry: 174, 177, 178
Johnson, Francis: 14, 15, 16, 17, 18, 35, 36, 38, 42, 50, 62, 63, 64, 65, 66, 67, 68, 86, 88, 166, 168, 174, 188, 211, 226
Jones, Captain Christopher: 97, 98, 99, 100, 121, 122, 126, 135, 253
Judson, Adoniram Jr.: 157
Judson, Adoniram Sr.: 157
Julian Calendar: 213

K

L

M

W

Y